FROM CANTON RESTAURANT TO PANDA EXPRESS

ASIAN AMERICAN STUDIES TODAY

This series publishes scholarship on cutting-edge themes and issues, including broadly based histories of both long-standing and more recent immigrant populations; focused investigations of ethnic enclaves and understudied subgroups; and examinations of relationships among various cultural, regional, and socioeconomic communities. Of particular interest are subject areas in need of further critical inquiry, including transnationalism, globalization, homeland polity, and other pertinent topics.

Series Editor: Huping Ling, Truman State University

Stephanie Hinnershitz, *Race, Religion, and Civil Rights: Asian Students on the West Coast, 1900–1968*

Jennifer Ho, *Racial Ambiguity in Asian American Culture*

Haiming Liu, *From Canton Restaurant to Panda Express: A History of Chinese Food in the United States*

Jun Okada, *Making Asian American Film and Video: History, Institutions, Movements*

David S. Roh, Betsy Huang, and Greta A. Niu, *Techno-Orientalism: Imagining Asia in Speculative Fiction, History, and Media*

FROM CANTON RESTAURANT TO PANDA EXPRESS

A History of Chinese Food in the United States

HAIMING LIU

RUTGERS UNIVERSITY PRESS
New Brunswick, New Jersey, and London

Library of Congress Cataloging-in-Publication Data
Liu, Haiming, 1953–
   From Canton Restaurant to Panda Express : a history of Chinese food in the
United States / Haiming Liu.
        pages cm. — (Asian American studies today)
     Includes bibliographical references and index.
     ISBN 978–0–8135–7475–2 (hardcover : alkaline paper) — ISBN
978–0–8135–7474–5 (paperback : alkaline paper) — ISBN 978–0–8135–7476–9
(ePub) — ISBN (invalid) 978–0–8135–7477–6 (Web PDF)
        1. Chinese restaurants—United States—History. 2. Chinese Americans—Food—
United States—History. 3. Chinese—Food—United States—History. 4. Food
habits—United States—History. 5. Cooking, Chinese—History. 6. United States—
Ethnic relations. 7. United States—Social life and customs. I. Title.
     TX945.4.L58 2015
     641.5951—dc23

                                                                    2014049319

A British Cataloging-in-Publication record for this book is available from the
British Library.

Visit our website: http://rutgerspress.rutgers.edu

Manufactured in the United States of America

To Aiping, Jeff, and my late father

CONTENTS

ACKNOWLEDGMENTS

I am grateful to many people and organizations that provided assistance, advice, and encouragement at various stages of this book. I published my first article on Chinese food in America in the *Journal of Asian American Studies* in 2009. I want to thank the journal and the two anonymous readers for their valuable comments. I published "Chop Suey as an Imagined Authentic Chinese Food" in the *Journal of Transnational American Studies* the same year. I want to thank the journal, the anonymous readers, Gordon Chang of the Advisory Board, and Shelley Fisher Fishkin of the Editorial Team of the journal. I published "Kung Pao Kosher" in the *Journal of Chinese Overseas (JCO)* in 2010. I must thank Tan Chee Beng, former editor of *JCO*, and an anonymous reader for his or her harsh but insightful comments, from which I benefited tremendously. I published "Flexible Authenticity: Din Tai Fung as a Global Shanghai Dumpling House Made in Taiwan" in *Chinese America: History and Perspectives* in 2011 and received valuable comments from the journal's committee members. Several chapters in this book are revised versions of the above articles.

I want to acknowledge that E. N. Anderson's *The Food of China* (1988) has significantly impacted my understanding of Chinese food history. Joanna Waley-Cohen's *The Sextants of Beijing: Global Currents in Chinese History* (1999) has deepened my knowledge of Chinese history. Donna R. Gabaccia's *We Are What We Eat: Ethnic Food and the Making of Americans* (1998) has shaped my conception of American food culture and history. Elizabeth Sinn's *Pacific Crossing: California Gold, Chinese Migration, and the Making of Hong Kong* (2013) has greatly enriched my comprehension of Hong Kong and California in the nineteenth century. My special thanks also go to John M. Liu of the University of California, Irvine, who was my mentor when I was a Ph.D. student at UC Irvine. I am indebted to Gilbert Hom of the Chinese Historical Society of Southern California, who has shared with me valuable information on Chinese Americans, including Chinese pioneers in manufacturing frozen foods in the 1940s.

I want to express my deep gratitude to California State Polytechnic University, Pomona, which provided me with two course releases and two minigrants at various stages of my writing. My dean M. G. (Peggy) Kelly, chair S. Terri Gomez, and other colleagues are extremely understanding and supportive in my research. Friendship with Wei Li, Zong Li, Jinqi Ling, Yuan Shu, Fenggang Yang, Philip Yang, and Min Zhou in the field of Asian American studies is a great asset in my professional life. Xiao-huang Yin of the Occidental College has read the introduction and discussed with me at length on how to improve it. He is always a supporter of my research and publications. I also want to thank Xiaojian Zhao, whose critical suggestions have pushed me to sharpen my thoughts on food history. She is a great friend. Da Zheng has also read the introduction and provided valuable suggestions. As a good scholar and friend, he has shared with me information on Chinese food in America. Zuoyue Wang, both a friend and Cal Poly Pomona colleague, has critically read several chapters of the manuscript and has been kindly supportive of me in numerous other ways. Jing Hu, another Cal Poly Pomona colleague, has also read a chapter and provided comment on the cover design. Huping Ling, editor of the Asian American series at Rutgers University Press, is a strong advocate for this book. I cannot thank her enough for her support. I also greatly appreciate two readers' meaningful suggestions and sincere criticism.

When I was a Fulbright scholar in the American Studies Program, Faculty of Arts at the University of Hong Kong (HKU) in the 2012–13 academic year, Kendall Johnson, Tim Gruenewald, and Ann Kwan Tsang were great hosts to me. Fulbright staff both in Hong Kong and the United States, and previous Fulbright scholars Wing-kai To and Monica Chiu, answered tons of my questions. I was able to accomplish several chapters in my ocean-view flat at 25 Sha Wan Drive. Staying in Hong Kong has considerably deepened my understanding of Cantonese food. I shared my research with HKU faculty and students, and delivered public lectures and presentations based on my manuscript. I received a warm response and meaningful inquiries from my HKU students and colleagues. I have fond memories of my stay at HKU.

I express my deepest appreciation to Rutgers University Press for accepting my manuscript. Katie Keeran and Leslie Mitchner are supportive but demanding acquisitions editors. I am grateful to their professionalism in the review and revising process. Carrie Hudak was very helpful in the prepress matters when I was preparing the final version of the manuscript. It is delightful that Marilyn Campbell, the prepress editor of my former book, worked with me again. Robert Burchfield has played an indispensable role as my copyeditor. I am extremely happy that this is my second book with the press.

Sadly, I suffered family death and illness when writing this book. I was able to rebound in my research because I have many reliable friends in North America, China, and Hong Kong. They are a great help in times of need. My family has long been supportive and understanding in my career. My wife and son read most of the chapters and gave me their input. They actually know and love food better than I do. Without their support and love, this book would have been impossible.

NOTE ON ROMANIZATION

This book uses pinyin to Romanize Chinese names and terms from Chinese-language sources, except for a few popular names such as Canton, Cantonese, and Hong Kong based on the Wade-Giles spelling.

FROM CANTON RESTAURANT TO PANDA EXPRESS

INTRODUCTION

Food has followed every wave of Chinese immigrants to the United States, from the mid-nineteenth century to today. Food tradition reflects the social background, lifestyle, and cultural values of both early and contemporary Chinese immigrants. Thus Chinese restaurant history in the United States is more than a story of food migration and change. It reveals who Chinese immigrants are; what challenges they have encountered; and how they have survived, struggled, and succeeded in their American experience. The American food market is both a meeting ground for different ethnic cuisines and a field of racial politics in which Chinese food culture has met with curiosity, prejudice, and even hostility. Yet through engagement and creative adaptation, Chinese immigrants have made Chinese food a vital part of American culinary culture.

Chinese restaurant history, at least before the 1960s, reflects more Chinese adaptation to America than what Chinese eat in China. The Chinese restaurant business has a long history in the United States, and its food, cooking, and operation illustrate the constant and continuous linkage between Chinese Americans and China.[1] Departure from the old country does not mean a break from the past for Chinese immigrants but the beginning of a new life in America. Chinese American food culture and restaurant business are a transnational history and should be understood as such. The goal of this book is not to chronicle the Chinese food and restaurant business in America but to explore a deeper meaning embedded in the Chinese restaurant experience.

Restaurant and food operations were among the earliest economic activities pursued by pioneer Chinese immigrants in California. Though modest in number, early Chinese restaurants were the "best eating houses" during the gold rush. Chinese restaurants' yellow silk flags, their famous commercial mark, attracted many customers. The first Chinese restaurant was established in 1849. With 300 seats and English-speaking bartenders, Canton Restaurant was a landmark food institution in San Francisco during the gold rush. While American "forty-niners" rushed to the mining fields, Chinese pioneer immigrants foresaw other opportunities for making money.

Forty-niners from China were restaurateurs, tradesmen, or investors who migrated to California not to dig gold but to engage in trade. Equally eager to strike it rich, Chinese forty-niners seemed more rational, calculating, and patient in making money. Trade was their profession. As merchants, they established import and export companies, brought in commodities for daily needs, and ran restaurants, tool shops, warehouses, herbal pharmacies, grocery stores, lodging houses, and many other retail and service businesses in San Francisco. Then they sponsored and encouraged waves of immigrants from their home regions in Guangdong Province, South China, to join the gold rush, to become the pioneer agricultural laborers, and to build the Central Pacific Continental Railroad.[2] As the historian Kevin Starr put it: "No Asian group played a more important role in the establishment of the state [California] in the nineteenth century than the Chinese. Chinese were more than immigrants. They were founders."[3] Rather than a desperate escape from poverty and hunger, Chinese migration to the United States began as a transplanted social network of entrepreneurs who brought with them trade, business, and people. Collectively, early Chinese immigrants were far more stable and rooted in California than most gold rush "sojourners" who came to the state merely for gold.

Food culture was an ethnic marker. Though Chinese restaurants were one of the pioneer food businesses in San Francisco, the city had only a small number of Chinese restaurants in the last three decades of the nineteenth century, when all kinds of food and restaurant businesses were thriving there. In 1882, the year that the U.S. Congress passed its first Chinese Exclusion Act, there were only fourteen Chinese restaurants in San Francisco. In comparison, there were 175 Chinese laundries. The restaurant business was one of the oldest professions in China. Chinese cuisine was one of the best in the world. However, the Chinese food business failed to carve a big niche in the city's restaurant market.

This was not a culinary failure. Anti-Chinese sentiment reached its peak during the last three decades of the nineteenth century. Several Chinese exclusion laws were passed between 1882 and 1904. Food culture in America was also tainted by racial ideology. Chinese food tradition was stereotyped. Rice became a racial symbol of Asian inferiority; beef consumption represented white American superiority. A century-long racist image of Chinese eating rats made many white Americans suspicious of the Chinese diet. Food was used as a tool in racial ideology. Eating in a Chinese restaurant could be culturally embarrassing or socially awkward for a middle-class white family. American society judged Chinese food through racial rather than culinary criteria.

The Chinese restaurant businesses made a rebound in the form of chop suey houses after Li Hongzhang's visit to the United States in 1896. Li was China's most important diplomat during that time. While racial discrimination against the Chinese was intense, American businessmen were still keenly interested in China trade and the Chinese market. American media had daily coverage about Li's visit. When the media reported that chop suey was Li's favorite food, the American public underwent a craze for Chinese food. Chop suey became an imagined authentic Chinese dish. Chinese immigrants quickly capitalized on the legend. They changed chop suey's ingredients, flavor, and method of preparation to fit the palate of Americans. They grasped the opportunity to expand their restaurant business outside of Chinatown.

Chop suey houses soon proliferated across the country. Based on chop suey, a simple rural dish, Chinese immigrants generated a series of Americanized Chinese meals such as beef chop suey, chicken chop suey, chow mein, and egg foo yong. From 1900 to the late 1960s, chop suey houses were synonymous with Chinese restaurants in the United States. Modified Chinese food became rooted in American society and constituted an important part of the American restaurant market. However, this is not an example of Chinese "assimilation" into American society. Instead, chop suey became a tool or a strategy for Chinese immigrants to create an occupational niche for themselves during the Chinese exclusion era. It represents a creative adaptation of Chinese Americans to American society.

The popularity of chop suey houses also reflected a dynamic interaction between Chinese food and American customers. While Chinese food was being transformed, reinvented, and even altered by American popular taste, Chinese restaurant businesses at the same time helped shape the American diet. It was an interesting process of cultural negotiation. Though popular, chop suey symbolized cheap exoticism in the eyes of many American customers. It succeeded mostly as a bargain ethnic food. American customers readily accepted it as a "foreign" food made in the United States. Its success reflected mainstream Americans' social expectations of Chinese cuisine. Rather than a culinary wonder, chop suey is a meaningful social construct in racial America.

Yet chop suey houses embodied not only Chinese ethnicity but also metropolitan Americanness. A Jewish man recalled his childhood in New York in the early twentieth century: "I felt about Chinese restaurants the same way I did about the Metropolitan Museum of Art—they were the two most strange and fascinating places my parents took me to, and I loved them both."[4] By historical chance, Chinese Americans and Americans Jews shared residential proximity in New York City at the turn of the twentieth century. Both groups explored ways to adapt to American society. Through frequenting Chinese restaurants, Jewish immigrants and their descendants became more metropolitan and more adapted to American urban life. Chinese food helped them gradually break away from their religious, restrictive, and symbolic dietary rules of the Old World. For many American Jews, eating Chinese food has become a weekly routine, a

Christmas tradition, and a childhood memory. It is rare but significant that the food of one ethnic group has evolved into an expressive form of another group's identity. This meaningful episode of American ethnic history reflects how the Chinese reached out to other cultures through food and how Jewish immigrants longed for a new identity.

The Chinese restaurant business began to change after World War II following the return of the U.S. servicemen from Asia and a restaurant boom in America. But a significant new turn took place in the 1970s. After the Immigration and Nationality Act of 1965, hundreds of thousands of Chinese immigrants came to the United States from Taiwan and Hong Kong, and later mainland China. Upon their arrival, chop suey houses gradually lost their appeal. Chinese restaurants started to serve authentic Chinese food. In Chinese culinary culture, authentic food means regional cuisines. China has no national food. Different geographical areas have different food products, local flavors, and famous dishes in their culinary culture. Between eight and ten regional cuisines are best known across the country, such as Guangdong, Hunan, Sichuan, Shandong, and Shanghai. In the 1970s and 1980s, the most popular Chinese food in New York was Hunan cuisine. However, few American customers knew that those Hunan restaurants in New York, New Jersey, Washington, D.C., or other areas on the East Coast were established by immigrants from Taiwan rather than Hunan Province in southwest China.

The popularity of Hunan restaurants in Taiwan and then in America is an interesting piece of Chinese Diaspora history. After the civil war in China ended in 1949, nearly two million Nationalists and their followers fled to Taiwan. Their arrival changed the social landscape of the island. The Nationalists and their families came from a variety of geographical regions of China. For them, food evoked memories of home and specifically the culture of their home regions. As a result, Hunan, Sichuan, Shandong, Shanghai, and many other Chinese regional cuisines were reproduced based on the collective memory of those Nationalists and their families. Though there was no political contact for decades across the Taiwan Strait, thousands of restaurants featuring Chinese regional flavors appeared in Taiwan. Cultural preservation was simultaneously a process of cultural reproduction. When Hunan cuisine spread from Taiwan to the United States, it was both a Chinese regional and a Chinese Diaspora food. Embedded in Hunan restaurants is the remigration experience of post-1965 Chinese immigrants from Taiwan.

Food represents an important aspect of contemporary Chinese American culture. Instead of wholesale assimilation, post-1965 Chinese immigrants have selectively maintained some of their native cultural traditions such as food. Food expresses ethnic solidarity and cultural traditions. The restaurant is an institution where Chinese socialize and pass on food traditions to younger generations.

Food culture of contemporary Chinese Americans reflects a seemingly paradoxical adaptation strategy. It is not only possible but also increasingly preferred for many immigrants to maintain their Chinese ethnic tradition while becoming Americans. With numerous restaurants, grocery stores, and ethnic strip malls visibly congregating and rooted in the San Gabriel Valley of Southern California, the transnational and multicultural identity of Chinese Americans is no longer an abstract idea but a solid and tangible reality. In food and restaurant operation, we see how transnational culture is deeply ingrained in the contemporary Chinese American community. Moreover, the flourishing of Chinese restaurant businesses in the metropolitan areas of the United State shows how new immigrants have enriched American culinary culture and how food choices continuously expand in the American restaurant market.

With more than 40,000 Chinese restaurants across the country in the early twenty-first century, Chinese cuisine has become an important component of the American food market. But the first and so far only full-service, sit-down Chinese restaurant that is a publicly traded stock company on Nasdaq is P. F. Chang's China Bistro, which was actually established by Paul Fleming, a white American restaurateur who used to own four Ruth's Chris Steak House franchises. As a full-service, sit-down restaurant, P. F. Chang's is in the same price range as Olive Garden, California Pizza Kitchen, or the Cheese Cake Factory. It caters mainly to middle-class mainstream American customers, and seldom locates in or close to a Chinese American community. In the shadow of its success, we ponder the question of who owns culture. Culture seems hereditary or primordial and is often considered as a genetic soft power of a community or an ethnic group. In reality, culture, especially restaurant culture, is a "public domain" in which every participating agent, organization, or corporation could have access to or even own it. Chinese Americans have no controlling power or patent rights to their own food in the American restaurant market. When food becomes a commodity, it is no longer an inherited culture. Corporate America could easily appropriate it. Food is both a culture and a commodity.

If P. F. Chang's is a case of a mainstream America food business embracing authentic Chinese culinary culture, Panda Express shows how Chinese restaurateurs have integrated American fast-food concepts into their business. It is the fastest growing and the largest fast-food Chinese restaurant chain in the United States. Established in 1983 by Andrew and Peggy Cherng, an immigrant couple from Taiwan and Hong Kong, Panda Express started in Southern California, the birthplace of the American fast-food industry. McDonald's, Carl's Jr., and In-N-Out are some of the big names that can trace their origins to this area. However, running a Chinese fast-food restaurant is far more challenging than running a McDonald's or a Burger King restaurant. As one food critic put it, "Panda Express is a real innovation. Where most attempts at Chinese fast food have settled for egg rolls, rice, and chow mein, Panda Express offers orange-flavored chicken, tofu with black mushrooms, beef with broccoli, and many other dishes conceived by Chinese chefs and prepared on site by trained cooks."[5] Like P. F. Chang's, Panda Express caters mainly to non-Chinese customers. It has affected the contemporary American palate almost as much as chop suey did in the first half of the twentieth century. The rapid growth of Panda Express has made Chinese food a visible option for American customers in the fast-food restaurant market.

Today, Chinese restaurants can be found in almost every city in the world. Local restaurant customers in New York or Southern California probably have more options in choosing different regional flavors of Chinese cuisine than Chinese customers in any midsize city in China. But authenticity in Chinese food is a complex issue, as shown in Din Tai Fung, a Shanghai-style dumpling house that originated in Taiwan. This internationally renowned restaurant has stores in the United States, Japan, Australia, and Hong Kong, as well as in Shanghai, Beijing, Guangzhou, Shenzhen, and a number of other cities in mainland China. Settling down in Shanghai, the birthplace of Shanghai steamed dumplings, can Din Tai Fung claim its own products as more authentic than products of 100-year-old native stores like Longxiang Restaurant? Who represents the genuine Shanghai dumplings? As Din Tai Fung shows, food authenticity is a fluid and flexible concept. This is especially true considering how Chinese cuisine has become a global phenomenon. The culinary identity of Din Tai Fung and many Chinese restaurants in the United States is simultaneously local and national, Taiwanese and Chinese, Diaspora and transnational. It confirms Tu Weiming's conception of cultural China as both a unified and fractured entity.[6]

There are nine chapters in this book. Chapter 1, "Canton Restaurant and Chinese Forty-niners," documents how Chinese migration to the United States in the nineteenth century began as a transplanted social network of entrepreneurs who brought over settlement and livelihood to the country. Chapter 2, "Flags of Yellow Silk," describes restaurant and food operations as one of the earliest economic activities pursued by pioneer Chinese immigrants in California. Chapter 3, "Chinamen Live on Rice," analyzes why San Francisco had only a small number of Chinese restaurants in last three decades of the nineteenth century when the food and restaurant business was thriving in the city. Chapter 4, "Chop Suey in Racial America," discusses how and why Chinese restaurant businesses made a rebound in the form of chop suey houses during the Chinese exclusion era. Chapter 5, "Kung Pao Kosher," focuses on Chinese food and the formation of the identity of American Jews. Chapter 6, "General Tso's Chicken Made in Taiwan," explains how Chinese regional cuisines spread to Taiwan and then to the United States. Chapter 7, "The San Gabriel Valley as a Chinese Food Capital," discusses how transnational culture is deeply ingrained in the contemporary Chinese American community. Chapter 8, "Who Owns Culture?," examines the meaning of P. F. Chang's China Bistro as a full-service restaurant chain and Panda Express as a fast-food chain, both of which cater mainly to non-Chinese customers. Chapter 9, "Din Tai Fung's Dumplings as Diaspora Chinese Food," discusses Chinese cuisine as a global food phenomenon.

1 · CANTON RESTAURANT AND CHINESE FORTY-NINERS

MERCHANTS AS THE PIONEERS

On November 19, 1849, 300 Chinese gathered at Canton Restaurant in San Francisco. At their meeting, they selected Selim E. Woodworth, a merchant and former state senator, as their adviser and arbitrator.[1] Through Woodworth, they later purchased a large piece of land in Tuolumne County as a center for mining and agriculture.[2] A restaurant with a capacity of 300 seats was huge by any standard at that time or even today. Early California journal and newspaper articles often mentioned this gathering as the beginning of Chinese migration. Canton Restaurant was the first Chinese restaurant in North America. The 300 guests were the first Chinese arrivals from Guangdong, China, during the gold rush. Food importation and restaurant operation were among the earliest economic activities pursued by pioneer Chinese immigrants. With good service, tasteful food, and competitive prices, Chinese restaurants brought to San Francisco material comfort and a taste of urban life. Eating a Chinese meal was a great attraction that many gold rush miners did not want to miss when they came to the city.

As I searched through historical California journal articles, newspaper reports, and some travel accounts and put fragmented pieces together, significant facts emerged about the early Chinese restaurant business in California. Through food and restaurant history we gain a new understanding of Chinese migration in the nineteenth century. Pioneer Chinese restaurants in San Francisco are more than just a part of food history. They reveal many aspects of early Chinese migration that we still have not fully discovered. Restaurant business informs us about how Chinese migration began, who the first pioneer Chinese immigrants were, what their social background was, and how they participated in and contributed to American society. Many existing scholarly and journalistic writings from that time described early Chinese immigrants as illiterate peasants and greedy "sojourners" driven away by hunger, poverty, and social unrest from a poor, conservative, and backward China. While European immigrants came to seek liberty, freedom, and a new life and became settlers, Chinese immigrants were only interested in digging gold, making some quick cash, and then rushing back home. In American immigration historiography, Chinese immigrants were typically labeled as "aliens" and "sojourners" who had no intention and interest of staying in America. Chinese immigrants were "strangers from a different shore."[3]

In contrast to the stereotypes, pioneer Chinese immigrants were men of wealth and ambition. Their arrival in San Francisco signaled the beginning of Chinese migration as a transnational flow of people, commodities, and cultural traditions. Following in their footsteps, there would be steady and continuous waves of Chinese immigrants from all social classes. Many more Chinese would come to join them and engage in all kinds of economic and social activities, and make the United States their newly adopted country. With 300 seats, Canton Restaurant was anything but a transient or quick-cash business. A restaurant of this size required a reliable supply of food ingredients, an adequate cash flow to maintain its operation, and good chefs to prepare decent meals. It needed experienced managers and waiters to serve customers, as most of its customers were not necessarily Chinese. Like Chinese warehouses, grocery stores, pharmacy and herbal shops, or lodging houses, Chinese restaurant businesses were often a long-term investment by a wealthy merchant or a group of wealthy merchants exploring the food market in this emerging port city.

As the 300 guests selected an American adviser for future economic endeavors, those participants at the Canton Restaurant meeting in November 1849 were obviously not laborers but merchants who were interested in opportunities outside of China. They had capital to invest, and intended to stay and do business in California. According to the historian Elizabeth Sinn, one of the Chinese forty-niners was Norman Assing (also spelled as As-Sing, whose Chinese name is Yuan Sheng), who left Hong Kong on the *Swallow* on May 6, 1849. He was the first named Chinese passenger "among all the thousands who made that journey but who were merely referred to anonymously as passengers." Assing was a Xiangshan (it is called Zhongshan, a city in Guangdong Province today) native and grew up in Macau. He traveled to New York in 1820 and might have been naturalized as a U.S. citizen in North Carolina during his stay on the East Coast. He returned to China and then came back to the United States in 1849. He was the owner of Macau and Woosung Restaurant, another famous Chinese restaurant in San Francisco during the gold rush. While running the restaurant, he was also operating a trading company.[4] Assing was one of the first few hundreds of Chinese arrivals in San Francisco who were not here to dig gold in the mining fields but to strike it rich through trade and business.

When gold was discovered in California, soldiers of the Mexican-American War (1846–1848) deserted the battlefields for the goldfields. Sailors of all nationalities in San Francisco abandoned their ships. Two-thirds of the American men in Oregon raced southward in search of gold.[5] American forty-niners were typically young, able-bodied males who were adventurous, restless, and desperate. Many of them were not necessarily poor but were hardly settlers. The gold rush was not a migration movement that encouraged people to develop a sense of home in California. A small percentage of miners made a fortune through mere luck. But many were bitterly disappointed after months of exhaustive travel and hopeless digging in the field. William Swine, for example, left Youngstown, New York, in April 1849 and reached California by land in late November. Even before digging, Swine wrote to his brother George: "For God's sake. Think not of it. Stay at home." Digging could not make money, he concluded, only trade could. In November 1850, Swine boarded a ship in San Francisco to go back home with no cash left in his pocket. "I have got enough of California," Swine wrote to his wife, "I am coming home as fast as I can."[6] Rootless, homesick, often suffering from hunger, and surviving in a lawless social environment, many American forty-niners were eager to return home.

While forty-niners from the East Coast or other parts of the world rushed to California for a dream of quick gold, Chinese forty-niners had more practical economic goals. Being merchants in social class, they were a different kind of pioneer in California. They were interested in making money through trade rather than digging gold. James O'Meara wrote in 1884: "Among the thousand[s] of pioneers flocking to California during the Gold Rush were Chinese in San Francisco. It is enough to know that in the fall of 1849 the Chinese in San Francisco numbered several hundred. They were not laborers who came; not of the coolie class, at least. Very few of them went into the mining district."[7]

Rather than a desperate escape from poverty and hunger, Chinese migration to the United States began with a transplanted social network of entrepreneurs who could run retail and service businesses and bring over commodities for daily needs. O'Meara specifically pointed out that Chinese forty-niners were

> men of means enough to pay their own way and here they mainly embarked in mercantile and trading pursuits, in different degrees. A few were mechanics, but as these could not compete with Americans and Europeans, they dropped into other employment. While it had been not [an] infrequent thing to see Americans and foreigners of Caucasian blood working at rough jobs in carpentering, at other trades, and even digging in the banks in San Francisco, in 1849—some of these men educated to professions or accustomed to luxury—not Chinamen was seen [sic] as a common laborer. Some hired out as servants and cooks, but the number was small. Trade seemed to be their element, their ambition, their choice.[8]

In 1849, the Chinese community in San Francisco consisted mostly of merchants, traders, grocers, herbalists, warehouse owners, and, of course, restaurant operators. They came from Canton, the capital city of Guangdong Province, South China. The city was a famous international trading center long before the gold rush in California. Many Chinese forty-niners had rich experiences in the import and export trade. They had mingled with Westerners before. As merchants, they were here to develop trade and establish businesses such as boardinghouses, tool stores, herbal medical shops, or restaurants. A rapidly growing population in the mining area and San Francisco as an emerging port city probably attracted the pioneer merchant Chinese more than the gold. When other forty-niners rushed to the mining fields and focused only on digging gold, Chinese forty-niners saw other opportunities for making money. With restaurants, lodging houses, and grocery or hardware stores, they served both Chinese and non-Chinese customers. They encouraged and facilitated continuous waves of Chinese immigrants. Equally eager to strike it rich, Chinese forty-niners seemed more rational, calculating, and patient in making money. They brought with them trade, business, and laborers. They made San Francisco a better place for settlement.

The Chinese migration flow trickled from a few dozens in 1848 to a few hundred in 1849.[9] In the first three months of 1849, vessels from China never carried more than ten passengers. Then in August, sixty-two Chinese arrived. On October 15, the British ship *Amazon* disembarked 101 Chinese passengers in San Francisco.[10] Those few hundred Chinese immigrants were mostly merchants who could speak some English, had capital to establish businesses, and would function as sponsors, job brokers, potential employers, or social networks to encourage their fellow Chinese to join them in the near future. Quickly the number of Chinese immigrants jumped from a few thousand in 1851 to 20,000 in 1852.[11] In that year, ocean transportation between Hong Kong and San Francisco was significantly improved. Many ships began to carry 500 to 600 passengers. Some ships could reach San Francisco from Hong Kong in thirty-five to forty days, while others took forty-five to sixty days. Obviously, many Chinese arrivals in 1852 were labor immigrants ready to enter the mining fields. By then Chinese merchants had already established boardinghouses, grocery stores, herbal shops, restaurants, and, more important, a social and communication network to facilitate a rapidly growing migration flow from Guangdong Province to California.

Chinese forty-niners represented a general pattern of Chinese migration. Merchants tended to be the pioneer immigrants. They established businesses, and then encouraged people of lesser means or labor immigrants to join them in the new country.[12] Such a pattern sustained a momentum in migration movement, developed a sense of roots and community for later waves of immigrants, and established a social network among Chinese immigrants. Following the merchants, there were Chinese of different social classes. But they were not coolie laborers as white American labor unions labeled them in the 1870s. Elizabeth Sinn pointed out that even E. T. Bush, American consul in Hong Kong in 1851, strongly rejected the suggestion that Chinese immigrants leaving for California from Hong Kong were coolie laborers. The British governor of Hong Kong, Sir John Bowring (1854–1859), was also keen to clarify that many Chinese immigrants were merchants. They were in fact "a superior class."[13] Chinese migration to Canada, Australia, Southeast Asia, or elsewhere in the nineteenth century or earlier often followed a similar pattern.

There was a long tradition of migration and ocean travel in Guangdong and Fujian. Cantonese merchants had dealt with Westerners for centuries. It was not surprising that the Chinese merchants arrived in San Francisco shortly after gold was discovered in California in 1848. Long before the gold rush, American merchants in New England lobbied the U.S. government to acquire California for the purpose of the China trade. Trade between American merchants in New England and Chinese merchants in Canton, China, in the 1790s brought American merchants' attention to California, which was geographically a lot closer to Asia than to the East Coast.[14] Their goal was accomplished when California became a U.S. territory after the Mexican-American War. Chinese merchants in Canton were also familiar with the China trade. When gold was discovered, and more and more people rushed toward California, they saw opportunities and quickly established their commercial base in San Francisco. They knew that the city would become a significant Pacific link in the China trade.

As the historian Sandy Lydon pointed out, for Chinese immigrants, California was not the end of the continent but the nearest shore of a land stretching eastward. "Seen from our perch above Hawaii it is the European presence in California which becomes extraordinary (and even tenuous)."[15] During the migration process, some Chinese stayed in the new country while others returned home. But there were always new arrivals to join the process. Like European immigrants, many Chinese were sojourners. Going back home rich was a Jinshan ke, or a Golden Mountain, man's dream. Families left behind were waiting for their return. However, some people soon saw the new country as home away from home and wanted to stay. Many sojourners would be settlers when they became more familiar with the country and when the social and racial environment improved.

CANTON AS A METROPOLITAN CITY

Pioneer Chinese immigrants were mostly Cantonese. When gold was discovered in California, it quickly drew the attention of Cantonese merchants. As a metropolitan city in South China, Canton had been an international trading center for centuries because of the maritime trade. The Qing government established the famous "Canton System" during 1757–1842. According to this system, the imperial government designated Canton as the only port city open to foreign trade before the Opium War (1839–1842).[16] The "Thirteen Hong" merchants were the only merchants who could conduct international trade. Many American missionaries and businesspersons were working and living in Canton in the eighteenth and nineteenth centuries. Boston businessman John P. Cushing, for example, became a long-term business partner of Wu Binqian and other "Thirteen Hong" merchants. Wu was the wealthiest Hong merchant at that time. Cushing himself returned home as a wealthy merchant after living and doing business in Canton for decades.[17]

In distance, Canton was a lot closer to San Francisco and took much less time to reach than coming from New York or Boston. It was about thirty-five to forty-five days by ship from Canton or Hong Kong to San Francisco in the mid-nineteenth century. Long before gold was discovered in California, Cantonese merchants were involved in the maritime trade with Europe, South America, and Japan for silver, and with Siam, Malaya, the Philippines, and Indonesia for pepper, coconut oil, rice, brown sugar, copper, wood, and sea slugs. Compared with the maritime trade route between Acapulco, Mexico City, Philadelphia, New York, Boston, and the South Coast of China in the seventeenth and eighteenth centuries, the trip from Canton to San Francisco was a lot easier and closer.

As a metropolitan city in China, Canton was a well-known name among Westerners. Tea, silk, porcelain, and furniture as highly demanded commodities were exported overseas in large quantities from here. It was an era when average families in London spent 10 to 15 percent of their income on Chinese tea and wealthy families in North America drank more tea than coffee in elegant porcelain tea sets made in China. In the early gold rush days, there were Chinese merchants who built large tea warehouses in San Francisco and amassed "snug fortune." They were regarded by Americans as "the aristocrats of their race."[18] It was not surprising that Chinese forty-niners named their first restaurant in America after the city of Canton.

In his book about Canton, missionary doctor John G. Kerr observed that close to the Hong merchant residential and Western merchant office area, there were fruit stalls, tobacco shops, and, of course, large and fancy restaurants. Several fine teahouses with gardens were also found there.[19] In Canton, teahouses served not just tea but also all kinds of food and pastries. English clergyman John Henry Gray described teahouses in Canton as large saloons with big kitchens where cooks "remarkable for their cleanliness" were daily engaged in making all kinds of pastry. Gray also observed that restaurants in Canton were generally very large establishments, consisting of two to three stories with a public dining room for common customers and several private rooms upstairs for wealthy patrons.[20] The restaurant business was an important part of metropolitan life in Canton.

Canton was a much bigger and more prosperous city than San Francisco in the 1840s–1850s. Before the gold rush, San Francisco was a small fishing village called Yerba Buena. It became a rapidly growing port city only after hundreds of thousands of transient Americans and immigrants of other nationalities arrived.[21] Canton Restaurant appeared shortly after the gold rush began, which illustrates how Chinese merchants promptly responded to business opportunities overseas. In addition to restaurants, pioneer Chinese merchants also opened many retail shops and service businesses in San Francisco and established a foothold in California for later fellow immigrants. Many of them readily arrived due to the close sailing distance between Guangdong Province and California. Guangdong's geographical location, unique economic position, and cultural traditions explain why early Chinese immigrants in North America were mostly Cantonese.

While many disappointed American forty-niners never developed a sense of home in California and deserted it as abruptly as they hurried toward it from the East Coast, Chinese pioneers seemed to be far more persistent in pursuing business opportunities and gaining a foothold in San Francisco. During the early days of the gold rush, the city often suffered from fires. Chinese businesses, including restaurants, could be easily destroyed. According to a *Daily Alta California* report in 1850, several Chinese restaurants were burned out by a fire, but they again commenced operations after being rebuilt. "In passing down Jackson Street yesterday, we saw our celestial friend Ahi, industriously employed in putting up a spacious frame covered with blue nankeen. He was surrounded by a crew of Chinamen all working away, sawing, planning, hammering, nailing, and busying themselves in the most delightful manner, all [in] their native costume."[22] The *Daily Alta California* report provided a concrete and vivid example to show the confidence of Chinese pioneer immigrants in operating service businesses in San Francisco. In the nineteenth century, fires were common in San Francisco because the city did not have fire stations. Rebuilding businesses from fire damage could be a challenging job. Chinese proprietors' "delightful manner" in rebuilding their restaurants after a fire showed their eagerness to continue the business and their confidence in the restaurant market in this emerging city. Due to the geographical proximity, they had no problem getting regular supplies of all kinds of food commodities and ingredients, restaurant furniture, equipment, or dinnerware. They could bring in building materials, tools, and laborers from Canton and Hong Kong if they needed to rebuild their business or develop new ones. They made the city a comfortable place for the miners to rest and relax. Chinese immigrants liked San Francisco. It was their major North American link to home, a gateway to other parts of the United States, and certainly a steppingstone to many business opportunities. Calling San Francisco "Da Bu" (Big Port City), the Chinese made it their first North American home base.

ADAPTATION TO AMERICAN SOCIETY

Among the early Chinese restaurateurs, Norman Assing (Yuan Sheng) was probably the most famous. He was the owner of Macao and Woosung Restaurant on the corner of Kearney and Commercial Streets, about a block from Portsmouth Plaza. As Elizabeth Sinn documented, Assing was a forty-niner. While running a restaurant, he also operated a trading company.[23] Books and journal articles on early Chinese immigrants often mentioned his name or carried anecdotes about him.[24] The *Daily Alta California* once mentioned that Assing caught a thief in his house, chained him all night, and then brought him to the police station the next day. Consequently, he himself was arrested by the police for taking the law into his own hands.[25]

But Assing learned fast from his American experience. As a restaurant businessman, Assing used food to develop friendship with white Americans. He frequently gave banquets to entertain local politicians and policemen at his Macao and Woosung Restaurant.[26] In fact, interaction and socializing between early Chinese immigrants and white Americans was common. As Asian American studies scholar Xiao-huang Yin documented, Chinese merchants like Assing often dined with local civil leaders, and donated money to local schools, fire companies, police, or public charities in order to develop and improve their relationship with mainstream American society.[27] They were very adaptable people in the new environment. According to O'Meara, "The recognized chief of the Chinese was old Norman As-Sing, a sallow, dried, cadaverous, but active and keen old fellow, who kept a Chinese cake and confectionery shop on Kearny Street, just south of Clay, across from the old City Hotel adobe, and there became rich. . . . His dress was a singular mixture of the Chinese and American." Though Assing maintained his queue, he covered it with a cap. In fact, many other Chinese did the same thing. "He was quick to prove to the Americans his love for their land and themselves—he said nothing of their gold; it was not necessary that he should refer to it."[28] Based on O'Meara's description, Assing often mingled with Americans and understood well the newly arrived white Americans' mentality. They took for granted that California was their land and digging gold was their exclusive right. That was probably why Assing did not appear interested in "their" gold, but did express his love for "their" country.

However, as a pioneer Chinese merchant immigrant, Norman Assing knew his rights and often claimed to be an American citizen, naturalized in Charleston, South Carolina, and converted to Christianity.[29] Assing was not the only Chinese who understood the importance of U.S. citizenship. In late 1854, a Chinese named Chan Yong applied for American citizenship, but his application was denied by the federal district court in San Francisco.[30] Yung Wing (Rong Hong), the first Chinese student at Yale, probably obtained his citizenship as early as 1852. Wong Chin Foo (Wang Qingfu), a prolific activist-writer on the East Coast, applied and received his U.S. citizenship in 1874. According to Sucheng Chan, at least fifteen Chinese immigrants in New York applied and obtained citizenship since petitions for naturalization during the 1870s were reviewed by local courts. Several dozens of other Chinese in California may have also become citizens before 1878, when the U.S. circuit court in California declared Chinese ineligible for citizenship.[31]

Due to American missionary influence in China, some of the Chinese merchants had already adapted to Western culture. Tong K. Achick, another respected Chinese merchant, was a graduate from the famous Morrison School founded by British missionaries in Macao, had become a Christian, and picked up the English language there. Following the example of Assing and Achick, many Chinese immigrants were taking English-language lessons in the evening at Christian churches after they arrived in America. As early as 1852, there were a few Chinese who boldly cut off their queues and grew their hair in the Western style.[32] In 1855, a tea merchant, Ah The (Ya Ti), and his fiancée, Say Sung (Song Si), were married by Judge O'Bailey, which was the first Chinese wedding in San Francisco.[33] Meanwhile, many Chinese began to adopt American lifestyles and did not necessarily eat only in Chinese restaurants. A. W. Loomis observed in 1868: "California Chinese are frequently seen calling for the cup of coffee and cigar, . . . instead of the tea cup and the long pipe with the mild Chinese tobacco."[34] There were many examples of how Chinese immigrants learned and adopted Western ideas and ways of life shortly after they arrived in America.

Ever since their arrival, Chinese merchants like Assing demonstrated their interest in and commitment to American society. They actively organized the Chinese community to become involved in the social life of San Francisco. On October 29, 1850, they participated in the grand parade to celebrate California becoming a state. Immediately following the Guard of Honor and the veteran soldiers were thirty "China Boys" dressed in white shirts and blue pants, and representing the thirty American states. On February 1, 1851, they held their first Lunar New Year party and invited many Western guests. Two years later, they held a grand Lunar New Year celebration to entertain the entire city. On February 23, 1852, when the city celebrated George Washington's birthday, 200 Chinese joined the parade and marched in colorful costumes. They performed lion dances and Chinese music through the march. In the evening, they enlivened the city with their first firecrackers in America.[35] Significantly, they accepted and embraced those American national and public traditions not as individuals but as a community. Contrary to the stereotypes, Chinese immigrants were very adaptable people. Their different cultural background did not prevent them from fitting into American society.

Meanwhile, Chinese merchants did not hesitate to go to Sacramento, to meet with and voice their protest to Governor John Bigler in person about his racist remarks against the Chinese.[36] For example, when Bigler made a speech that called the Chinese "coolie laborers" who should be excluded, they responded quickly with a letter of protest. As a community leader, Assing joined other prominent Chinese in resisting prejudice and racial discrimination against the Chinese. In the letter, Norman Assing, Hab Wa, and Tong Achick pointed out that many Chinese were educated, wealthy, and open-minded people. Compared with the Chinese, working-class Irish immigrants could be considered as "coolies" in China. They claimed in the letter: "If the privileges of your laws are open to us, some of us will, doubtless, acquire your habits, your language, your ideas, your feelings, your morals, your form, and become citizens of your country."[37] Written in smooth English, in an eloquent and dignified tone, and published in the mainstream newspapers, the letter again informed us about what kind of people these early Chinese merchants were. Though they still wore their Manchu queue under their Western or Mandarin hat, they were receptive to Western ideas, adaptable to modern culture, and willing to learn and speak English. They may still have maintained some of the core Chinese values such as ancestor worship or food habits, but they would not hesitate to become U.S. citizens. Their point was quite clear: American society was not fair; U.S. laws did not allow them to become citizens; the hostile racial environment prevented Chinese immigrants from becoming full participants in American civil society.[38]

Early Chinese immigrants were not a transient people. They formed a vigorous community full of social activities and cultural traditions. While learning and adopting American values and customs, the Chinese continued to practice some of their own and quickly established a growing and stabilized transnational community. On October 18, 1852, the first Cantonese opera troupe, Hong Fook Tong (Hong fu tang), with 130 people, arrived and performed in a Western theater in San Francisco. The tickets, ranging from $1.00 to $6.00, quickly sold out. On December 23, 1852, the first Chinese theater, with a 1,000-seat capacity and colorful decorations, opened on Dupont Street. The Hong Fook Tong performed their last Cantonese opera there on March 23, 1853.[39] Also in 1852, the first Chinese joss house was built, where religious immigrants could pray. In 1854, the first Chinese-language newspaper was published. Being a transplanted immigrant community, the Chinese were not rootless. Their cultural traditions and social networks bonded them together, gave them a collective identity, and also helped them develop a sense of home in the new country.

2 · FLAGS OF YELLOW SILK

FLAGS OF YELLOW SILK

American food historians generally regard Ritz Old Poodle Do and Tadich Grill, established in 1849 and 1850, respectively, as the oldest restaurants in San Francisco. However, several Chinese restaurants appeared at the same time. In their book *Eating in America*, Waverly Root and Richard de Rochemont wrote: "It was also at this time and place that the American Chinese restaurant got its start."[1] Though they mentioned the Chinese only briefly, they at least acknowledged that Chinese restaurants were part of the earliest culinary businesses in San Francisco.

Canton Restaurant was not the only Chinese restaurant in San Francisco in the early days of the gold rush. By 1850, there were at least four Chinese restaurants on Pacific, Jackson, and Washington Streets.[2] In 1851, there were seven of them in the city. Besides Canton Restaurant, there were also Tong Ling's on Jackson Street, Kong Sing's on Montgomery Street, Wang Tong's on Sacramento Street, Wo Hi's on Kearney Street, Macao and Woosung Restaurant at the corner of Kearny and Commercial Streets, and another restaurant on Pacific Street.[3] Among them, Canton Restaurant and Macao and Woosung Restaurant were named after Chinese cities.

Both Macao and Canton were Chinese cities where Westerners arrived and lived long before the gold rush. Bordering Guangdong Province to its north, Macao had been a Portuguese enclave since the sixteenth century. In the early nineteenth century, many British and American missionaries arrived in Macao first. Then they entered Canton and other places of China. Canton, as mentioned earlier, had been an international trading center for centuries. Woosung was a river town and a port guarding the entry of the city of Shanghai. During the Opium War, the British navy captured Woosung and occupied Shanghai for a short time. Using such city names, the owners of Canton Restaurant and Macao and Woosung Restaurant attempted to attract non-Chinese customers.

Like other local businesses, Chinese restaurants were housed in wooden structures, painted white with green trim. But Chinese restaurateurs used flags of yellow silk as their own commercial identity to get the attention of American customers. Bayard Taylor, a reporter for the *New York Tribune*, wrote that on Dupont Street, together with French, German, Peruvian, and Italian restaurants, there were "three Chinese houses, denoted by their long three-cornered flags of yellow silk. The latter are much frequented by Americans on account of their regard to quantity. Kong-Sung's house is near the water, Whang-Tong's on Sacramento Street, and Tong-ling's on Jackson Street."[4] He also pointed out that the Chinese also owned one of the four hotels at that time. They summoned the customers by the sound of their gongs.[5] Chinese restaurants almost unanimously displayed three-cornered flags of yellow silk outside of their business. Some also added Chinese calligraphy.

Early Chinese restaurateurs may have gotten the flag idea from Westerners in China. In Canton, European and American business office buildings and warehouses often flew national flags. The Norwegian flag was yellow. The British flag was designed like the Chinese word "rice." The American flag had many stars on it. In the nineteenth century, Cantonese and later Chinese in other places usually referred to the United States as a "flower flag country." Flying the national flag was a symbol of nationalism in the West and reflected the imperialist idea that "trade follows the flag." However, the triangular flag of yellow silk was not a Chinese national flag but just a cultural symbol. Yellow silk was a forbidden fabric in feudal Chinese society, especially during the Qing Dynasty (1644–1911). When made into a robe, a jacket, or a vest, this color and material represented a sign of authority and privilege. It was reserved for the emperors, royal families, or a few trusted and respectful high-ranking government officials. In China, yellow silk was rarely used as a commercial sign for a restaurant or any other business. But there was no such restriction overseas. Using it as their commercial icon, early Chinese restaurateurs developed a sense of collective identity. In their eyes, yellow silk was probably more symbolic than anything else of Chinese culture.

In terms of location, pioneer Chinese restaurants were not far away from each other. In his comprehensive study of the early Chinese community in San Francisco, the historian Yong Chen pointed out that Chinese businesses clustered mainly on the two blocks between Kearny and Stockton Streets and Sacramento and Jackson Streets during the mid-1850s. A China quarter was emerging there.[6] In February 1856, the *Oriental* listed five new restaurants—Ping Heung Low on Dupont, east side near Sacramento; Yuen Chan on Dupont, east side corner of Commercial; Me Heung Low on Dupont, west side near Washington; Tsu Chan on Dupont, east side near Washington; and Tsuen Chan on Jackson, north side near Dupont.[7] When the Chinese restaurants stayed close to each other, they formed a visible Chinese dining area that could be recognized by local residents and gold rush customers from the mining fields. At that time, the formation of a China quarter was not driven by racial discrimination but developed for business purposes. The congregation reflected the restaurateurs' business strategy.

Chinese restaurants attracted customers not only by their flags but also by offering good food and better prices than other restaurants. Tsing Tsing Lee established the Balcony of Golden Joy and Delight, a restaurant even bigger than Canton Restaurant that could seat as many as 400 customers. For a dollar, customers could eat anything they liked and whatever they wanted. This restaurant sold meal tickets at $20 for twenty-one tickets. As Joseph R. Conlin pointed out, "Chinese eating houses displayed triangular yellow silk flags and offered 'all you can eat' meals at a fixed price and this attracted western miners when their funds were low."[8]

THE BEST EATING HOUSE

William Shaw, a miner in the gold rush, recalled in 1851: "The best eating houses in San Francisco are those kept by Celestials and conducted in Chinese fashion. . . . The dishes are mostly curries, hashes, and fricassees served up in small dishes and as they are exceedingly palatable I was not curious enough to enquire as to the ingredients."[9] "Chow-chow, curry, or tarts" were what American customers remembered about Chinese food. There is no record of the content of the chow-chow or curry dishes. Those "curries, hashes, or fricassees" could be dishes such as chopped beef or pork boiled on a slow fire, or sliced meats and vegetables quickly stir-fried from a wok. Though they may not know exactly what they ate, most American customers liked Chinese food and spoke highly of Chinese restaurants, especially when they compared them with American ones. James Ayers's memoirs of the gold rush emphatically stated that "the best restaurants—at least that was my experience—were kept by Chinese and the poorest and dearest by Americans."[10]

The restaurant business did not have a long history in the United States. Generally speaking, restaurant service in America was rudimentary in the first half of the nineteenth century. Some hotels or lodging houses provided food, and many hotel guests just came for meals. Usually all the guests ate at one long, common table.[11] There was no menu or service. Guests grabbed food put down on the table on a first-come first-served basis. If they were late, they could miss their meals but still get charged. Some hotels used a gong to wake up guests in the morning for breakfast time.[12] Most Anglo-Saxon Americans did not have much interest and experience in running a restaurant business. Home-cooked meals at a well-to-do American home were usually better than meals in a restaurant.

In comparison, the restaurant business had a long history in China. Early Chinese merchant immigrants were familiar with restaurant operation and knew how to deal with Western customers. When restaurant meals were rare and out-rageously expensive in San Francisco during the early gold rush days, Chinese restaurateurs quickly grabbed the opportunity and established their food busi-nesses there. Canton Restaurant, Macao and Woosung Restaurant, and the other Chinese restaurants were larger in scale and more professional in operation than their Western counterparts at that time. The food, service, and prices in Chinese restaurants often impressed American customers.

In mid-1849, William Redmond Ryan, a British immigrant in San Francisco, observed that among the various immigrants flocking into the city, there were numerous Chinese who came with all kinds of merchandize and prefabricated houses. "The houses they brought with them from China, and which they set up where they were wanted, were infinitely superior and more substantial than those erected by the Yankees." According to his description, "Houses that cost $300, sell readily for $3,000; and the demand is constantly increasing. At least 75 houses have been imported from Canton, and put up by Chinese carpenters; and all chairs in private families are of Chinese manufacture." Ryan also wrote about Canton Restaurant:

> I once went into an eating house kept by one of these people, and was astonished at the neat arrangement and cleanliness of the place, the excellence of the table, and moderate charges. The Chinese venture was styled the "Canton Restaurant," and so thoroughly Chinese was it in its appointments and in the manner of ser-vice, that one might easily have fancied one's-self in the heart of the Celestial empire. The bar-keeper—though he spoke excellent English—was Chinese, as well all the attendants. Every item that was sold, even the most trifling kind, was set down, in Chinese characters, as it was disposed of; it being the duty of one of the waiters to attend to this . . . [which] he did very cleverly and quickly.[13]

Ryan was obviously amazed at the comfort and well-prepared food provided by Canton Restaurant.

In Ryan's description, the bar keepers and waiters of Canton Restaurant per-formed like well-trained staff of a contemporary upscale restaurant or four-star hotel who could take care of every single detail in their service. Chinese restau-rants in China had no bars. Whether customers ordered wine, liquor, or food, they consumed it at a dining table. Canton Restaurant provided a bar, apparently to target American and European customers. Being a widely traveled person, Ryan was deeply impressed by the savvy business skills of Chinese waiters. In his opinion, this Chinese restaurant looked trendy, elegant, and much more refined than other restaurants in San Francisco. Its nice eating environment made Amer-ican customers feel as if they were living in a metropolitan city in China. He complimented the good service and cleanness of Canton Restaurant as typically

Chinese and seemed to think that Chinese restaurants in general were higher in standard compared with their American counterparts.

In addition to Canton Restaurant, William Ryan also mentioned two other Chinese restaurants in San Francisco. One was kept by Kang-sung and the other by Want-tong. Ryan emphasized that both of them offered "very palatable chow-chow, curry, and tarts."[14] By the 1850s, American miners "ventured into Chinese kitchens willing to try something other than fried eggs and beans. Many viewed Chinese 'Hangtown' fry (a relative of what we know today as Egg Foo Yung) as a cheap alternative to American meals, dished up by Chinese cooks."[15] Digging gold was a rough life. When visiting San Francisco from mining areas, many gold rush miners wanted to eat in Chinese restaurants. It was one of the few city luxuries they would not want to miss during their stay in San Francisco. Most Anglo-American miners' immediate reaction to Chinese food was that it was good and more palatable than Western food. Some of them had probably never seen such nice food and sophisticated service before. Charles Plummer, a miner, wrote to his father in New England in 1851: "Those who come here now Know nothing of 'life in California' as we found it, for now the country not only abounds in the comforts of life but many of the luxuries are among us. Of the contributors of the latter, the Chinese are at the head. There are many of them here, and they are very good citizens."[16]

As California had just become a state in 1850, Plummer took for granted that the Chinese were citizens because they were the pioneers during the gold rush and founders of San Francisco as an emerging metropolitan city. Ryan used similar term to describe them. He wrote: "The Chinese had all the air of men likely to prove good citizens, being quiet, inoffensive, and particularly industrious."[17] Both Plummer and Ryan viewed the Chinese as valuable members of American society and appreciated that they brought civilized life to the frontier miners. Chinese commodities such as furniture, semifabricated houses, stores, lodging houses, and restaurants made San Francisco a great place to live. But the Chinese could not automatically become U.S. citizens when California joined the Union. U.S. naturalization acts, first passed in the 1790s, only granted citizenship to "free, white men."

CROSS-CULTURAL FOOD PRACTITIONERS

In food and restaurant operation, Chinese immigrants were cross-cultural practitioners. Big or small, fancy or down-to-earth, Chinese restaurants served all customers. Some Chinese restaurants provided both Chinese and Western food. Many Cantonese had seen Westerners before. A few of them had probably worked as servants or chefs for British and American businessmen and missionaries in Canton. Once in California, Chinese restaurant operators quickly learned how to cook English dishes such as mutton chops or grilled steak, and how to make coffee for white American customers. Bayard Taylor wrote: "the grave celestials serve up their chow-chow and curry, besides many genuine English dishes; their tea and coffee cannot be surpassed."[18] In food operation, Chinese immigrants seemed more adaptable than any other groups in adapting to American society.

The food historian Donna Gabbacia pointed out: "Beginning with the Gold Rush, the Chinese of San Francisco had gained considerable cross-cultural experience serving up all manner of 'English' dishes in cheap restaurants and cafes for miners. Later, Chinese chefs often managed the kitchens of prestigious San Francisco French restaurants as well. They also busied themselves trying to sell Americans variations of their own homeland dishes."[19] In general, Chinese immigrants were more familiar with Western culture compared to what Westerners knew about Chinese culture. There were, for example, Chinese chefs working for wealthy American families and Chinese cooks for American restaurants and white laborer camps.

Whether as restaurateurs, chefs, family cooks, or other specialists, early Chinese immigrants were professional in their food operation and cooking, adaptable in social manners, and experienced enough to serve all kinds of customers. Some Chinese restaurants provided "beefsteak," "hash," and boiled potatoes, which were typical food of Anglo-Americans. Chinese restaurants provided knives, forks, and spoons. Coming from a city where British and Americans had lived and worked for years, Chinese restaurateurs and cooks were familiar with Western food habits. They were pioneers in cross-cultural business practices.

During the early gold rush days, food was expensive. According to Alexander McLeod, bean soup could cost $1.50; sauerkraut, $1.00; hash of low grade, $2.00; hash, $2.50; beef of Mexican prime cut, $1.50; beef with one potato, $1.25; plain baked beans, 75 cents; greased beans, $1.00; drinks, coffee, or tea, $1.00.[20] Chinese restaurants were competitive in price because Chinese supplies from Guangdong arrived in California readily following the immigrants. Among many other good things, William Ryan noticed the "moderate charges" of Canton Restaurant in his description. Eldorado Taylor wrote that the Chinese restaurants were "much frequented by Americans" on account of their excellent cookery and prices.

In comparing prices, James O'Meara also wrote: "While one could consume a square meal for 1 dollar at a Chinese restaurant, other establishments would charge 1–2 dollars per dish often costing up to 5 dollars per dinner. It was also cheaper to board in Chinese restaurants; 16 dollars per week vs. 20–30 dollars per week elsewhere."[21] As everyone was busy digging gold, and farming in California did not develop until after the 1860s, food prices were high. With their wide trade networks and sophisticated business skills, and the relatively short geographical distance between San Francisco and Canton, early Chinese merchant immigrants regularly imported food commodities from China, which enabled their restaurant businesses to be operated at a low cost. J. H. Bates, in his travel notes about California, observed that Chinese imported most of their own food from China.[22]

During the gold rush era, Chinese and non-Chinese clients used the same menu and consumed the same kind of food prepared by Cantonese chefs in Chinese restaurants. Occasionally some American customers would even try expensive Chinese dishes such as bird's nest or sea cucumbers. In 1853, the Chinese merchant Key Chong hosted a dinner at Hong Far Low for some American journalists. The menu included bird's nest, sea cucumbers, and mushrooms that cost $3 a pound. "The whites in attendance were often flummoxed as to what they were eating." But they liked most of the dishes they tasted. In 1857, four white Americans spent $42, an astronomical sum for post–gold rush San Francisco, on a sumptuous and memorable Chinese dinner that included sea fish maws, sea cucumbers, crab balls, ducks' hearts, and many other delicacies.[23] The dinner could be seen as a bold culinary adventure taken out of curiosity for them or their belief that Chinese delicacies were worthy of their money. For whatever reason, what they consumed seemed tasteful to them, as there were no complaints after this costly dinner. The Chinese did not have to change the method of cooking and ingredients of their dishes to fit Americans' tastes. All Chinese dishes were genuine Cantonese food as it was cooked in China. There was, at that time, no Americanized Chinese food such as chop suey.

In most circumstances, American customers were not familiar with Chinese food but accepted Chinese restaurant food with ease. Both Ryan and Shaw, for example, found Chinese food "exceedingly palatable." Though American miners did not know the names of Chinese dishes, they were happy with the service, prices, and quantity of food at Chinese restaurants. Most of them did not care what the ingredients were or how Chinese meals were prepared. James O'Meara observed: "Just what it was the guests at the Chinamen's restaurants ate was always a sort of Dundreary puzzle. The beefsteak was certainly cheap and 'bully,' for it would cost more than the whole meal at another restaurants. Hash was indeed a venture in the dark. . . . But there were two dishes in which they excelled, rice and potatoes; although the desire for the former was rather subdued by the pronunciation of the celestial waiter."[24]

As southerners in China, Cantonese immigrants pronounced "rice" as "lice." American customers understood it and had no problem ordering Chinese food. A Chinese meal usually consisted of staple food (*fan*) and supplementary dishes (*cai*). Rice was often a staple food for southern Chinese, while a potato could be *fan* or *cai* depending on how it was cooked. If Chinese restaurants boiled it and served it with some salt, it was a staple food. If Chinese cooks sliced potatoes thin like French fries and stir-fried them with chopped meats, the potatoes were cooked as a dish in a Chinese way. O'Meara referred to it as a dish. It was probably the case. Stir-fried potato was a common dish in many areas in China.

CHINESE OPERATIONAL SKILL

Early Chinese restaurateurs functioned smoothly in the international atmosphere in California. The efficient management seen in the Chinese restaurant businesses both puzzled and impressed their American customers. James O'Meara wrote: "It was a strange scene that presented itself in those restaurants. Quick, though imperfect in catching in the pronunciation of the order given, the Chinese waiters would repeat, parrot-like, whatever the call might be. The freak of the waggish miner who would order 'roast elephant on half shell,' would be sounded in his presence, so that no mistake should be made, 'roas' tellephun hap sell,' were shouted, 'collid mock-sup,' in sober earnest, in the best 'pigeon English' the attendant could command."[25] American forty-niners often referred to their gold rush experience as "seeing the elephant." Here O'Meara may have merely been describing a miner's ordering of roast beef or pork. The Chinese waiter had no problem understanding it and repeated it aloud in his Cantonese pidgin English.

Alexander McLeod made similar observations on the English-language ability of Chinese waiters. He wrote: "Chinese waiters were quick, though imperfect in catching the pronunciation of the English words spoken in giving your order. They repeated the order to the cooks in the kitchen, who would unscramble the Chinese-English. Errors were seldom made in the orders. . . . Whenever the Chinaman mixed with the American, he soon picked up sufficient English to understand what was wanted, and soon the china boys in the restaurants were able to hold their own with the rough miners."[26] McLeod was not a sympathetic writer when he described Chinese immigrants. But he at least acknowledged that early Chinese immigrants quickly picked up some English and could smoothly serve all kinds of American customers, including the rough miners. They were socially adaptable in California.

In O'Meara's observation, Chinese waiters, when taking an order, would repeat it aloud so that no mistakes would be made and potential conflicts between customers and the restaurants could be avoided. They actually did so because that was a routine practice in restaurant operation in China. Cantonese restaurateurs simply brought over the practice, and the waiters followed it, except using English. Restaurant businesses existed in Chinese society for centuries, and restaurant operation skills followed Chinese immigrants to America. In his account of a big restaurant in the thirteenth century in Hangzhou in East China, Jacques Gernet wrote:

Hundreds of orders are given on all sides; this person wants something hot, another something cold, a third something tepid, a fourth something chilled. . . . The orders, given in a loud voice, are all different, sometimes three different ones at the same table. Having received the orders, the waiter goes to the kitchen and sings out the whole list of orders, starting with the first one. The man who replies from the kitchen is called the Head Dishwarmer, or the Table-setter. When the waiter has come to the end of his list, he takes his tray to the stove and then goes off to serve each customer with the dish ordered. He never mixes them up, and if by any unlikely chance he should make a mistake, the proprietor will launch into a volley of oaths addressed to the offending waiter, will straightaway make him stop serving, and may even dismiss him altogether.[27]

Gernet's account described Chinese restaurant operations in the Song Dynasty (960–1279). This had been standard practice in Chinese restaurants for hundreds of years. Such professionalism or operation skill could be seen in many restaurants in Chinese cities. Naturally, it also followed the Cantonese immigrants when they opened restaurant businesses in America.

FOOD CULTURE FOLLOWING THE CHINESE

As more and more Chinese went to the mining areas, some Chinese proprietors followed the immigrant miners and established restaurants wherever the Chinese mining population was significant. Outside of San Francisco, a historical account of Tuolumne County in California recorded that a Chinese man named Ah Chi opened a restaurant in Sonora around July 1850.[28] The first documented Chinese businesses in the Chinese quarter in Stockton "were two restaurants on the waterfront catering to both the white and Chinese trade" in 1851.[29] Initially, some Chinese mining immigrants carried food themselves. As their number increased, merchants began to establish grocery stores, herbal shops, and restaurants. Such businesses served both white and Chinese customers. Chinese camps or quarters in the mining areas always had those three retail businesses. As Mary Coolidge pointed out, the Chinese "were highly valued as general laborers, carpenters, and cooks; the restaurants established by them in San Francisco and in the mines were well kept and extensively patronized."[30] Chinese restaurants in the mining areas may not have looked as fancy as Canton Restaurant, but most camping areas with Chinese immigrants had Chinese restaurants. They were flexible mobile eateries that followed the miner customers.

Chinese miners either ate in Chinese restaurants or bought food products from Chinese grocery stores and cooked their own meals. Chinese food habits and culture allowed them to easily survive in the mining areas. They could eat boiled rice or dried noodles as their staple food with cooked vegetables, salted fish, or meat as dishes. Such meals were easier to cook than baking a loaf of bread or roasting a chunk of beef. Tea and herbal medicines could also keep them healthy.

In order to meet the needs of Chinese restaurants and the growing Chinese immigrant population, the importation of food commodities obviously began as soon as Chinese forty-niners arrived. By the 1860s, Chinese were paying $500,000 duty on imported goods such as sauces and dried oysters.[31] As Elizabeth Sinn documented, exported commodities from Hong Kong to California in 1849 included only 690 piculs of rice but 536 cases of brandy, 190 cases of gin, 510 cases of wine, and 2,827 piculs of sugar. (Picul in Chinese is "dan 担 or 石." One picul is equal to 60 kilograms.) Such commodities obviously served the needs of non-Chinese communities.[32] As the Chinese immigrant population was rapidly growing, they began to import even more commodities. In 1852, Jardine, a trading company in Hong Kong, delivered 13,333 bags of rice and 837 packages of tea to San Francisco.[33] An even more obvious commodity was opium from Hong Kong, which began to arrive in San Francisco in 1853.[34] According to Robert Spier, imported items from China in 1852 included many traditional Chinese food products such as rice, dried oysters, shrimp, cuttlefish, mushrooms, dried green vegetables and been curd, bamboo shoots, sausages, sweetmeats, duck liver and kidneys, water chestnut flour, and many other items.[35] The most important food product was probably rice, which was continuously imported from Hong Kong or Canton to California until the early twentieth century.[36] While rice was a major staple food in the South, flour was its counterpart in the North. Chinese dishes could include all kinds of vegetables cooked with or without meats. Rice and other Chinese food products arrived in San Francisco in "sacks, earthen jars, glass bottles, and woven baskets" and were sufficiently delivered to the mining areas in their original containers.[37] Chinese dietary habits followed the immigrants.

Chinese restaurants did use some fresh meats and vegetables from local suppliers. Farming was an important occupation for Chinese immigrants. Coming from Guangdong, a southern province where people grew many kinds of vegetables and fruits, Chinese immigrants brought with them some plants from China and also learned how to grow many of the local plants. As early as the 1850s, some Chinese immigrants began to grow potatoes, sweet potatoes, wheat, rice, and many kinds of vegetables and fruit trees, and started raising hogs and poultry for food supplies in the mining area. According to Sucheng Chan, there were twenty-three Chinese pig-raisers in Calaveras County in 1860, and they slaughtered $42,650 worth of pigs in 1859–60.[38] "In 1870, San Francisco had over a hundred Chinese truck gardeners; by 1880 Chinese truck gardeners were also prominent in Los Angeles and in the upper Sacramento Valley."[39] By then, Chinese truck gardeners supplied food products to both Chinese and American communities at large. "Truck gardening and vegetable peddling not only were the two agricultural roles Chinese immigrants took up earliest, but were also the ones in which they have remained the longest."[40] When the famous Polish writer Henryk Sienkiewicz traveled in California from 1876 to 1878, he observed how the Chinese were dominant in truck gardening and sales. He wrote that "all the fruits and vegetables, raspberries and strawberries, under the care of the Chinese gardeners grow to a fabulous size. I have seen strawberries as large as small pears, heads of cabbage four times the size of Europeans heads and pumpkins the size of our wash tub. . . . Yet the whole of San Francisco lives on the fruits and vegetables bought from the Chinese."[41]

In the area surrounding San Francisco, the Chinese were also pioneers in developing shrimp and fish drying businesses in San Rafael, San Bruno, and San Mateo. They introduced the use of funnel-shaped traps for shrimping and fishing. At first, their market was their own countrymen and women in California and China. Once established, they also delivered fresh bay shrimp to San Francisco restaurants. In 1880, half of all California fishermen were Chinese.[42] There is a large body of evidence that indicates the Chinese community became rooted in California shortly after they arrived.

Like any immigrant group, some Chinese returned home while others stayed. But collectively, Chinese immigrants were far more stable in California than most gold rush "sojourners" who came to California merely for gold. Their restaurants, herbal pharmacies, grocery stores, lodging houses, and many other businesses became a visible part of the American West Coast social landscape. As the historian Kevin Starr put it: "No Asian group played a more important role in the establishment of the state in the nineteenth century than the Chinese. Chinese were more than immigrants. They were founders."[43] The pioneer Chinese immigrants brought with them capital, vision, business experience, and social networks. They arrived with their own cultural traditions. But they were willing to learn from others and indeed adopted many American ways of life. They were open-minded, sociable, and outward-looking people.

The legacy of the early Chinese restaurant business in America cannot be measured simply in terms of the number of Chinese restaurants. Rather, it rests on the lasting impact and influence it had as a part of the Chinese American experience and in shaping the history of the state of California. In 1853, the Chinese merchant Key Chong hosted a dinner at Hong Far Low at 713 Grant Avenue to entertain some curious American journalists. The restaurant was later moved to 723 Grant Avenue. This legendary Chinese restaurant lasted in San Francisco until 1960.[44] It is unfortunate that the intense racial discrimination against the Chinese in the last three decades of the nineteenth century prevented greater Chinese migration to the United States and limited the spread and growth of Chinese food culture in California and other parts of the United States.

3 · "CHINAMEN LIVE ON RICE"

A CHINESE FEAST

On August 17, 1865, thirty elite Chinese merchants of San Francisco held a grand banquet at the Hang Heong Restaurant at 308 Dupont Street for thirty-five local American merchants. Attending were also four special guests from the East Coast: Schuyler Colfax, congressman from Indiana and Speaker of the House; William Bross, the lieutenant governor of Illinois; and Samuel Bowles and Albert Richardson, two noted newspapermen. The banquet began at 6:00 p.m. shortly after Chinese Six Companies' leaders greeted their American guests. The feast served more than 325 dishes including sharks' fins, stewed mutton, roast duck, rice soup, rice with duck eggs, pickled cucumbers, bamboo soup, bird's nest soup, stewed seaweed, stewed mushrooms, fried fungus, reindeer, scorpion eggs, watermelon seeds, fish in scores of varieties, many kinds of cake, and fruits ad infinitum.[1] While feeding their American guests with almost an unlimited list of dishes, Chinese merchants socialized with them in fluent English.

In early California journals and newspapers, reports on Chinese food habits were not rare. But most descriptions of Chinese food were impressionistic in nature and often biased in tone. Readers could hardly tell what exactly Chinese ate. The above account was much more specific than "curries, hashes and fricassees chow-chow, curry, and tarts." It at least gives us an idea of what a Chinese banquet looked like or what a fine Chinese restaurant in San Francisco could serve in a feast at that time. For many centuries, ordinary people in China ate better than ordinary people in England. Chinese elites ate a lot better than British elites.[2] Confucius (551–479 b.c.) was a scholar as well as a gourmet. His attitude and philosophy on food are still valued by the Chinese today. Even Robert Fortune (1812–1880), a nineteenth-century British merchant who was very prejudiced against Chinese culture, acknowledged that "the poorest classes in China seem to understand the art of preparing their food much better than the same classes at home."[3] China had developed a rich and sophisticated food culture long before Cantonese immigrants arrived in San Francisco during the gold rush.

Cantonese immigrants referred to themselves as Tang people because their ancestors migrated from North China to South China during the Tang Dynasty (618–907). By then, Chinese people had been familiar with many types of grain crops, vegetables, and meats. Steaming, boiling, roasting, stir-frying, and broiling were common cooking methods. Spices and spice ingredients included salt, wine, vinegar, green onion, onion, ginger, and many others. Boiled millet, baked flour cakes, noodles, boiled rice, rice porridge, steamed bread, or boiled dumplings were popular food items in a family meal. Meat stews, vegetable soups, and stir-fried vegetables were common dishes. The kitchen cleaver and chopsticks were two important tools in Chinese cooking and eating. Chopping and cutting by a kitchen cleaver made meat or vegetable pieces small enough for people to pick them up with chopsticks from plates and bowls.

As mentioned earlier, Chinese diet followed a *"fan-cai"* concept, which means a meal consisting of cooked grain crops as staple food (*fan*) with cooked vegetables and meats as dishes (*cai*). Having a meal in Chinese was to *"chi fan"* ("eat rice"). Cooked rice, noodles, dumplings, steamed bread, or baked pancakes were all staple food items of *fan*, though people in South China consumed mostly rice. *Cai* was complimentary. Its ingredients, cookery, flavor, and combination were an unlimited list of recipes and endless inventions. As Joanna Waley-Cohen pointed out, "the most fundamental principle underlying Chinese cuisine, and its most distinct characteristic, is the *fan-cai* principle. *Fan* denotes rice, but in this context encompasses all grains. *Cai* denotes the dishes made to flavour the *fan*, and is of secondary importance. All Chinese meals consist of different combinations of *fan* and *cai*."[4]

Meat was not available every day. Ordinary people, however, were able to eat eggs, poultry, fish, pork, mutton, or other meats from time to time. Food vendors were everywhere in Chinese cities. Wealthy families hired cooks in their kitchens, and a good meal would consist of chicken, duck, fish, and pork. Royal court banquets could have several hundreds of different dishes. Though Tang writings were more famous for poetry, "two menus have survived from the early eighth century. One is a list of fifty-eight courses."[5] By the Tang Dynasty, the *fan-cai* concept was firmly established in Chinese food culture.

The Song Dynasty (960–1279) marked a breakthrough in farming and a peak in Chinese culinary culture. Farming tools and technology were considerably improved. Agricultural knowledge spread across the country through printed books. Grain crops such as rice, wheat, millet, corn, and potatoes, and a variety of vegetables and fruit trees, were efficiently planted and harvested. Rural families raised pigs and chickens. Fishing was a profession and trade. In Chinese food history, soybeans, wheat, rice, proso millet, and foxtail millet were the earliest cultivated and consumed crops and were consequently classified as the five sacred grains. Among the five, rice became increasingly important in the Sung Dynasty because of its proteins and vitamins. Thus "mi fan" ("cooked rice") was a synonym of "fan 饭" in Chinese.

Though *fan-cai* was a national diet concept, China had no national cuisine. Food traditions were a result of Chinese understanding of local ecology, environment, and farming resources. Different climates, soil conditions, water resources, and local cultures shaped different local food traditions. The complexity of China's physical landscape led to the development of a variety of regional cuisines. Eight of them ranked among the top cuisines across the country. Each cuisine had its own unique flavor and famous gourmet dishes. Food markets consisted of eateries featuring a variety of flavors from other regions. During the Song Dynasty, Kaifeng and Hangzhou were capital cities. In addition to all kinds of retail stores, inns, hotels, teahouses, theaters, and food and grocery shops, both cities had fine restaurants featuring regional cuisines and brand-name dishes. The French scholar Jacques Gernet pointed out that Hangchow had restaurants specializing in Sichuan, Shandong, and Hebei flavors and even in Muslim food.[6] Translocal restaurant businesses characterized the Chinese food market from ancient times.

During the Ming Dynasty (1368–1644), Chinese food culture reached a new level with more options and varieties in staple foods and meat and vegetable dishes. Big cities had fine restaurants. Royal palace and elite families hired professional chefs to cook gourmet cuisine based on numerous recipes.[7] Nutrition, health, tastefulness, and famine were all elements in the development of Chinese food culture. More books were published on food and medicine in the Ming Dynasty than in any previous dynasties. While *Yin shi xu zhi* by Jia Ming was a classic cookery book, Li Shizhen's *Ben Cao Gang Mu* was an encyclopedia on numerous herbs with medicinal effects. Though the novel *Jin Ping Mei* (The Plum in the Golden Vase) in the late Ming Dynasty is more famous for its explicit depiction of sexuality, it also contains numerous descriptions of gourmet food.

Generally speaking, the Chinese people had no taboos on what to eat. Many Cantonese, for example, claim that in their food culture, almost anything alive was edible. The Chinese were also open to foods from other cultures. As the anthropologist Eugene N. Anderson put it, "The Chinese have rarely been uninterested in new foods, and their position between the fantastic vegetational riches of Southeast Asia and the ancient agricultural cradle of the Near East has been the world's best for borrowing."[8] For nutritional purposes, elite and wealthy people began to consume rare foods like sea cucumber, shark fins, birds' nests, or ginseng. But they were actually imported from overseas. Sharks' fins, sea cucumber, and birds' nests had no flavor. Ginseng tasted bitter. They became nationally known in China because of their real or alleged nutrition elements. To alleviate hunger, poor people ate root crops like potatoes or sweet potatoes, both of which were transplanted from Europe and North America. Such root crops became popular especially during famine times as they could yield larger quantities and feed more people.

Though the emperors and noble families of the Qing Dynasty (1644–1911) came from an ethnic minority background, they had no prejudice against mainstream Chinese food when they were in power. Culinary luxury for the new royal families and high-ranking government officials followed the old tradition. In fact, the Qing royal families, government elites, and wealthy merchants were even more demanding of gourmet cuisine. More than any previous dynasties, Qing's writings were filled with descriptions of food and gourmet cuisines. In 1792, poet and retired official Yuan Mei authored *Sui Yuan Shi Tan* (Recipes of the Sui Yuan Garden), which was a collection of over 300 recipes representing the best dishes from several regional cuisines.[9] A picky and elite eater, Yuan showed how Chinese cuisine and cooking was a fine art. His work is a valuable and rare classic in food history.

Cao Xueqin, Yuan's contemporary and the author of *Hong Lou Meng* (*The Story of the Stone*) published in 1791, was also interested in food. This greatest novel in Chinese literature contained numerous descriptions of Chinese delicacies. Food was a favorite and frequent topic among female characters in the story. Food and food metaphors were not necessarily rare in English literary writings, but few British writers described food in the same detailed and delightful manner as Cao Xueqin did in his novel. We could hardly imagine that female characters in Jane Austin's novels would discuss food in the same enthusiastic and pleasant way as the female characters do in Cao's fiction. Watching how the Bennet sisters pass around a huge plate of boiled potatoes in the 1995 television series *Pride and Prejudice*, Chinese audiences could hardly believe this was what a British well-to-do family ate for a Sunday dinner.

Food was an important part of Chinese culture. Whether they were high-ranking government officials, famous scholars, wealthy merchants, or ordinary people in China, the Chinese were all proud of their fine culinary tradition. From Lunar New Year celebrations to weddings, funerals, religious rituals, or government functions, no Chinese social event would be considered complete without fine dining. The Hang Heong Restaurant dinner was one of the many banquets that Chinese merchants in San Francisco held for American merchants, politicians, and journalists in the 1860s and 1870s. They were proud of their rich culinary culture and wanted to socialize with Americans on the basis of their food. In his 1868 article on the restaurant business in San Francisco, Noah Brooks wrote that Chinese "are social and cheerful in their habits. They seized every possible occasion for a feast and the restaurants of the race

in this city are almost constantly lighted up with the banquets of their numerous customers."[10]

ANGLO-AMERICAN TASTE

In food tradition, British people preferred bland and simple meals. Bread,
roasted meat, milk, butter, and some fruits or nuts would make a good dinner
for a well-to-do family. As Daniel J. Boorstin wrote, "In western Europe, until
about the middle of the nineteenth century the mainstays, and in some places
nearly the exclusive items in the diet, were various forms of cereal, mainly bread,
supplemented now and then by salted meat. Milk, fruit, and vegetables were
frills, eaten for novelty by those who could afford them and when and where
they could be found fresh. Nourishment was measured by quantity: the poor suffered not because they ate mostly bread, but because they did not have enough
bread."[11] Similar to their British counterparts, Anglo-Americans had a monotonous diet. Their meals usually consisted of big chunks of meat, bread, and potatoes. Deep-fried meats or potatoes in lard or butter were considered delicious
food. Roasted fatty animal joints, boiled whole fowls with some salt and pepper, boiled potatoes, and boiled vegetables for hours until they became paste
were normal and decent food for wealthy or middle-class American families in
the first half of the nineteenth century. As the food historian Harvey Levenstein
pointed out, "The United States may have won its political independence from
Great Britain in 1783, but during the hundred-odd years that followed, Americans never liberated themselves from the British culinary heritage."[12]

Before Chinese immigrants arrived in California, British and American missionaries and merchants had lived in Canton for decades. Though Canton was
a city with numerous restaurants, teahouses, and all kinds of eateries, Western
expatriates seldom ate out and developed no appetite for Chinese food. Early in
the nineteenth century, wealthy Cantonese merchant Pan Zhengwei (Paunkei-
qua) invited Bryant Parrott Tilden, a resident American merchant, to dinner in
his mansion. Of the twenty-two courses, Tilden was not interested in bird's nest
soup, chopped meats, and cooked vegetables. He looked for big boiled joints
of meat, fried whole fowl, and potatoes. He was disappointed when he found
his host did not serve them. He felt even more helpless when he was provided
only with chopsticks.[13] Food habits were hard to change for anyone, as they were
shaped through years of history. But it was also rare for any people not to have
any curiosity or interest in another people's food when living among them.

When the *Empress of China*, the first American trade ship to China, arrived
in Canton in August 1784, Captain John Green and his business agent, Samuel
Shaw, were invited to a dinner by Chen Zuguan, a leading Thirteen Hong merchant, in his mansion. Green and Shaw were deeply impressed by the beautiful

garden, elegant furniture, and dinnerware. But the host had to serve his American guests French food and wine because they "could not stomach dishes prepared by Chen's chefs."[14] After eating salted beef and pork, boiled potatoes, and dried cabbages every day for six months on the ocean, a Chinese feast still did not appeal to them. They were keenly interest in the China trade but could not care less about Chinese food.

At the Hang Heong Restaurant banquet, Samuel Bowles only tasted a few dishes and left earlier with another unhappy guest. Both of them found Chinese food repelling and wanted to have a square meal in a good American restaurant. Their appetite was back when they saw mutton chops, squabs, and fried potatoes at an American restaurant across the street.[15] Though Chinese merchants were confident of their gourmet food, using food to socialize with Westerners was not effective.

BEEF AS AMERICAN FOOD

Anglo-Americans were different from their British ancestors in one way. They consumed much more meat and sugar than did the British. Before 1860, pork was the major meat for Anglo-Americans. The country was then nicknamed as "The Republic of Porkdom." But it was beef that finally shaped the American diet. Beef became a valuable food in Anglo-American meals because it had been a pricey and preferred meat on the dining tables of elite British families. In the mid-1880s, white Americans revered beef above all meats as they believed it was the most preferred food by elite British families. When the supply of beef became plentiful, many of them began to despise pork, a major meat for Americans before the first half of the nineteenth century. Middle-class American families "shunned fresh and salted pork, and deigned only to eat an occasional slice of smoked ham. Although low price induced them to consume much more pork than it did the rich, in middle-class eyes pork ranked far below not just beef, but lamb, poultry, and game as well."[16] During the Golden Age of American beef, beef quickly ascended to the top of all preferred meats. Mutton ranked second, poultry rated the third, and pork was disdained. The ranking was not based on culinary or nutritive considerations but on the monotonous British food tradition. "People of plenty" did not treat meats equally.

In 1817, the first cargo of British cattle was imported. That was when farmers on the East Coast began to raise them. Wealthy American families ate beef at all three meals. Luxury hotels offered roast beef or beefsteak even for breakfast. In the 1860s and 1870s, most American restaurants and hotels served French cuisine. For breakfast, however, luxury hotels often provided their guests with the so-called American Plan. Beefsteak was the most visible item in such breakfasts among broiled chicken, broiled salmon, liver, bacon, kidneys, lamb chops, tripe, clams, omelets, cold cuts, many kinds of potatoes, beans, breads, and so on.[17] When the American West became new cattle fields, beef began to shape the urban working-class American diet.

In the late 1860s, cowboys drove millions of wild Texas Longhorn cattle to Cheyenne, Wyoming, or Abilene, Kansas, where railroads were available. After Joseph G. McCoy sent his first twenty carloads of cattle from Abilene to Chicago in September 1867, those isolated, unsettled villages became booming cattle towns.[18] In 1881, Gustavus Franklin Swift organized a sufficient transportation system that could ship freshly slaughtered beef from Chicago to East Coast cities in refrigerator cars.[19] That year was labeled as the "year of cheap beef." After that time, beef prices declined; Chicago became the American capital of meats; and numerous working-class white American families were able to afford more beef than ever in their meals. The 1880s were regarded as the "Golden Age of American Beef."

Within a few years after 1876, ten million cattle were shipped to Chicago from the cattle towns in Kansas. Millions of ordinary Americans began to eat beef daily—something that only wealthy British families could afford. As Daniel J. Boorstin put it, "Americans would become the world's great meat eaters. In the Old World, beef was the diet of lords and men of wealth. For others it was a holiday price. But American millions would eat like lords—because of the efforts of American Go-Getters in the half-charted West."[20] Cheap beef satisfied ordinary Americans' stomachs as well as their expectation of being "people of plenty." In his classic book *People of Plenty: Economic Abundance and the American Character*, David M. Potter believed that material abundance had impacted the national character of Americans tremendously.[21] With abundant beef in their meals, Americans viewed themselves as people of extravagance and the decades of the late nineteenth century as the "age of excess." Eating beef made them believe that they ate better than their counterparts in Europe and a lot better than people in Asia or other parts of the world. The abundance of beef was part of the white American Dream and a symbol of their American democracy.

Meat of Texas Longhorn cattle was far from being palatable compared with imported beef from Europe or beef from East Coast farms. Upper-class Americans still preferred the latter two. But it was the quantity rather than the quality that mattered. The significance of Texas cattle meat was social rather than culinary. Beef abundance did not generate more recipes and new dishes in American cuisine. Steak, stewed beef chunks, or later ground beef for hamburgers remained major forms of consuming beef for a long time. In food culture, Anglo-Americans believed in quantity and homogeneity rather than in variety and diversity. Cheap beef further reinforced this belief.

"CHINAMEN LIVE ON RICE"

Though beef abundance did not generate many American recipes, it strengthened Americans' prejudice against other people's food. For a long time, Anglo-American foodways predominated in American society. Euro-centric food was a culinary as well as a social criterion on what was proper to eat. The difference between the grain-based Chinese diet and meat-centered Anglo-American food habit became a matter of racial debate. In the criminal trial of a race riot in 1865, the lawyer defended his white client's criminal behavior against the Chinese by pointing out to the judge, "Why, Sir-r-r, these Chinamen live on rice, and, Sir-r-r, they eat it with sticks!"[22] The remark seems ignorant today. But it was delivered as a serious argument against the Chinese at that time. Food mattered in racial stratification. In racial rhetoric, Chinese was an inferior race because the Chinese people consumed rice as a staple food and used chopsticks as "uncivilized" eating tools.

Interestingly, high-class Chinese people had their own opinions about the fork and knife in Western food culture. A Qing government official once told a correspondent of the *London Times*: "In remote ages, before we became civilized, we used knives and forks as you do, and had no chopstick-case, but it is a remnant of barbarism—we never use it. We sit down to table to eat, not to cut up carcasses."[23] In his opinion, the use of chopsticks was not only a different way of eating from using forks and knives but also displayed the thoughtful food preparation and cookery process of Chinese meals.

In the 1860s, many working-class American families could not afford beef in their daily meals, but they knew beef was preferred meat on rich people's dining tables. To have beef in daily meals was a desired lifestyle. In their opinion, beef represented the standard of the American diet. Rice represented an inferior Asian diet. In 1902, Samuel Gompers, a leader of the labor movement and president of the American Federation of Labor, published a famous anti-Chinese pamphlet entitled *Some Reasons for Chinese Exclusion: Meat versus Rice, American Manhood versus Asiatic Coolieism—Which Shall Survive?*[24] In Gompers's pamphlet, Chinese immigrants were portrayed as "scabs in the American labor force" because of their rice-based diet. In order to win votes from the union organizations, American politicians joined racial campaigns against the Chinese. Senator James G. Blaine delivered his anti-Chinese message by attacking Chinese food culture. "You can not work a man who must have beef and bread, and would prefer beef," he said, "alongside of a man who can live on rice. In all such conflicts, and in all such struggles, the result is not to bring up the man who lives on rice to the beef-and-bread standard, but it is to bring down the beef-and-bread man to the rice standard."[25] When racial discrimination against the Chinese became intense, food was viewed as an inextricable part of Chinese racial identity. In racial rhetoric, rice became a symbol of Chinese ethnicity.

Racial ideology shaped Americans' perception of food. For a long time, many white people believed rice "was the main dependence of certain not very progressive Eastern peoples—especially of the Chinese."[26] In the 1910s, when the New York City government tried to encourage white working-class families to eat more rice than potatoes, local residents denounced the use of "China's men's food" for American workmen. During the 1917 food riot, when New York mothers protested against hunger, they complained about shortages of eggs, milk, and sugar and the use of rice as hunger food. They felt degraded if they had to eat rice. In Boston, several hundred white workers stormed into a grocery store and shouted, "We want potatoes! We want potatoes!"[27] Nutrition-wise, potatoes may contain more vitamins than rice, but Americans' popular perception of rice was more a matter of taste than an issue of protein or vitamins. Baked potatoes with butter, sour cream, gravy, and bacon was not a healthy daily diet anyway.

Ironically, Americans in the Deep South did grow and eat rice, and even exported it to Britain. Carolina Golden rice was a legendary food in the Deep South for a long time. In 1685, a storm-wrecked ship from Madagascar stopped by the Charles Towne harbor in Carolina. Local colonists helped the captain repair the ship. To express his gratitude, the captain left them some rice seeds. Marshlands in Carolina and Georgia were fertile, wet, and soft, which may not be good for other crops but was ideal for planting rice. Since then, rice became a major crop in the two states. In 1700, 80 percent of this high-quality rice was exported to England and Europe, while 20 percent was consumed by local wealthy families. Planting and harvesting rice was labor intensive and done mostly by slave laborers. It was a rich person's food. Poor whites and black slaves could not afford rice. By 1726, the Port of Charleston shipped at least 4,500 metric tons of Carolina Golden rice to Europe. By the Revolutionary War, rice was a major agricultural export crop for the American colonies.[28] The Golden Rice brand later became the standard of high-quality rice in Europe and North America. In the Deep South, rice was a high-end, delicious grain food for the privileged planters. When not associated with the Chinese, rice was recognized for its nutrition and value. Rice ranked lower than the potato only when it was used as a racial label for the Chinese.

"ROUGH ON RATS"

If rice was a marker of Chinese ethnicity, rat eating has been a century-long racial profile imposed on the Chinese. As early as 1853, the *Daily Alta California*, a usually sympathetic local newspaper toward the Chinese, carried an article with a nasty description about the Chinese diet:

If there is one class of nasty foreigners . . . more ill-favored, unfortunate, and for-lorn among us, than another, it certainly must be the Chinese. The length and breadth of popular sentiment against them in California, is as a wide gulf, separat-ing them more and more every day from the hope of obtaining established rights and privileges as citizens in the State. The depth of degradation to which they are fallen in public opinion is as the bottom of a deep pit. . . . They are sunk immea-surable lower than the native Indians, in the estimation of the miners. . . . Rats, lizards, mud-terrapins, rank and indigestible shell fish, and such small deer, have been and continue to be, the food of the "no ways partickler" Celestial, where flour, beef, and bacon, and other fare suitable to the stomachs of "white folk" abound. It is not to be wondered at, therefore, that the habits of the Chinese in California should excite ineffable disgust, and turn the stomachs of the stoutest Anglo Saxon.[29]

The *Daily Alta California* report was not even close to describing the real food served in the pioneer Chinese restaurants in California. In reality, what "turned the stomachs of the stoutest Anglo Saxon" was not Chinese food but the arrival of an increasing number of Chinese immigrants ready to enter the mining fields. When Chinese immigrants were seen even "lower than the native Indians in the estimation of the miners," the real intention of this piece of racial rhetoric is revealed. It demanded that Chinese immigrants not enter the mining fields. Dig-ging gold should remain white folks' right only.

Rat eating was a century-long stereotyped image of the Chinese diet. As Hunter Rose put it, "A popular fallacy with 'Western barbarians' is the belief that the Chinese consider rats, mice, cats, snakes, and such-like vermin and rep-tiles, edible delicacies." But since the hunger-driven French "were glad to fall back upon kitten-cutlet, horse-haricot, and puppy-pie, why should the fact of indigent Chinese sustaining existence upon similar food be deemed such a dis-gusting trait in the national character?"[30] Hunger food could be anything for any people during a famine. Western journalists' and missionaries' writings about Chinese food culture in the eighteenth and nineteenth centuries, however, often deliberately described rats or cats as preferred food for the Chinese. The *Daily Alta California* report was a convenient repetition of such writings. As the Chi-nese immigrant population in California was rapidly growing, biased and racist attacks on Chinese culture became increasingly intense. Alexander Young wrote: "Superficial artists have insisted that the reason why the Chinese are attached to California, notwithstanding the ill-treatment to which they have been subjected there, is the abundance and superior quality of the rats of the golden gate."[31]

The rat-eating image was so prevalent that many innocent Americans took it for truth. In the 1860s, when Mark Twain was working as a journalist for a news-paper in Nevada, he was once invited by a Chinese grocery store owner, a Mr. Ah

Sing, to a dinner and reported: "He offered us a mess of birds'-nests; also, small, neat sausages, of which we could have swallowed several yards if we had chosen to try, but we suspected that each link contained the corpse of a mouse, and therefore refrained." However, Twain did not hesitate to eat "chow-chow with chop-sticks in the celestial restaurants" and concluded that the Chinese were "a kindly disposed, well-meaning race," and "only the scum of the society . . . abused or opposed them."[32]

Louis Beck's book on New York's Chinatown described the first experience of a white American customer who tried a chop suey dish in a Chinese restaurant. "He is certain it has rats in it, for the popular superstition that the Chinese eats rats is in-bred. He remembers his schoolboy history, with the picture of a Chinaman carrying around a cage of rats for sale." But when he tasted one mouthful after another of his order, all he declared was "great, great."[33] In 1915, a Chinese caterer at the Panama-Pacific Exposition promoted his dishes by sarcastically assuring the customers that "the dainties sold at his counter were guaranteed to be safe from such ingredients as preserved mice or unborn birdlings."[34] While humorously rejecting the rat-eating stereotype about the Chinese, the salesman displayed a good understanding of American racial attitudes toward Chinese culinary culture.

Food is an important component of Chinese culture and an expression of Chinese identity. Chinese merchants, intellectuals, diplomats, and ordinary people often defended Chinese food culture in public. When San Francisco Chinese restaurateur Assing mingled with Americans in his social life and was confronted with the rat-eating inquiry, he "simply explained that famished Chinese might possibly prefer rats to death, but for his own part, he preferred rice, and ducks and fish."[35] As a merchant who grew up in Macau and had traveled to the East Coast before he came to San Francisco, Assing understood well that duck and fish were common food items in Western cuisine.

In April 1877, pioneer Chinese civil rights activist Wong Chin Foo gave a lecture on Chinese culture at Steinway Hall, New York. Wong had a sharp tongue. When he had to deal with a provocative inquiry from the audience about the Chinese eating rats, he quickly snapped: "I never knew that rats and puppies were good to eat until I was told by American people."[36] Making public lectures for a living, Wong's English was fluent. His speeches and writings were often witty and sarcastic. He was provocative himself. In 1883, Denis Kearney, an Irish American and a leader of California Workingmen's Party, and also a renowned Chinese exclusion advocate, came to New York City to speak at Cooper Union, where Wong had delivered several speeches. Wong challenged Kearney to a duel. When asked how by a journalist, he said with a cigar in hand: "I give him his choice of chopsticks, Irish potatoes, or Krupp guns." The joke was loaded with sarcastic implication and meaningful facts. Potatoes were a major food for the poor in Ireland. As a Chinese, Wong obviously viewed it as a hunger food. He also knew that Westerners often made fun of Chinese chopsticks. In his joke, Wong frankly told his opponent that Chinese hands could not only handle chopsticks but also the powerful German Krupp cannons.[37]

"Rough on Rats" was probably the most notorious racist commercial on Chinese eating habits in the nineteenth century. Promoting a pest control product on a trade card in 1897, the advertisement featured a Chinese man with his mouth open ready to eat a rodent. It personified the product in the Chinese man being an effective rodent exterminator. The commercial reflected an intense racial sentiment against the Chinese in the late nineteenth century. "The Chinese Must Go!" was the most extreme political slogan in the white labor movement in California.[38] In the advertisement, "They Must Go" implied the Chinese rather than the rats. Racist propaganda against the Chinese was often creative and persistent. It repeatedly degraded Chinese food culture by claiming that rats, cats, or dogs were preferred meat in the Chinese diet. The image of eating rats has been one of the most ugly and vicious racial profiles of the Chinese.

When Chinese exclusion became a public agenda, racial prejudice reached every corner of American society. Racial rhetoric on Chinese food culture even influenced American children. Some of them grew up learning and passing around racist rhymes on Chinese eating rats. Edgar Snow, the author of *Red Star Over China*, was one of the few American journalists who interviewed and wrote about Chinese Communist leaders in the 1930s. When the Communists relocated themselves from the South to the North through the famous Long March, the Red Army's soldiers and commanders often suffered from hunger. They ate everything edible, including wild animals, grass roots, herbs, tree bark, or even belts made of leather. But they never ate rats. Snow had a different image of the Chinese when he was a child. At school, he was taught and often sang a chant that many American children were familiar with:

Chinaman, Chinaman,
Eat dead rats!
Chew them up
Like gingersnaps!

This is only one of the most notorious popular songs in American society about Chinese eating habits. Snow was also once assigned to look for a photograph showing a Chinese hen laying on an egg on a dung heap.[39] In the 1920s, American popular magazines reiterated the popular myth that the Chinese could not be assimilated because of their food traditions. Their delicacies were rats and snakes, and their national dish was chop suey or chow mein.

In 1944, the musical *Meet Me in St. Louis* became a hit movie in America. A children's rhyme sung by Judy Garland in the movie stayed alive throughout the 1950s. It went as follows:

Chinkie, Chinkie Chinaman,
Sitting on the fence;
Trying to make a dollar
Out of fifteen cents.
Chink, Chink, Chinaman
Eats dead rats;
Eats them up
Like gingersnaps.[40]

The rhyme exemplified an image of Chinese being stingy in money issues and nasty in food habits. Ironically, Judy Garland was a frequent customer at General Lee's Restaurant in Los Angeles's Chinatown in the 1930s.

The rat-eating stereotype still haunts Chinese restaurants today. As recently as January 29, 2007, the New York television station CW 11 (WPIX-TV Channel 11) broadcast a news story about New Food King, a Chinese restaurant run by a Fujian immigrant in Brooklyn, alleging that it had served mouse meat in a takeout order by a local customer. Before the alleged mouse meal had been professionally tested, the station broadcast the news with statements like "nasty dining experience" or "rodent slathered in garlic sauce." The customer said: "I will never eat Chinese food again." Following the news, the restaurant received several dozens of racist phone calls "ordering" mouse meat and telling the owners to "go back to China." For a restaurant, it would cost more labor and money to catch a rat than to order chicken meat for food supply. This racist report illustrates the lasting power of the rat-eating image as a racial profile.

Chinese Americans in New York City responded quickly. They invited the city's health agency to conduct an immediate inspection. The agency did so on February 2, and the restaurant easily passed the inspection. Chinese Americans also organized protest demonstrations in front of the CW 11 office building. Instead of offering an apology, CW 11 sent the same journalist, Chris Glorioso, to cover the protests. On February 5, about 500 Chinese Americans protested against the vicious report in front of CW 11's office building. The station refused to apologize. On February 26, over 2,000 Chinese Americans, representing several dozens of different community organizations, held a demonstration again in front of the CW 11 office building, demanding an apology and protesting the stereotypes. The station again refused to apologize.[41] In a few weeks, the angry protesting voices of the Chinese quieted down. Most of the Chinese restaurants in New York continued to receive a constant flow of all kinds of American customers. The controversy reflects an ironic aspect of the Chinese restaurant business in America. While stereotypes of Chinese culinary culture have long and widely existed in American society, Chinese food has continuously been popular with American clients.

Only a few weeks later, on February 23 of the same year, the Associated Press published another piece of news with a startling title, "'Rats Gone Wild' in NYC Restaurant." Ironically, the report was about a mainstream chain restaurant. The news reported: "A dozen rats were caught on video scurrying around the floor of a New York City KFC/Taco Bell restaurant early today, running between counters and tables and climbing on children's high chairs. News crews flocked to the windows of the Greenwich Village neighborhood restaurant, which hadn't opened for the day."[42] By midmorning, the footage was all over the Internet and television news shows, with onlookers giving a play-by-play from the sidewalk as the rodents moved about. Though the rats were videotaped and the clipping widely spread via the Internet and television coverage, the news did not make people think of KFC/Taco Bell as a rat-server and associate mainstream Americans' diet with rat-eating. The report was factual rather than sensational.

SLOW GROWTH IN A GILDED AGE

The Chinese restaurant business experienced stagnant growth in the last three decades of the nineteenth century, when the food and restaurant business was thriving in the United States. The San Francisco restaurant industry in the late 1860s was very different from that of the 1850s. The continental railroad, partly built by the Chinese, brought massive waves of Americans from the East Coast to the West Coast and quickly changed San Francisco, which became an attractive metropolitan center in the American West. In his article of 1868, Noah Brooks wrote that restaurants in San Francisco were "numerous, plenteous, inviting, and even cheap." A good dinner with soup, fish, salad, two or three entrées, vegetables, roast, dessert, fruit, coffee, and wine cost only a $1.50 at a nice restaurant. At such a dinner, "the fish is hot and crisp from the fire; the entrees are those Frenchy side-dishes hot and spicy, . . . the vegetables have the flavor of nature. . . . The same repast would cost four times as much in any of the Atlantic cities."[43] The restaurant business was thriving in San Francisco because many new settlers were single men who were living in hotels or lodging houses and had to eat in restaurants. As the prices were low, middle-class families began to frequent restaurants that provided private rooms for family parties. Tourists were another major source of customers. Every year, thousands of them came from other parts of the country to see the city that became increasingly famous for its restaurants.

According to Waverly Root and Richard de Rochemont, a turning point in the San Francisco restaurant industry was the opening of the Palace Hotel in 1875, the world's greatest hotel in the opinion of many San Franciscans.[44] The hotel marked how San Francisco had developed into a metropolitan city from a mining town. In fact, it was a period when wealthy investors built grand hotels and French-inspired restaurants to feed and accommodate newly status-conscious travelers everywhere in the United States.[45] By the 1870s, San Francisco had a prosperous restaurant business that featured many different flavors. There were restaurants that offered "baked beans garnished with crispy pork" from New England, Indian-meal pudding, the corn pone of Virginia, the chicken gumbo of New Orleans, the "side-meat" of Missouri, or New York's chicken pie.[46]

More important, there were large quantities of fresh fruits and vegetables in San Francisco restaurants, which made them different from those on the East Coast. "For six months in the year strawberries are common, and at all seasons there is an abundance of fresh fruits of some sort. Grapes and pears that grace only the table of the very wealthy in Atlantic cities, are lavished here in unstinted profusion."[47] While French cuisine was predominant, the city also offered good German, Italian, Danish, Greek, Balkan, Yugoslav, Russian, Spanish, and Caribbean restaurants.[48] In the American food history, immigrants were far more motivated and far more enthusiastic than native-born Americans in engaging in the restaurant business. Pioneer famous restaurants in the United States were often established and operated by immigrants. In San Francisco, Tadisch, a seafood restaurant, was founded by a Yugoslav immigrant in 1850. Jack's, a restaurant established in 1864, served French cuisine. Schroeder's, founded in 1893, served German cuisine.[49] These restaurants became culinary landmarks in San Francisco in those decades.

However, the growth of the Chinese restaurant business in San Francisco was surprisingly slow in the last three decades of the nineteenth century. There were already seven to eight Chinese restaurants in 1849. After almost thirty years, there were still only eleven Chinese restaurants in 1878. Then the number jumped to twenty-eight in 1881 but dropped again to thirteen or fourteen in the following year.[50] In those decades, only a few isolated high-end Chinese restaurants occupied multistory buildings with elegant decorations and typical Chinese business names in Chinatown. In his article, Brooks noted the "oriental" appearance of those high-end Chinese restaurants that had "large circular openings for exit and entrances, dispensing with doors, hanging gaudy scrolls of gilded, painted and lettered paper about the rooms, and fitting up a carpeted platform."[51]

Brooks was not very positive about the food that those restaurants provided. He wrote: "They cook chickens and ducks nicely though queerly, the bird being first split clean in two; but almost everything has the same taste of nut oil. . . . Shark's fins, stewed bamboo, duck's eggs boiled, baked, and stewed in oil, pork disguised in hot sauces, and other things like these, are the standard dishes of a Chinese bill of fare, though they have an infinite variety of sweetmeats which are really palatable, and of sweet cakes, which are inviting in their quaint, odd forms and decorations."[52] Brooks's comment on Chinese sweetmeats indicated that some Chinese foods actually fit American tastes.

As Harvey Levenstein pointed out, "Sweet or sweet and sour condiments were particularly popular as accompaniments for meats, and as sugar prices declined in the nineteenth century they soared in popularity. Cucumbers, onions, and other vegetables were preserved in sugar, salt, and vinegar."[53] The "infinite variety of sweetmeats" mentioned by Brooks was actually cha shao, or barbecue pork, beef, or even fish in Cantonese cuisine. In fact, cha shao meat is still popular among the Chinese today. A contemporary version close to the Chinese "sweetmeats" in the nineteenth century is the barbecue meat used in the sandwiches in Lee's Sandwiches Restaurant, one of the largest Vietnamese fast-food chain restaurant businesses in California today.

Though Chinese restaurants were one of the earliest businesses in San Francisco, Chinese cuisine failed to carve a wide niche in the city's fast-growing restaurant market. Chinese restaurants remained modest in number while Chinatown in San Francisco was expanding in the last three decades of the nineteenth century. In the 1850s, the Chinese quarter occupied only two blocks between Kearny and Stockton Streets and Sacramento and Jackson Streets, and formed a "Little China." In 1860, the Chinese population in San Francisco reached 2,719. Ten years later, the Chinese population exploded to 12,022, and by 1879, it had more than doubled, rising at least to 30,000. As the historian Yong Chen documented, Chinatown by 1885 occupied twelve blocks from California Street on the south, Kearny Street on the east, Broadway on the north, and Stockton on the west. The San Francisco city directory listed 942 Chinese businesses in 1882.[54] By then, Chinatown in San Francisco became the largest Chinese community in North America.[55]

The 1882 *Directory of Principal Chinese Business Firms in San Francisco*, another historical source, listed 175 laundries (16.6 percent located in Chinatown), 77 general merchandise stores, 62 grocery stores, 40 cigar factories, 31 shoe factories, 23 clothing factories, 22 drugstores, 19 cigar stores, 18 dry goods stores, 16 butchers, 16 tailors, 14 Chinese restaurants, 11 jewelers, 11 barbers, 10 slipper factories, 8 pawnbrokers, 4 undertakers, 3 newspapers, 2 beancake stores, 2 employment offices, 1 photographer, 1 toy store, 1 variety store, 1 watchmaker, and so forth.[56] Chinatown had become a vigorous economical entity in the late nineteenth century. As the *Directory* indicates, there were 175 Chinese laundries but only fourteen Chinese restaurants.

The list was a significant footnote on the continuous deteriorating racial environment for the Chinese. When the Chinese first arrived in the American West, they could be found in almost every sector of the American economy—trade, retail business, mining, farming, fishing, light industry, manufacturing, garment

and shoe factories, truck gardening, railroad construction, chefs, domestic servants, and waiters. They were also making their living in many different places
in the American West. Racial tensions changed that. From the 1860s, Chinese
immigrants began to taste the bitterness of a rapidly growing white American
population and their racial hostility toward them. In 1862, Leland Stanford
became the first Republican governor in California. Being an astute politician,
Stanford smelled an increasing anti-Chinese sentiment among the white laborers. Labeling the Chinese as "coolies," white labor activists organized citywide
Anti-Coolie Clubs in San Francisco in the same year. In his inaugural speech,
Stanford delivered a strong anti-Chinese message, though he employed a large
number of Chinese laborers in his own railroad construction business and made
a huge fortune from their labor.[57] In his private life, Stanford actually liked Chinese food and often consulted Li Po-tai, a famous Chinese herbalist in San Francisco, for his health problems.

Between 1860 and 1870, the white American population in San Francisco
increased by 88 percent, and most of them came after the American Civil War
in the mid-1860s. Newly arrived white Americans from the East Coast brought
with them unrealistic dreams about good jobs, better pay, and cheaper houses
in California. Many became disappointed when the Golden State suffered a
serious economic depression in the 1870s. Using the Chinese as a scapegoat
for the economic problems, Republicans and Democrats in California "vied
with one another in the virulence of their anti-Chinese resolutions."[58] By 1876,
both major parties had adopted anti-Chinese clauses in their national plat-
forms.[59] In 1870, the San Francisco city government passed a Cubic Air Ordinance that targeted mainly Chinese immigrants and required them to meet a
lodging requirement of 500 cubic feet per person when renting apartments.
In 1873, the city passed a Pole Ordinance that forbade persons from walking
with bamboo poles on the street. Only Chinese used bamboo poles to carry
their packages when walking on the street. Between 1873 and 1884, the city
passed fourteen ordinances concerning Chinese laundry businesses, requir-
ing them to pay more taxes unless they used horses to deliver laundry to their
customers.

In 1877, 6,000 working men in San Francisco elected Denis Kearney as the
president of Workingmen's Party. His campaign slogan was that "the Chinese
laborer is a curse to our land, is degrading to our morals, is a menace to our liber-
ties, and should be restricted and forever abolished, and the Chinese must go."
In 1879, the California constitutional convention adopted a resolution that no
corporation should hire Chinese and that no state, county, municipal, or other
public institutions should hire Chinese. Finally, the anti-Chinese movement
became a national phenomenon. In 1882, the U.S. Congress passed its first Chinese Exclusion Act.

As the 1882 *Directory* indicated, Chinese immigrants engaged mainly in two kinds of ethnic enclave businesses. The first kind served mainstream American society, while the second kind catered to the needs of Chinese customers. Products and services by shoe factories, cigar factories, or laundry shops were essentially consumed by non-Chinese clientele outside of Chinatown. On the other hand, grocery stores, pharmacies, and restaurants primarily served Chinese customers. While the first kind of ethnic businesses reflected how the Chinese were pushed into segregated ethnic occupations, the second kind represented ethnic solidarity and shared cultural traditions.

Similar lifestyles, social values, and kinship networks bonded the Chinese together. Of the second kind of ethnic businesses, a grocery store or drugstore was probably more important for an ordinary Chinese than a restaurant. Many immigrants, especially laborers, ate at home and cooked their own meals more often than eating in a restaurant. They visited grocery stores far more frequently than they did restaurants. There were also more pharmacy (herbal medicine) stores than restaurants because San Francisco public hospitals were not open to the Chinese. Herbal medicine was not only a familiar traditional therapy to many Chinese but often the only health care available to them. Thus the 1882 list had more grocery stores and drugstores than restaurants.

Laundries constituted the largest number of Chinese businesses. June Mei documented that the number of Chinese-owned laundries in San Francisco grew to about 300 by 1876, employing some 1,500 workers. Another 1,500 or so Chinese worked in white-owned laundries.[60] Takaki also noted that by 1870, there were 2,899 Chinese laundry workers in California, 72 percent of all laborers in this occupation. Twenty years later their number had more than doubled to 6,400, or 69 percent of all laundry workers. Takaki concluded that the Chinese laundryman personified the forced withdrawal of the Chinese into a segregated ethnic-labor market.[61] Paul Ong pointed out that laundry work was a relatively lucrative business from the very beginning. Start-up costs required little capital investment beyond an iron, an ironing board, and a scrub board. It also demanded little knowledge of English and could be carried out in an inexpensive location, since the custom then was to pick up and deliver the clothing to an individual's home.[62] In comparison, investment in one restaurant was equivalent to "twenty to thirty or even more laundries put together." While starting a laundry cost between $350 and $1,600, starting a restaurant cost $16,000 to $24,000 in the 1880s.[63] In part because of these differences in start-up costs, there were more Chinese laundries than Chinese restaurants. Chao also pointed out that the gap was due to the fact that most laundries were located outside of Chinatown, while over 95 percent of all the Chinese restaurants listed between 1848 and 1906 had Chinese names and Chinatown addresses, which meant the clientele was predominantly Chinese.[64]

However, the slow growth or the small number of Chinese restaurants was not a location or money issue. There were smaller and cheaper restaurants in Chinatown that did not need huge capital investment. For white Americans, eating Chinese food was a different consuming activity from using a Chinese laundry. The social status of laundrymen was low. Laundry operation bore an obvious menial service character. Customers and laundrymen were clearly from two different social classes. Though the service was performed by the Chinese, it was not a skill they brought to the United States from China. There was no laundry profession in Chinese society. Chinese immigrants learned the trade anew. It was the American racial environment that channeled them into this occupation. White Americans felt comfortable using a Chinese laundry service; it was also a job that many of them did not want to do themselves. Chinese laundry shops proliferated in the last three decades of the nineteenth century.

Patronizing a Chinese restaurant was a different matter. Customers not only used Chinese service but also consumed Chinese food. A restaurant was a public eating place. Food was part of Chinese culture and an ethnic marker. High-end Chinese restaurants often exemplified sophisticated cuisine traditions. Eating in a Chinese restaurant, especially in a high-end restaurant, would imply accepting Chinese food culture. It could be culturally embarrassing or socially awkward for a middle-class white family to do so at that time. During the 1870s and 1880s, many white American residents in San Francisco shunned Chinese restaurants.[65] Tourists from the East Coast were advised to be cautious about Chinese restaurants in Chinatown. B. E. Loyd's 1876 guide to the "lights and shades" of San Francisco described the Chinese as "penurious eaters" who often held banquets where exotic and rare and sometimes disgusting food items were served.[66] Some tourist guidebooks recommended that tourists ask no questions about the ingredients of Chinese food.[67] At the turn of the twentieth century, many tourists hired guides when visiting Chinatown and looked for the eccentric lifestyle of the Chinese. Chinatown became an ethnic amusement park of fake Chinese culture.

While the Chinese restaurant business experienced little growth, many Chinese men worked as cooks for white American families. June Mei noted that there were about 4,500 Chinese who were hired as domestic servants by American families in San Francisco in 1877.[68] Most of them cooked while doing other house chores. Sucheng Chan also noted that Chinese cooks were especially prevalent in the Sacramento Valley, where hundreds of them worked for farm owners and town dwellers in the late nineteenth and early twentieth centuries. Some began at an early age and quickly learn to speak English. They often took care of other family chores while working as a chef.[69]

In order to assist the Chinese to become familiar with Anglo-American cuisine, special cooks prepared literate Chinese men at the turn of the twentieth century. The *Chu shut ta chuan* (Chinese and English Cookbooks 厨术大全), for example, was published to aid the employer "who desires good things to eat" but suffers frustration because he is unable to talk "to the Chinese cook or because his Chinese cook does not know the methods of preparation." The cookbook provided bilingual recipes for forty-one American puddings, thirty-five cakes, twenty-five soups, sixty meats, and forty vegetables. There was not a single recipe for Chinese food among them.[70] Though not trusting Chinese food, white families hired Chinese as their cooks to make American meals. When one white American woman hired a Chinese cook in 1866, she said, "What a blessing he was. What bread and coffee and nice broiled steak he gave us, and no fuss nor noise. He staid nearly a years [*sic*], then left for higher wages."[71] Many white families liked Chinese cooks and believed that most Chinese immigrants made good cooks through learning a little English and reading a bilingual recipe book. Domestic cooking was a menial service occupation. Not every Chinese man was a talented cook. Chinese being cooks obviously fit white Americans' perception of Asian status in American society.

4 · CHOP SUEY AND RACIAL AMERICA

THE ORIGIN OF CHOP SUEY

In the early hours of a morning in 1917, John Doe, a white laborer, strolled into the Dragon Chop Suey House on 630 West Sixth Street, Los Angeles, and ordered chicken chop suey. A grinning Japanese waiter soon placed a steaming bowl before him. "I won't eat it," barked Doe. "There's no poultry in it." The police squad was called in. Annoyed but entertained by this early morning incident, they offered to act as a jury, but each officer demanded a bowl of chop suey as a sample meal. The Japanese owner declined the demand, and Doe was free to go.[1] The story tells of a silly dispute between a customer and a proprietor, but it also shows how popular chop suey was as a restaurant food in American society.

After growing slowly in the last three decades of the nineteenth century, the Chinese restaurant business made an amazing rebound in the American restaurant market in the 1900s. Chinese food became popular again in the format of chop suey meals. From 1900 to the 1960s, chop suey was synonymous with Chinese food in the United States. Chinese restaurants had names such as China Garden, Oriental Inn, Cathay Tea House, and Moon Café. But they were all chop suey houses that served Americanized Chinese food like chop suey, egg rolls, and chow mein. Many Americans loved Chinese food. President Dwight Eisenhower was a lifelong personal fan of chop suey in Washington, D.C. American Jews are well known for their persistent love of Chinese food.

In the format of chop suey meals, Chinese food carved a firm niche in the American restaurant market. Its popularity made restaurant operation a cornerstone business for Chinese Americans and provided them with many job opportunities when they had few options in other fields. Capitalizing on this popularity, some American entrepreneurs produced canned and frozen Chinese meals for American consumers. As a culinary icon in urban America, chop suey became a theme in several famous compositions from American jazz musicians Louis Armstrong and Sidney Bechet. Artists John Sloan, Max Weber, and Edward Hopper all created memorable art works on Chinese restaurants. This chapter documents how chop suey emerged as a popular ethnic food in urban America and explores its multidimensional significance in food history.

In 1888, Wong Chin Foo, a pioneer Chinese American journalist, described chop suey in his article for *Cosmopolitan* as the following: "A staple dish for the Chinese gourmand is Chow Chop Suey, a mixture of chicken's livers and gizzards, fungi, bamboo buds, pig's tripe, and bean sprouts stewed with spices. The gravy of this is poured into the bowl of rice with some [sauce], making a delicious seasoning to the favorite grain."[2] Wong lived by writing and making public speeches. He often spoke about Chinese culture and published many articles about Chinese life in America. If chop suey had caught his attention, it was obviously a popular dish in New York's Chinese restaurants for both Chinese and non-Chinese customers. In fact, American journalists had already mentioned chop suey a couple of years earlier. After trying a Chinese meal at Mong Sing Wah's restaurant in a courtyard behind 18 Mott Street, one of them wrote: "Chow-chop suey was the first dish we attacked. It is a toothsome stew, composed of bean sprouts, chicken's gizzards and livers, calf's tripe, dragon fish, dried and imported from China, pork, chicken, and various other ingredients which I was unable to make out. Notwithstanding its mysterious nature, it is very good and has formed the basis of many a good Chinese dinner I have [had] since then."[3] The description anticipated chop suey's growing popularity.

Early Chinese immigrants were mostly Cantonese. "Chow chop suey" was Cantonese pronunciation. In Mandarin, it should be "chao za sui." "*Chao*" is a verb in Chinese meaning to stir fry. "*Za sui*" means animal intestines. In other words, "chao za sui," or "chow chop suey," in Chinese food culture was a dish of stir-fried animal intestines. "*Za*" in Cantonese pronunciation was close enough to the English word "chop" and was misunderstood as such. Thus American customers mistakenly assumed "chop suey" was a dish in which chicken or pork was chopped into fine, delicate pieces in its cookery. But "chow chop suey" was not a delicacy in Chinese cuisine. Using animal intestines rather than prime meat, restaurants usually served "chow chop suey" as a cheap dish, though some restaurants might cook a featured dish with animal intestines. The Chinese seldom wasted any part of butchered livestock.

Wong's description in 1888 revealed some basic ingredients in the original format of "chow chop suey," which included animal intestines. In North China, however, this dish did not use bamboo shoots. Wong also noticed that the mixed and stir-fried ingredients were made into gravy and poured on the cooked rice. In China, most restaurants did not use gravy when cooking "chao za sui," or "chow chop suey." In rural Cantonese meals, cooked rice could be accompanied with a topping made of all possible ingredients—vegetables mainly or a tiny bit of meat—mixed with gravy. The purpose of the topping was to help the eater gulp down the rice when there was no formal dish at a meal. In Cantonese, this type of meal was called "song 餸." There is no such equivalent word in North China, though the word is still widely used in Hong Kong.[4] Some Cantonese referred to "song" as "gai jiao fan," meaning rice with a topping. It was not a formal Chinese meal that followed the *fan-cai* concept. This could have been an early form of a chop suey dish in America—rice with a gravy topping. Scholars and people interested in early Chinese American food culture are still debating and often disagree with each other about the origin of chop suey. A well-known Hong Kong doctor, Li Shu-fan, for example, insisted that chop suey was invented in China and existed as a popular dish in Taishan in the 1890s.[5]

Chop suey may have its culinary roots in China as Dr. Li or people holding similar opinions have argued. However, the popularity of chop suey owed more to its social origin rather than its culinary origin. Of the many legends about the origin of chop suey, most have the dish originating in the United States rather than in China. On the West Coast, the most popular story about the invention of chop suey is that it occurred during the gold rush. The late Chinese American historian Iris Chang cited this West Coast legend in her book *The Chinese in America*. During the gold rush, a group of drunken American miners entered a Chinese restaurant in San Francisco one late night just as the shop was about to close. The owner, in an effort to avoid a confrontation, decided to serve them. He quickly threw together a handful of leftover table scraps to stir-fry. The dish tasted good. When asked what it was, the cook replied "chop suey."[6] Another book on Chinese Americans also cited this legend and emphasized that chop suey quickly appeared on the business signs of every Chinese restaurant in the American West. Following the incident, every city with a population over 25,000 would have one or more chop suey houses.[7]

A different West Coast story about chop suey's origins relates to Chinese immigrants when they were building the continental railroad. According to this legend, a Chinese immigrant was hired as a cook for his fellow Chinese laborers working on constructing the railroads. But he did not know much about cooking. In a hurry, he just put rice, vegetables, and a little bit of meat together and cooked them in a wok. When asked what it was, he replied that the dish was called "chop suey."[8]

On the East Coast, most stories about chop suey were associated with Li Hongzhang's visit to the United States in 1896. Li was the most influential government official of China in diplomatic affairs at that time. The legend claims that Li did not touch much of Western food and preferred to go to Chinatown for his meals, where he was honored with sumptuous banquets and receptions during his visit. In Chinatown, his favorite dish was chop suey.

None of these stories should be treated as historical facts. The gold rush story is a folk tale. Early California journal and newspaper articles on Chinese restaurant food during that period never mentioned chop suey. Regarding the one that claimed chop suey was Li Hongzhang's favorite food, the historian Renqiu Yu has convincingly pointed out that the New York legend was a fiction. Li never ate in Chinatown.[9] He actually stayed away from Chinese communities during his visit. He was keenly aware that the Chinese were treated as an inferior race in America and did not want to mix with Chinese Americans. Though these stories are not factually "accurate," they seem historically "logical" because they all contributed to the invention of chop suey and they are all related to the Chinese experience in the United States. But the rise of chop suey was a result of Chinese adaptation to the racial environment of American society. Its Chinese culinary roots played no role in its popularity in America. Chop suey is not a culinary wonder but a meaningful social construct.

THE RISE OF CHOP SUEY HOUSES

Though the legend of chop suey's New York origin is a fiction, Li Hongzhang's visit did help promote the fame of chop suey. As the highest-ranking Chinese official to visit the United States in the nineteenth century, Li received a royal reception and great media attention during his American trip. American journalists and diplomats were also traveling with him on his ship. News reports about Li included detailed descriptions of what he ate. One report mentioned that Li brought his own cooks, who prepared for him seven meals daily when traveling across the ocean. His meals included sharks' fins and birds' nests.[10] Another report said that when he attended a dinner hosted by ex-secretary of state J. W. Foster, "Li drank sparingly of champagne during the banquet, and ate a little ice cream, but touched no solid food."[11] In still another report, when Li hosted a dinner at the Waldorf Astoria for U.S. diplomats who had served in China, he "let the veal and grouse pass untouched." Then his Chinese servant brought him his "real dinner," which consisted of "boiled chicken, cut up in small square pieces; a bowl of rice, and a bowl of vegetable soup." The report claimed: "For the first time in the history of the Waldorf, Chinese chefs have prepared Chinese dishes in Chinese pots, pans, and skillets. And the dishes they have cooked have created more curiosity and consternation than the presence of the great Viceroy himself."[12] Instead of providing realistic coverage of Chinese food culture, American media's scrutiny on what Li ate delivered an exotic and mysterious image of Chinese food.

While American news reports explored the "Oriental" lifestyle of a high-ranking Chinese official, Chinese immigrants discovered a business opportunity for Chinese food. Chop suey had already received more attention than other

Chinese dishes from American customers and the media before Li's visit. In his article "Chinese Cooking" published in the *Brooklyn Eagle* in 1884, Wong Chin Foo wrote that chop suey "may justly be called the 'national dish of China.'"[13] Media coverage about Li's visit further promoted American public curiosity and interest in Chinese culture and food. Thousands of New Yorkers flocked to Chinatown during Li's visit. For most of them, that was the only place where they could feast their eyes on "exotic Chinese culture." Even the mayor of New York City, William L. Strong, paid a visit to Chinatown on August 26, 1896, probably for the first time during his term of office. As a result, Chinese restaurants and stores did a thriving business during this period.[14]

In 1898, ten years after Wong Chin Foo's article, the journalist Louis Beck published his book *New York's Chinatown*. He observed that there were at least seven high-end Chinese restaurants in New York's Chinatown. They were located on the upper floors of "gorgeously decorated and illuminated buildings," with Chinese lanterns "suspended in reckless profusion from every available point. . . . The eating rooms are kept with scrupulous cleanness, and no unusual dirt will be found in the kitchens." Their menus were thirty-dishes long, ranging from shark's fin, an expensive $2 dish, to the 75-cent fried duck's foot and the 15-cent chop suey. Beck also noticed the popularity of chop suey. In his observation, chop suey consisted of "A Hash of Pork, with Celery, Onions, Bean Sprouts, etc."[15] Beck's version of chop suey was very different from the one described by Wong. Meat replaced intestines. Celery, onions, and bean sprouts became major vegetable ingredients. Most contemporary descriptions of chop suey are similar to Beck's observation. *Webster's Dictionary*, for example, defines chop suey as "a dish prepared chiefly from bean sprouts, bamboo shoots, water chestnuts, onions, mushrooms, and meat or fish and served with rice and soy sauce."[16] By 1898, this dish had been shaped in its American form.

Chop suey's marketability was due to its modest price. Beck reported that a typical chop suey joint in Chinatown was crudely decorated and had no tablecloths. Waiters cared more about getting a sale than receiving a tip. But both the place and waiters appeared clean.[17] A *New York Times* article in 1903 stated: "Chop suey enthusiasts declare that to get the dish in perfection, it is still necessary to go to the stuffy little places in Chinatown, where less attention is paid to appearances than is required in the newer resorts uptown. . . . Furthermore it is cheaper in Chinatown. A heaping dish of chop suey is served for 15 cents."[18] Outside of Chinatown, chop suey cost a little bit more. In a better-decorated Chinese restaurant, "a heaping dish of suey, with a cup of tea, a bowl of rice, costs 25 cents without mushrooms and 35 and 40 cents with them. But from the gourmet's point of view, the mushrooms (canned after a Chinese fashion) are supposed to be the principal feature of the dish."[19] Though mushrooms may not have been a major ingredient in American meals, this was a period of time when canned foods began to be used in American restaurants and homes. The use of canned mushrooms was obviously a key ingredient in chop suey meals and was well liked by American customers—"the cranberry sauce to the turkey" in Beck's words.

In Beck's description, Chinese restaurants catered to all kinds of American customers, including African Americans. He pointed out that "black Americans were among the earliest fans of eating Chinese. . . . Their [Chinese restaurants'] average daily receipts are estimated at $500, of which come $25 from Negroes, who seem to delight in frequenting the lower class places."[20] "Early menus offered a number of dishes that would have been familiar to the traditional black palate, including collard greens, pig's feet, and barbecued pork. . . . While the wait-staff may have whispered slurs in their native language, there is no record of any overt ethnic tension in New York's first Chinese restaurants."[21]

Chinese immigrants are known as laundrymen and restaurant operators in American history. As mentioned in the previous chapter, the laundry business became an important menial service occupation for the Chinese much earlier than restaurant operation. In the 1890s, the Chinese population in the city of New York reached 13,000, though only 4,000 lived in Chinatown while the rest were scattered throughout the city. About 8,000 Chinese were doing laundry work in the vicinity of New York.[22] Li's visit in 1896 provided an opportunity for the Chinese to make restaurant operation another feasible economical niche. When the American media "cooked up" chop suey as Li's favorite food, it became a hit dish in Chinese restaurants. Building on this momentum, motivated Chinese restaurant proprietors began to take chop suey out of Chinatown and opened establishments in non-Chinese communities.

NEW YORK GOES CHOP SUEY MAD

According to the 1903 *New York Times* article, the first Chinese who opened a chop suey house outside of Chinatown was a man named "Boston." He closed his restaurant at Doyer Street in Chinatown and opened it on Third Avenue and Rivington Street. "He did so well that soon many other Chinese followed him."[23] Charley Boston, also known by the name of Lee Quong June (or Li Quen Chong), was a thoroughly Americanized wealthy Chinese merchant, and a leader of the famous On Leong Tong in New York's Chinatown.[24] Little information is available on whether Boston was truly the first chop suey proprietor outside of Chinatown. But the report was significant. Boston's restaurant marked the beginning of Chinese immigrants moving outside of Chinatown in another major economic pursuit.

When Boston's restaurant became an immediate success, other Chinese followed suit, as they were anxious to squeeze into the New York restaurant market. Chop suey houses soon mushroomed in New York City and were particularly attractive to those customers who were active in the nightlife. Competition from newly established chop suey houses soon forced Boston to relocate his restaurant to Seventh Avenue, near Thirty-Fourth Street. Then more chop suey houses appeared, pushed past him, and opened everywhere from the wealthy Long Acre district to Harlem, a tourist site and a neighborhood into which African Americans from the South and black immigrants from West India began to move. "The result has been the establishment within a few months, of one hundred or more chop suey places between Forty-fifth Street and Fourteenth Street, and from Bowery to Eighth Avenue. A large number of these are in the Tenderloin."[25]

When Liang Qichao, a reformist leader and a famous Chinese intellectual, visited the United States in 1903, he was surprised to notice that there were more than 400 chop suey houses in New York alone.[26] Though Liang's estimate may not be accurate, New York City at that time experienced an explosive growth of chop suey houses. A *New York Times* article in 1900 exclaimed: "Judging from the outbreak of Chinese restaurants all over town, the city has gone 'chop-suey' mad."[27] In 1901, W. E. S. Fales, a returning American diplomat from China, also observed: "There is a growing taste on the part of New Yorkers for Chinese dishes. Chinese restaurants have sprung up all over the city, and they are well patronized, especially at night. The dish mostly in demand is chow chop suey, a most delicious concoction, if properly prepared."[28]

As a former vice consul in Xiamen (Amoy), China, Fales offered to teach American housewives how to cook chop suey in his *New York Times* article. He wrote, "For the benefit of those who do not care to go to a Chinese restaurant, let me give the recipe, so that it can be made by any intelligent house wife." Fales's recipe mentioned chicken livers and gizzards, but his major ingredients were "one pound young, clean pork, cut into small pieces, half an ounce of green root ginger[,] two stalks of celery." For cookery, Fales advised: "Sautee this in a frying pan over a hot fire, adding four tablespoonfuls of olive oil, one tablespoonful of salt, black and red pepper to taste, dash of cloves and cinnamon. When nearly done add small can of mushrooms, half a cup of either bean sprouts or French green peas, or string beans chopped fine, or asparagus tips."[29]

Fales's chop suey was a far cry from the rural dish chao za sui, the stir-fried animal intestines in China. It is doubtful whether he had actually tasted chao za sui as a Western diplomat in China. But his longtime diplomatic career in China made him appear like an authority on Chinese food. His recipe was actually an Americanized version of a Chinese dish. It would taste like an elegant Western dish that would no doubt fit the taste of middle-class American families. Fales's recipe and the popularity of chop suey among Americans only indicated that chop suey had symbolic Chinese roots. Its culinary base was in the United States.

Eating out in New York City was a social trend at that time. The city's night-life generated more sales for restaurant business. According to the 1903 *New York Times* article, once or twice a week, or even more often, many New Yorkers had a "hankering" for chop suey. But they did not want to go all the way to China-town for chop suey meals after theater hours. Some had safety concerns about eating Chinese food in Chinatown at night. Many wanted to stay in the theater district. Middle-class bachelors often hoped to encounter actresses after the per-formance. Italian and other ethnic restaurants had already been established in the theater district to serve a fast, nightlife crowd of New Yorkers.[30] As a result, a well-known man in the Broadway café set, who used to bring parties of well-dressed night-lifers into Chinatown frequently to have a chop suey treat, sug-gested to Charley Boston that he open a chop suey house outside of Chinatown. The man guaranteed the success of such an undertaking.[31] When moving out of Chinatown, a chop suey house could cater to more nightlife customers for social gatherings.

Chinese restaurant proprietors proved to be shrewd businessmen outside of Chinatown. The chop suey house in Harlem, for example, was "a far cry" from the one in Long Acres, an upper-scale neighborhood in uptown Manhattan. The latter was under "the light of multi-colored lanterns, and amid the silk and bam-boo decorations that are quite luxurious from an Oriental point of view." Called a "resort" by the 1903 *New York Times* article, the chop suey restaurant in Long Acres competed with other high-end American restaurants across the street, and "claimed the most exclusive patronage of the town." Its clients were appar-ently those middle- or upper-class Americans who were active in the nightlife. To cater to their eating habits, chop suey houses in the uptown area opened only at night. "This resort, like a great many others of its kind that thrive within ten blocks of it toward any point of the compass, is not open in the daytime. Only the cheaper sort of places, much further down town, are open before nightfall, and they do business very much in the style of American restaurants that are compelled to serve early breakfast."[32] However, the decoration, floor plan, and interior and exterior design of a cheaper chop suey joint outside Chinatown and the work uniforms of its cooks and waiters looked very similar to other less expensive New York restaurants.[33] The goal of chop suey proprietors was not to attract Chinese customers or the fluctuating tourist business but to build a reli-able local clientele. They wanted to make their restaurants part of metropolitan New York's social life.

Chop suey businesses served all social classes and all racial groups. Whether opening in an upper-scale area or a poor neighborhood, chop suey houses usu-ally had no safety issues. According to the 1903 *New York Times* article, Chinese chop suey houses were as safe as any other restaurant along upper Broadway or the avenues that ran parallel to it. The article emphasized that the owners were not involved in any illegal activities, unlike some of the other restaurants open at night. It quoted a few police officers who spoke favorably of the chop suey houses in regard to safety issues. The article pointed out: "Many persons who have seen this crop of chop suey establishments have jumped to the conclusion that opium smoking and kindred vices usually associated with Chinamen have been going [on] there with the tacit consent of the police."[34] In addition to the "resort" chop suey restaurants, there were also a couple of chop suey houses in the uptown area that were exclusively frequented by African American clients who "were afraid to go to Chinatown" but "developed an extreme fondness for chop suey" because it had a lot of chicken meat.[35] Though these chop suey restaurants were not as fancy as the one in Long Acres, they were clean and safe.

As an ethnic food, chop suey provoked and satisfied American curiosity and taste. The 1903 *New York Times* article on chop suey noted the importance of using soy sauce in cooking this dish. Though the article still pointed out that no two Chinese cooks made it exactly alike, its author wrote: "Everything seems to depend on the mushrooms and the mysterious black or brown sauce that is poured over the stew. . . . That sauce they put on it is a powerful steadier, whatever it may be. A man who likes the dish seldom gets through one portion of chop suey after a night out without feeling a second one."[36] The mysterious black or brown sauce was actually Chinese soy sauce made of soybeans, which has existed in Chinese culinary culture since ancient times. It was a common seasoning in Chinese cookery. Soy sauce added flavor to a chop suey dish whether its meat was beef, chicken, or pork. If soy sauce was regarded as a key element responsible for chop suey's success, it indicated that the flavor of Chinese cuisine was not a problem for many American customers.

While popular, chop suey was often viewed as an exotic and mysterious food. The *New York Times* article of 1903 further stated: "Innumerable attempts have been made to get Chinamen to tell what chop suey is made of. Chinese cooks have been hired by families, but never seemed to be able to impart the secret of the dish to others. When Americans asked the Chinese cooks about the chop suey recipes published in books and periodicals, they often smiled knowingly without making any response."[37] In fact, chop suey was anything but a mysterious dish. Chinese cooks were fully aware of its humble origin and knew that the chopped meat and vegetable ingredients were different from the original chao za sui in China. They were creating a new dish under an old name just to fit American customers' palates. Animal intestines were abandoned. Meats and vegetables were chopped into thin pieces so that customers could conveniently use chopsticks or spoons in a chop suey meal. As a restaurant meal, its Chinese flavor did not totally disappear, though the Chinese *fan-cai* concept was completely gone. While being more and more Americanized and popular, chop suey houses became fast-food type of restaurants in the American food market.

On June 15, 1904, the *New York Times* reported that a Chinese man named Lem Sen claimed that "he was the original inventor and sole proprietor of the dish known as chop suey." Sen insisted that chop suey was no more a national dish of the Chinese than pork and beans: "There was not a grain of anything Celestial in it." With many legal documents to prove his claim and by hiring Rufus P. Livermore, a lawyer who had an office in the St. Paul Building, Sen threatened to obtain "an injunction in the Supreme Court restraining all Chinese restaurant keepers from making and serving chop suey." According to his own story, he was born in San Francisco and had never been to China. He had worked for many years in a Chinese restaurant in San Francisco, and was later employed in a "Bohemian" restaurant run by an American. "It was just before the arrival of Li Hung-Chang [Li Hongzhang] on a visit to this country that a real interest in things Mongolian and Celestial began. The owner of the restaurant suggested that Lem Sen manufacture some weird dish that would pass as Chinese and gratify the public craze at that time. Lem Sen says that it was then he introduced to the astonished world the great dish."[38] Though the news report was anecdotal in nature and Sen's claim looks like a prank, he did emphasize that chop suey was invented in America.

Following its popularity, American newspapers and magazines began to publish food review articles on chop suey. One article quoted a New York doctor who believed that chop suey was as "digestible again as a broiled lobster." The article recommended it as a healthy food especially for those who drank too much beer. According to the article, a dish of chop suey was the finest thing in the world for those customers who "have been taking a little more beer than they should, and want to feel all right in the morning." The sauce helped "steady the stomach. . . . The Chinese custom of serving tea with the go-to-bed meal is a splendid one." With a chop suey meal, a person after drinking beer "sleeps like a top."[39] However, it was probably the large amount of carbohydrates in the rice of chop suey meals that functioned as the real sobering agent. Tea was helpful too. Chop suey operators served tea mainly because they could not get liquor licenses due to racial discrimination. Liquor usually brought more sales and higher profits for restaurant businesses, especially during night hours. But for chop suey houses, tea was often the only beverage they could legally serve.

CHOP SUEY IN AMERICAN ART AND LITERATURE

While chop suey emerged and remained as one of the most visible racial/ethnic labels of Chinese Americans, it also embodied American metropolitan culture. In Sinclair Lewis's novel *Main Street*, we see an interesting scene of how middle-class Americans learned to accept Chinese food. The main character, Carol, used chop suey and chow mein as an entree food for her dinner party guests:

Before they were quite tired of the concert Carol led them in a dancing proces-
sion to the dining-room, to blue bowls of chow mein, with Lichee nuts and ginger preserved in syrup. None of them save that city-rounder Harry Haydock had
heard of any Chinese dish except chop sooey. With agreeable doubt they ventured through the bamboo shoots into the golden fried noodles of the chow
mein; and Dave Dyer did a not very humorous Chinese dance with Nat Hicks;
and there was hubbub and contentment.[40]

However, Lewis presented quite a nervous scene. Middle-class Americans were
still not sure if they should treat a Chinese dish as a party food or as a bargain-
priced ethnic meal.

Though Sinclair Lewis spelt the word as "chop sooey," "chop suey" was the
standard spelling and officially entered into the English vocabulary. According to
Imogene Lim and John Eng-wong, both *A Dictionary of Americanisms*, in its 1951
edition, and the *Oxford English Dictionary*, in its 1989 edition, included "chop
suey" and "chow mein" and cited examples of their usage as early as 1898 and
1903.[41] Since then, "chop suey" has been part of the English vocabulary.

As a culinary culture, "chop suey" denoted concoction and blending, and
attracted several American artists and musicians. John Sloan was a fan of Chinese food and often frequented chop suey houses. After one such visit, he
painted *Chinese Restaurant* in 1909, which featured a flamboyantly dressed
young woman feeding a cat while three other male customers looked on.
Twenty years later, Edward Hopper, who also often frequented Chinese restaurants, painted his masterpiece *Chop Suey*.[42] The restaurant in this famous
oil painting was not a street food joint in Chinatown but a stylish café where
middle-class Americans socialized. In the foreground, the painting features
two fashionable women facing each other. Behind them is a man in the shadow
looking down his cigarette, while a pretty woman looks at him with inquiring
eyes. On the table are a lonely purple, square-shaped clay teapot and an empty
greenish blue porcelain bowl. There are no teacups or food. The four guests are
sitting in silence. Outside of the large restaurant window is a bright red sign-
board with four big white letters, "S U E Y." While displaying a theme about
human loneliness in metropolitan New York, the central figures in the art are
two young women coming out to eat on their own. Restaurant life was no longer a man's world. Women were frequent guests in chop suey houses. In 1934,
the photographer Imogen Cunningham captured an image of Chinatown in
New York, although the scene does not look like Chinatown. None of the people on the street are Chinese. Merchandise on a horse-drawn cart was not Chinese food. But on the second floor of the street is a Chinese restaurant. It has
three visible "chop suey" signboards. In the photo, chop suey houses were part
of the social landscape in modern New York.

Jazz musician Louis Armstrong's "Cornet Chop Suey" was released in 1926 at the height of his career. He put "chop suey" in the title because of his lifelong passion for Chinese food. Sidney Bechet's "Who'll Chop Your Suey When I'm Gone?" in 1925 goes as follows:

Chop suey, chop suey!
Mixed with all the hokum and bally hooey.
Something real and glowing grand.
Sheds a light all over the land.
Boston, Austin, Wichita, and St. Louey,
Chop suey. Chop suey, chop suey! Chop suey, chop suey!

The song sang out the popularity of chop suey among ordinary Americans across the country. Together with Armstrong's music, Bechet's hit song reverberated and further boosted chop suey's rising fame. Being a theme of popular art and music, chop suey was more than an economic success. It was a cultural landmark in New York City that embodied the metropolitan American lifestyle.

THE GOLDEN ERA OF CHOP SUEY HOUSES

At the turn of the twentieth century, rapid urbanization created many office jobs for young people who had limited budgets and a short lunch time but preferred warm food. "The proliferation of a new lower-middle class of male and female office and shop employees after the turn of the century created a burgeoning market which neither the old saloons nor the higher-class restaurants could tap. Short lunch hours and expanding cities made going home for lunch impossible. Hot lunches were regarded as necessary and lunch pails were too working-class. As a result, new kinds of restaurants tried to fill the growing gap in the middle."[43] Chop suey houses were a good choice because they served cheap and warm food. Though highly Americanized, chop suey meals remained Chinese in one important way. They were fully cooked warm meals. Compared with the alternative of cold sandwiches and salads, many New York office workers liked chop suey because it was warm food.

In the 1920s, chop suey houses were especially attractive to women office workers. Edward Hopper's painting was based on his close observation of this phenomenon. The *New York Times* once reported: "It [chop suey] is vigorously vying with sandwiches and salad as the noontime nourishment of the young women typists and telephonists of John, Dey, and Fulton Streets. It rivals coffee-and-two-kinds-of-cake as the recess repast of the sales forces for West Thirty-fourth street department stores. At the lunch hour there is an eager exodus toward Chinatown for the women workers employed in Franklin, Duane, and

Worth Streets. To them the district is not an intriguing bit of transplanted Orient. It is simply a good place to eat."[44] Chinatown was close to their workplace and served chop suey meals with an authentic flavor at a lower price. Chop suey was not a mysterious food but a regular lunch option for these women patrons. Their word of mouth probably further spread chop suey's reputation among even more lunch customers. Some chop suey houses provided breakfast. One Chinese restaurant owner proudly said that in addition to a lunch business, he also had breakfast customers; chop suey seemed destined to become a necessity of New York life. When he retired, he said he wanted to take chop suey back to China.[45]

Chop suey houses spread from New York to other cities and states on the East Coast, such as Boston, Long Island, New Jersey, and Connecticut, as well as to the midwestern and western United States. In 1900, Chicago had only one Chinese restaurant. By 1905, it had forty Chinese restaurants, and only five were in Chinatown. By 1915, it had 118, and only six or seven were in Chinatown.[46] In 1900, there were but two or three Chinese restaurants in Los Angeles, frequented almost exclusively by Chinese. There were at least fifteen Chinese restaurants by 1910 when "Caucasian customers discovered that Chinese food was quite good and not all poisonous" as some had imagined. Several of these Chinese restaurants were outside Chinatown, and a few were in downtown Los Angeles.[47] By 1920, there were more Chinese who worked in the restaurant business than in the laundry business. As Ching Chao Wu documented, while 11,534 Chinese were laundrymen, 6,943 were cooks, 2,766 were waiters, and 1,688 were managers.[48] On the West Coast, interestingly, there were not only Chinese but also Japanese and Korean Americans who became chop suey proprietors. In the 1920s, one of the largest Chinese restaurants in the Los Angeles area was Crown Chop Suey Parlor in Pasadena, owned by a Japanese immigrant, a Mr. Kawagoye.[49] Surviving in the same racial environment, it was not so difficult for Japanese Americans or Korean Americans to learn how to cook chop suey and operate a Chinese restaurant.

Though San Francisco was the first city in which Chinese immigrants landed in America, the number of Chinese restaurants there was modest compared to New York City. In 1905, San Francisco had forty-six Chinese restaurants. The number grew to seventy-eight in 1925.[50] By then Chinatown had become a tourist attraction in San Francisco. The number of Chinese restaurants was growing more rapidly in San Francisco after the 1906 earthquake when Chinatown was rebuilt and when chop suey houses spread to the West Coast. But the food served in San Francisco's Chinese restaurants by then was very different from what was served in the 1860s and 1890s. Photographs of Chinatown taken after the earthquake show that Grant Avenue was peppered with bold chop suey signs. Chow mein or egg foo yong was advertised alongside chop suey.[51] The growth of chop suey houses took place at a critical moment. Prior to the quake, practically all San Francisco Chinese restaurants were located in Chinatown. After the quake, between 1905 and 1925, 35 percent of Chinese restaurants moved into non-Asian neighborhoods.[52] San Francisco, with the oldest Chinatown in America, was also losing its Chinese population. By 1920, only 7,744 Chinese remained in San Francisco—1.5 percent of the city's 506,676 residents.[53]

Chop suey restaurants boosted the tourist business in San Francisco and helped generate many employment opportunities for the Chinese. By 1938, San Francisco Chinatown drew close to one million visitors annually, where they left behind some $28 million, $5 million of which was spent along Grant Avenue. Between 1929 and 1949, the number of Chinese restaurants in San Francisco increased from 78 to 146.[54] Some restaurants tried to develop their specialty by serving stir-fried dishes, different types of noodles, or Cantonese dim sum food. Some other restaurant owners put a topping on their noodle dishes and advertised their business as a chop suey noodle shop. But they all had to offer chop suey, egg foo yong, and chow mein. Their business names, whether Peking Restaurant, Wong Coffee House, or Lee Noodle Shop, were all accompanied by chop suey signs or banners. After 1950, while the total population of San Francisco was decreasing, the number of Chinese residents and number of Chinese restaurants continued to climb.[55] Eventually, the city regained a large percentage of the Chinese population it used to have during the gold rush years.

With a growing number of chop suey houses in San Francisco, some Chinese merchants realized that it might not be the food but the "Oriental temperament" of their business that attracted mainstream American customers. In her research, Ruth Hall Whitfield pointed out that there were two types of chop suey houses: one type, located in the low-rent district, catered to low-income customers; the other, located in the theater district, catered to the after-theater crowd who liked the "pseudo-Oriental atmosphere" and the American dance bands. Some of the New York chop suey houses in the downtown area used this latter model.[56] Chop suey was essentially a cheap meal. To make more money and higher profits, the Chinese had to go beyond food service and further promote "Oriental exoticism" in their business. In the 1920s, cocktail bars, cafés, and nightclubs like Chinese Village, Twin Dragons, Chinese Pagoda, and Jade Palace began to appear in San Francisco's Chinatown. Live music and dancing performances rather than food became the major attraction in these restaurants. From the very beginning, such bars attracted tourist customers, especially white males. Many Chinese families in Chinatown became increasingly upset at seeing their neighborhood turned into an ethnic "theme park."

More ambitious merchants opened nightclubs outside of Chinatown. Some of them did not even serve Chinese food as they targeted mainstream customers. The most famous Chinese nightclub in San Francisco was Forbidden City, started by Charlie Low in December 1938 on Sutter Street outside of China-town.[57] In its peak days, the club was often fully booked. The customers were drawn there not by its food but by nude dances performed by Asian women. Among the celebrities who visited it were Bob Hope, Ronald Reagan, and many others.[58] The seductive and exotic image of Asian women was a major feature of such Chinese-run restaurants and nightclubs in those years. Forbidden City actually served mediocre Western food. What had been "upgraded" was not the food but the "Oriental atmosphere." Such restaurant operators knew that could play a key role in the success of their businesses.

CHOP SUEY BECAME CANNED FOOD

In the 1920s, chop suey began to appear on the dining tables of many Ameri-can homes. According to one article, "Chinese chop suey is so delicious that the hostess cannot make a mistake in placing it before her guest in such a luncheon menu as the following (which is equally as good a supper menu): Chop suey, Hot graham Rolls, Coffee, Orange soufflé."[59] Meanwhile newspapers and maga-zines also carried chop suey recipes due to the growing interest of American cus-tomers in Chinese food. Many housewives became interested in learning how to cook chop suey at home. From the 1910s to the 1950s, the *Los Angeles Times* and other newspapers often carried recipes on how to cook chop suey, rice, and other Chinese dishes.[60]

Chop suey was also used as a food for American soldiers. Joining spaghetti and tamales as "ethnic" dishes listed in the 1942 edition of the U.S. Army cook-book, chop suey and chow mein were staples of the military mess hall.[61] The biggest fan of chop suey in the army was Dwight D. Eisenhower. When he was a major stationed in Washington, D.C., in the 1930s, Eisenhower was a faithful customer of the Sun Chop Suey Restaurant owned by Jew Gam On on Colum-bia Road. He often took his wife and young son there. His patronage was inter-rupted during World War II and then resumed when he came back from the war. As president, Eisenhower continued to order his favorite food—chicken chop suey—there for his family from time to time. His request was simply that the chop suey be good and hot.[62] Eisenhower tended to stay with one dish such as chicken chop suey. He ordered it not as an exotic food but as a regular meal avail-able for average American customers.

When Jeno Paulucci, a well-known food business entrepreneur, served in the U.S. armed forces in Asia during World War II, he noticed that many of his fellow American GIs liked Chinese food just as much as he did.[63] Paulucci first began working in grocery sales and was quite successful at it. Born to poor Italian immigrant parents in Minnesota, Paulucci used to help his mother run a small grocery store when he was a child. After coming back home from his military duty, Paulucci could hardly forget chop suey and its popularity among his fellow servicemen. Then in 1947, at the age of twenty-nine, Paulucci borrowed $2,500 and purchased a Chinese food cannery.[64] Paulucci noticed that some Japanese Americans in Minnesota were growing bean sprouts, a basic ingredient of Chinese dishes. Realizing that celery was another principal ingredient in chow mein and chop suey, he visited Florida farms and discovered that celery was trimmed evenly to fit into crates for shipping and that he could purchase the trimmings. As a talented food entrepreneur, he saw the potential of Chinese food. "I felt here must be a tremendous untapped market for ready prepared Chinese foods for home use," he once said. "The food industry was missing the boat, allowing the restaurants to handle all the take-home business."[65] Paulucci's vision was to mass produce Chinese food and distribute it nationally.

By the 1950s, Americanized Chinese food became one of the major "national" food items in the United States. More and more Americans consumed it regularly. According to a *New York Times* article in 1955, the most extensively promoted and consumed "national" food items were Italian, Chinese, and Jewish. Most of the items were canned, but an increasing number were beginning to appear in frozen form. Sales of frozen and processed Chinese food in 1955 was predicted to reach $20 million and had increased 70 percent since World War II. There were now twenty-five Chinese foods in canned form.[66]

Paulucci's initial market was the Scandinavian-settled area of Duluth in northern Minnesota.[67] Chow mein was the first product offered by his future fast-food empire, Chun King Corporation. He canned and packed as much as he could sell and trucked his chow mein to nearby Duluth each night. It was in the unlikely market of Scandinavian-settled northern Minnesota that this Italian American businessman successfully promoted chow mein as a mass-produced frozen food. Paulucci used his mother's guidance for seasonings when he started his canned Chinese food business. In fact, his chicken broth and spicy flavor were based on recipes from his mother's kitchen. One of his later canned foods was actually marketed through the Michelina's brand named after his mother.[68] Adding his own spices and chicken broth, Paulucci made canned chow mein a national food in America.

In the 1940s, there were also Chinese American pioneers in manufacturing frozen foods. Two Wong brothers from Los Angeles's Chinatown manufactured frozen Chinese foods while operating their Grandview Garden Restaurant. They hired Thomas Yue, an exchange student from Tianjin, China, who had studied food production at Oregon State University, as their manager. In addition to their own brand, they manufactured products for other companies such as Morton's frozen pies. Their brother-in-law, Gordon Chun, later ran the company's operations.[69] It is not clear if their vision was similar to Paulucci's, but their company never reached the same level as his. In the 1950s, Chun King's competitors consisted of about fifteen other companies across the country, including La Choy Food Products, in Archbold, Ohio, a division of Beatrice Foods; Minsura Trading Company and Great China Food Products Company, in Chicago; Wong's Frozen Chinese Foods, in Los Angeles; Ruby Foo's Products and Chin & Lee Company, both in New York City; and Temple Frosted Foods Inc., in Brooklyn, New York.[70]

In 1957, Paulucci patented his canned Chinese food by packaging chow mein or chop suey in one can and vegetables in another.[71] In October 1963, Paulucci's Chun King Corporation purchased Chun Wong, Inc., based in Compton, California, a leading frozen convenience food packer on the West Coast since 1948.[72] Then he expanded his business across the country from its Minnesota base. The famous Chun King brand chow mein eventually grew into a manufacturing line that included egg rolls and other specialty products. The brand name reminds people of Chongqing, the war capital of China in the 1940s. Paulucci probably learned of this city when he served in the Pacific theater. By the mid-1960s, his Chun King brand merchandise became the top-selling canned Chinese food, and his canned chop suey and chow mein were distributed across the country. The Chun King Corporation sold 80 percent of the canned Chinese food in the national market when Paulucci sold the company for $63 million in cash in 1967 to the R. J. Reynolds Tobacco Company. In 1989, a food and beverage giant in Singapore purchased Chun King from R. J. Reynolds.[73] Kellogg's, Howard Johnson's, and many other companies were all once involved in producing Chinese food.[74]

CHOW MEIN AND WONDER BREAD

Mass-produced canned chop suey and chow mein reached the national market when "chop suey" and "chow mein" became household words in American food culture. Like chop suey, chow mein also entered into the English vocabulary. Beginning in the 1930s, the chow mein sandwich became a hit local food in Fall River, Massachusetts. Instead of ground beef, fried chow main was placed in between a hamburger-size bun. Many local restaurants, Chinese and non-Chinese, in southeastern Massachusetts served a hot chow mein sandwich with brown gravy.

Soon the food spread to Rhode Island. According to Imogene Lim and John Eng-Wong, the chow mein sandwich was so popular that some restaurants even offered meatless versions on Fridays for Catholic customers. Chinese restaurants used a kind of thin sauce because the customers requested that the gravy be strained for their meatless Friday diet. For the Depression-era youth, "the chow mein sandwich was a real treat," even cheaper than a regular Chinese meal, costing only 30 or 40 cents.[75] As a popular local food, both Chinese and non-Chinese restaurants placed chopped meat, celery, onions, and bean sprouts with gravy onto a hamburger bun or Portuguese bread along with chow mein noodles. Nathan's in the cities of Woonsocket and Pawtucket, Rhode Island, Lowe's and Woolworth's in downtown Providence, Rhode Island, and their fellow chain stores in the Fall River area and on Cape Cod all offered chow mein sandwiches. Like cream cheese rolls (egg rolls on the outside, cheese steak inside) in Philadelphia, the chow mein sandwich was a famous local dish in the New England area.

The St. Paul sandwich in St. Louis, Missouri, was another Chinese creation. Like a regular sandwich, the bread was slathered with mayonnaise; a pickle, sliced tomato, and iceberg lettuce could be added. But a deep-fried egg foo yong patty was the key to the sandwich. The egg foo yong patty consisted of several whipped eggs, bean sprouts, and minced white onions. If the customers wanted to go beyond the basic version, they could ask for additions such as shrimp, beef, chicken, or ham. According to Billy Luu, Park Chop Suey Restaurant's proprietor, the sandwich was created by his restaurant's former owner, Steven Yuen, who named it for his hometown, St. Paul, Minnesota.[76] Beginning in the 1960s, this sandwich became one of the most popular offerings by Chinese restaurants in St. Louis. Yuen's creation was featured in the PBS documentary "Sandwiches That You Will Like" in 2003. Though it started as a specialty in Chinese restaurants, many non-Chinese restaurants also offered it. Some American families simply ordered the egg foo yong patties without the brown sauce from a takeout restaurant. Longtime customers knew how to assemble the sandwich at home with white bread, brown sauce, pickles, mayonnaise, and lettuce. It had evolved into a familiar local food. When egg foo yong is sandwiched by Wonder bread, it has become a hybridized food, and it is difficult to decide whether it is Chinese or Western.

CHOP SUEY GOING TO CHINA

Americans eventually realized chop suey was only an imagined authentic Chinese food. In 1924, the *Los Angeles Times* carried an article entitled "China Has Most of the Things Chinese, But Chop Suey Isn't to Be Found There." According to the article, "China has played a little joke on the world. Its citizens in America have popularized chop suey as if that dish were characteristically Chinese. It is not. It is unknown in China."[77] An article in the *New York Times* in 1928 also noted that the dish was virtually unknown in China. While beef was a common ingredient in chop suey, the average Chinese did not consume beef frequently.[78] But Chinese restaurant proprietors knew what they were doing from the very beginning. When job opportunities were so limited for Chinese immigrants during the exclusion era, restaurant work became one of the few options available to them.

Though there was no chop suey in China, the dish did have an intrinsic linkage with its home country. Its imagined authenticity actually depended on this linkage. The story of chop suey as Li Hongzhang's favorite dish was widely circulated in various versions. When another *Los Angeles Times* article confirmed that China had no chop suey, it repeated the famous legend. According to the article, "Any of these meals I have yet to get a taste of chop suey. The truth seems to be that there is no such dish known in China although it is commonly served as Chinese throughout the United States." This article was actually commenting on the restaurant market in Canton, the hometown of many Chinese immigrants and a city with numerous restaurants. It was supposedly the birthplace of chop suey. Linking chop suey to Li Hongzhang, the article pointed out:

> It originated at a dinner that Prince Li Hung Chang gave in New York when he made his trip around the world. Prince Li carried his own chef with him, and the menu was strictly Chinese. One of the dishes especially delights the wife of the guest of honor and she asked Li what it was. Prince Li called in his chef, and the chef replied in Chinese that it was his own creation called "chop suey" which meant a mixture or hash. Prince Li then said in English: "It is a chop suey." The American woman spread the news of "chop suey," the wonderful dish.[79]

Though the American media discovered that there was no chop suey in China, its image as an authentic Chinese dish was already rooted in the American public imagination. The report repeated the Li Hongzhang legend. Being Li's favorite dish, American consumers would not think of this "wonderful dish" as a fake. The article finally concluded: "The name was taken up by the Chinese restaurants in America and today chop suey is the chief concoction that they serve."[80] Interestingly, while chop suey became less and less Chinese in its culinary format, it appeared more and more "authentic" as a Chinese food in the minds of the American public.

Entitled "China Disowns Chop Suey," a *Los Angeles Times* article in 1937 put yet another spin on the story:

> Chop suey, you know, considered all over the world, except in China, as being a typical Chinese dish, is not Chinese at all. The story is told the Viceroy Li Hung Chang, upon being pestered by American newspapermen during a meal as to the name of the dish he was eating, snapped "Chop Suey" (Literally "dirty mixed fragments") in his annoyance. The name stuck and Chinese restaurateurs, both in America and Europe, were quick to see the publicity value of the name.[81]

The report recognized again that chop suey did not exist in China but acknowledged that Chinese immigrants made it famous all over the world, except in China.

The food historians Waverly Root and Richard de Rochemont pointed out that American culinary history was so characterized by its cosmopolitan tradition that sometimes restaurateurs created foreign names for their cuisine. While chop suey "has gotten around the country, in restaurants or in cans," many Americans "who eat it certainly do not think of it as part of their native fare; yet it was invented in the United States and was unknown in China until very recently, when it began to be imported into that country for the delectation of the American visitors beginning to arrive there."[82]

Ironically, chop suey, as an invention of overseas Chinese, attempted to return home as it followed Western travelers to China and tried to settle in places where Americans congregated. A *Los Angeles Times* article in 1924 reported that searching China from end to end, one could not find a dish of chop suey, or a Chinese cook who knew how to prepare it, or a restaurant that appeared similar to a chop suey house in America except in the American quarter of Shanghai.[83] During World War II, when American soldiers went to China, they were searching around Chongqing, the wartime capital and a city in remote Southwest China, for real chop suey. Only a few local restaurants advertised: "We serve authentic San Francisco–style chop suey."[84] In China, or at least in such advertisements, chop suey was featured as an authentic American dish. Going back to its symbolic home, China, chop suey was promoted as a popular American food. After Japan was defeated and Shanghai regained its international life and prosperity, Westerners could find a neon sign in a main street that proclaimed: "Genuine American Chop Suey Served Here."[85] In the 1950s, Tokyo had many restaurants that offered Chinese dishes. But only a big restaurant that served American food offered chop suey.[86] Japanese customers knew that it was not a Chinese but an American food.

In 1928, a chop suey restaurant was also opened in Beijing. However, local Chinese customers failed to develop an appetite for the invention by their overseas brethren. The chop suey restaurant in Beijing soon closed. Compared with Shanghai, the influence of the Western community was much smaller in Beijing. Local Chinese had never heard of chop suey. "It was an American dish and there were not enough Americans in Beijing to support it."[87] Many Americans who liked Chinese food were shocked to learn that the only chop suey house in Beijing was closed and that average residents of any city in China knew nothing of chop suey.[88] Beijing was a metropolitan city that housed many good restaurants from other Chinese regions. Chop suey as an "authentic" Chinese American food was either too foreign or too strange for the local residents.

Chop suey eventually faded away from the American restaurant world. When a new wave of Chinese immigrants arrived with the 1965 immigration reform, the Chinese restaurant business experienced a new surge. The new immigrants preferred genuine rather than Americanized Chinese food. They brought in new tastes, created new businesses, and built new communities. Suburban Chinese neighborhoods emerged in Flushing, Queens County, New York, or Monterey Park and a host of San Gabriel Valley cities of Southern California, where thousands of Chinese restaurants have congregated. Few of them served chop suey. Genuine Chinese food has replaced Americanized dishes. Chop suey gradually lost its traditional appeal. But it had already accomplished its historical mission to establish a solid culinary bond between American customers and Chinese food. Without chop suey, it would have been a much more challenging task for contemporary Chinese restaurant businesses to enter the American restaurant market.

CREATIVE ASSIMILATION

Whether chop suey was a real or imagined favorite dish of Li Hongzhang, Chinese immigrants made it a true legend in food history. From a humble rural dish, Chinese immigrants generated a series of fast-food types of meals in their restaurant businesses. On the menus of Chinese chop suey houses were chicken chop suey, beef chop suey, pork chop suey, fish chop suey, vegetable chop suey, chow mein, egg foo yong, paper-wrapped chicken, and many other American Chinese dishes. While serving different types of meat chop suey dishes, vegetable ingredients routinely included bean sprouts, celery, bamboo shoots, water chestnuts, and mushrooms. Though not belonging to one restaurant business chain, Chinese proprietors developed standardized chop suey meals in order to promote the familiarity of Chinese food to the American public.

Popular as it was, chop suey essentially embodies cheap exoticism in the eyes of American customers. It succeeded mostly as a bargain-price food in racial America. Chop suey houses bore the menial service characteristics of an ethnic operation. If chop suey somehow indicated "assimilation," it was a case of "creative assimilation." It shows that the formation of Chinese American ethnicity was more than a simple blending of Western and Asian cultures. It reflects how Chinese Americans negotiated with a hostile racial environment, explored new opportunities, and creatively adapted their food culture to American society. While Chinese food was being shaped, transformed, and sometimes altered by American popular tastes, Chinese restaurant businesses at the same time helped shape the American diet. The adaptation was a two-way process.

Chop suey houses should be understood as a pioneer fast-food business in the America restaurant market. They were not big, corporate chains. Most chop suey houses were individually owned small businesses. The similar formula for cooking chop suey meals reflected a mentality shared by all Chinese food operators. They understood well that their food had to satisfy not only American customers' culinary tastes but also their social expectations of Chinese cuisine. The niche in the mainstream American restaurant market for Chinese food was not fine dining but cheap ethnic meals. Chop suey was the right format for such a niche. Embedded in the history of chop suey is how Chinese immigrants creatively found employment opportunities for themselves during the Chinese exclusion period.

When Li Hongzhang visited the United States in 1896, the Chinese Exclusion Act of 1882 had been extended for another ten years by the Geary Act of 1892. Li was fully aware of the unequal treatment of the Chinese in America, especially in California. In his comment on the Geary Act, Li pointed out that the law denied Chinese immigrants the same rights granted to other immigrants and that the Chinese Exclusion Act was a most unfair law. He asked American journalists: "Do not consider me as a high Chinese official, but as a cosmopolitan; not as a Mandarin, but as a plain citizen of China and of the world, and let me ask what you expect to derive from excluding cheap Chinese labor from America? Cheaper labor means cheaper commodities, and better commodities at lower price. . . . You are proud of your liberty and your freedom; but is this freedom?"[89] History is full of surprises.

Though Li's visit could not protect Chinese immigrants from Chinese exclusion laws, it did accidentally help promote chop suey as a famed Chinese food in America. Chinese restaurant businesses began to expand into mainstream American society shortly after Li's visit. Thus a Chinese immigrant writer wrote in 1948 that this Chinese dish was no longer a traditional Chinese food but a dish specially prepared for American people. "It is called Li Hong Chang Chop Suey; and the same dish has ever since that time been listed on the menu in that name—chop suey."[90]

5 · KUNG PAO KOSHER
American Jews and Chinese Food

AN UNLIKELY ETHNIC ROMANCE

Jewish immigrants' interest in Chinese food looked like an impossible ethnic romance. The two ethnic groups were very different from each other in food traditions. In Chinese food culture, almost everything alive could be edible, from flock animals to wild snakes. There were no taboos in the Chinese diet. Cookery was a flexible culinary art. In comparison, Jews had a highly restrictive and complex set of dietary laws regarding the slaughtering, processing, and preparation of food. Their dietary rules involved religious rituals. In the Jewish world, how food was prepared and eaten was closely tied to cultural and religious traditions. "God gave Jewish people 613 *mitzvot* (commandments)" and one of them was that "you shall eat to be satisfied and bless God as it gave you good land."[1] Food reflected their cultural beliefs, philosophy, and world outlook. As Gaye Tuchman and Harry Levine put it, of all the peoples whom Jewish immigrants and their children met, of all the foods they encountered in America, the Chinese were the most foreign, the most "un-Jewish." "Yet American Jews defined this particular foreignness not as forbidding but as appealing, attractive, and desirable."[2]

Chinese food has a unique place in the experience of American Jews. Jewish immigrants and their children have been the most enthusiastic and faithful American customers of Chinese restaurants since 1900. As did many other Americans, early Jewish immigrants liked Chinese food for its flavor and modest price. But different from other American customers, they found a deeper meaning in consuming Chinese food and incorporated it into their own culture. For many Jewish families in America, eating Chinese food became a weekly routine, a Christmas tradition, and a childhood memory.[3] It has been a practice of American Jews that spans over several decades and multiple generations. Eating Chinese food is an integral component of the identity of American Jews. Embedded in Jewish affection for Chinese food is the story of how two different ethnic groups discovered each other and embraced each other's culture in their adaptations to American society.

THE HISTORICAL CONTEXT

Chinese immigrants entered the United States in the 1840s during the gold rush in California, much earlier than Jewish immigrants. When chop suey houses in New York began to thrive and attract Jewish clients in the 1900s, the Chinese community had already been in the United States for half a century. During this period, however, the Chinese community was faced with serious racial discrimination. As mentioned previously, the first Chinese Exclusion Act in 1882 barred the entry of Chinese labor immigrants and their family members, and denied them naturalization rights. The law was extended in 1892 for another ten years, renewed again and applied to all U.S. territories in 1902, and was made permanent two years later. Under the shadow of Chinese exclusion laws, the Chinese population declined from over 100,000 in 1882 to 85,000 in 1920.[4]

Racial riots and bullying also drove Chinese immigrants into big cities like San Francisco, Los Angeles, and New York and pushed them into menial service jobs like laundries and restaurants. Beginning from the 1900s, the number of Chinese restaurants in New York and other metropolitan American was growing rapidly. Coincidentally, this was also a period when Jewish immigrants began to arrive in the United States in large numbers. Coming from Russia, Germany, Romania, Poland, Hungary, and other European countries, most of them landed in New York City. Roger Daniels pointed out that the number of eastern European Jews increased dramatically during the late nineteenth century, from perhaps 1.5 million to nearly 7 million. Many of them settled in New York City and other cities in the Northeast and Midwest. In the 1920s, they made up about a quarter of New York's population.[5]

While many European immigrants left their home countries because of hunger, poverty, and unemployment, Jewish immigrants were often driven away by anti-Semitism. Some political activists in the Chinese community expressed their sympathy toward Jewish people with fund-raising events. In 1905, the *New York Times* reported: "Under the auspices of the Chinese Empire Reform Association, a company of some forty Chinese presented 'King David' at Miner's Bowery Theatre last night for the benefit of the suffering Jews in Russia. Nearly $1,000 was realized."[6] According to the report, the performance drew so many people that many police were called in to maintain order. The Chinese Empire Reform Association (Bao huang hui) was a political organization that tried to reform the Chinese political system without overthrowing the Manchu emperor. The aborted reform in 1898 made its leaders like Kang Youwei and Liang Qichao the targets of political persecution by the conservative Qing government. As they were exiled overseas, the reformists naturally developed a sympathetic attitude toward those Jewish people who were forced out of their countries due to religious prejudice.

Jewish immigrants arrived in an era when the United States was going through rapid urbanization. New York City's population was rapidly increasing due to the immigration boom and large manufacturing and commercial activities. As New York was growing into a metropolitan city, eating out became trendy, especially during the decades of the 1910s and 1920s. Bank clerks, law firm associates, department store salesmen and saleswomen, secretaries, and even factory workers were all typical lunch patrons of various American and ethnic restaurants on weekdays. Families, couples, or groups of friends became dinner customers on Friday nights and weekends. With tasty food and low prices, Chinese restaurants were affordable eateries popular with all social classes and ethnic groups in New York City. Newly arrived Jewish immigrants joined this trend and began to patronize Chinese restaurants. By 1903, the *Jewish Daily Forward*, a Yiddish newspaper founded by Jewish immigrant scholar Abraham Cahan in 1897, coined a new Yiddishism: *oyesessen*, or eating out. "Oyesessen," the paper reported, "is spreading every day, especially in New York."[7] When eating out, Jewish immigrants often chose chop suey houses. Chinese food was cheap, warm, and delicious. Chinese restaurants were also in or close to their neighborhood.

When Jewish immigrants landed in New York, many lived in the Lower East Side just neighboring Chinatown in the city. By 1910, more than 500,000 "Jews were wedged into tenements in the 1.5 square miles of New York's Lower East Side."[8] On August 13, 1925, the *New York Times* carried a touching story about the friendship between John, a Chinese chop suey house waiter, and Norton Rubin, a three-and-half-year-old Jewish boy. "Nobody knew John's last name, nobody cared." In those decades, Chinese men were often referred to as "John" and Chinese women as "Mary." "The ways of the people to the east of the Bowery have encroached on Chinatown, and little Norton was one of those who toddled into a neighborhood that was alien but fascinating, with all the glamour of the unknown."[9] Under the Chinese exclusion laws, many Chinese immigrants were separated from their wives and children. Family life was rare in Chinatown. While Chinatown was declining, the Jewish and other immigrant populations were growing.

Little Norton probably reminded John of his own family or children. He adored the child and often bought him ice cream cones or lollipops. When not busy with work, John often waited at the Solomon Rubin store in the afternoon until the boy appeared and "ran into the arms of his Chinese admirer." The little visitor brought John pleasant diversion from his monotonous job of taking chop suey orders. As a result of this friendship, Norton's "speech became a polygot of Chinese, Jewish, and English. . . . The little boy came to know the Chinese of the section as well as he did his own people." One night, when the two disappeared for several hours, Norton's family became concerned and alerted the police station. After some search, officers found the two friends joyously laughing at a comedy in the Thailia Theatre. Pressured by Norton, who wanted something more than ice cream that day, John took him to movies for a special treat.[10] When placed into a larger historical context, the friendship between this Chinese waiter and Jewish child showed the geographical proximity and social interaction between the Chinese and Jewish immigrant communities in New York City. At the start of the 1900s and in the following decades, many Jewish immigrant families lived just next door to Chinatown. They often frequented Chinese restaurants.

IMAGINED SAFE TREYF

In Jewish culture, food, especially meat, should be processed and prepared according to kashruth (dietary laws), and such food was called "kosher." In the first decades of the twentieth century, there were 10,000 kosher butcher shops in the United States.[11] Food without following kashruth was "treyf." Chinese food was treyf but somehow appeared safe enough for Jewish people to eat. In reality, Chinese food was anything but kosher. Jewish dietary laws forbade consumption of pork, shrimp, and lobsters. In Chinese cooking, those were common ingredients and were frequently consumed. According to Louis Beck's 1898 book, *New York's Chinatown*, roasted pig was a regular dish among the Chinese because of their fondness of pork. He wrote: "Next to rice, pig's meat is probably the most popular dish of their ordinary diet. . . . Young pigs roasted whole are considered the acme of prepared meats. . . . They must be freshly killed and addressed with care. The skin must be thoroughly scraped and cleaned, and the entrails carefully removed. The entire carcass, including the head, tail and feet, with the tongue and ears, is used, each part being supposed to possess a particular relish which it imparts to the whole."[12] This was actually a popular Cantonese dish. Beck's description showed how Cantonese food and cooking traditions were transplanted in their original form. When Chinese restaurants served Cantonese immigrants, their food was far from being "safe treyf."

Another unkosher element in Chinese food culture was the use of animal intestines. According to kashruth law, slaughtering an animal should be performed by a single cut across the throat of the animal to a deep and precise depth with a sharp blade. Proper slaughtering should be swift and painless to an animal and end in the complete draining of the blood. Kosher rules forbade consumption of animal blood, though some Jewish people did eat animal organs. Even chop suey in its early form included ingredients like animal intestines. In Wong

Chin Foo's description in 1888, chop suey was "a mixture of chicken's livers and gizzards, fungi, bamboo buds, pig's tripe, and bean sprouts stewed with spices."[13] In stir-fried Chinese dishes, fresh intestines were not necessarily depleted of blood. That was all right in Chinese cooking. In fact, pork blood was often made into a *toufu* (tofu) kind of food to be stir-fried as a dish or slow-boiled as a soup. Many Chinese believed that this dish would help them digest any pig's hair that was not thoroughly removed during the slaughtering and skin-scraping process. It is still a popular dish in Guangdong.

Chinese cooking included boiling, steaming, stir-frying, stewing, slow boiling in a clay pot, deep-frying, baking, roasting, braising, poaching, and many other procedures. However, the most common way to make a dish was to chop or slice the meat or vegetables into small pieces and stir-fry them with a few drops of oil in a wok. Interestingly, it was this format of cooking that helped some Chinese dishes pass for "safe treyf." Chop suey and chow mein were dishes where Chinese cooks chopped or minced pork into small, thin pieces and stir-fried them with a variety of vegetables or noodles. In this kind of food preparation and cooking, offensive ingredients were often sufficiently disguised. Green onions, ginger, and garlic made the flavor of Chinese dishes especially appealing to Jewish patrons. Wonton became a favorite dish for many Jewish people because those tiny dumplings were filled with thoroughly ground pork, minced green onions, ginger, and salt, and boiled in chicken soup. Food preparation and the cooking process were the key in making Chinese dishes acceptable to Jewish immigrants and their children. Though Jewish customers knew that pork was part of chop suey, chow mein, and wonton, they still frequented Chinese restaurants.

Chinese food appeared to American Jews as "safe treyf" also because the Chinese seldom mixed milk and meat in cooking. Kashruth strictly banned such blending. Jewish culture did not allow consumption of young cows' meat together with their mothers' milk. Neither should young goats be cooked in their mothers' milk. If Jews ate meat, they should wait at least three hours before they could consume any dairy products, though it was sometimes permissible to eat fish and dairy products at the same time. A strict kosher family usually had two sets of pots, pans, and dinnerware for meat and dairy products, respectively, and cleaned and dried them separately in dishwashers or with towels. As mentioned above, cow's milk was rarely used in Chinese cooking. In fact, only well-to-do urban families could afford it as a nutritious drink for breakfast. Almost no Chinese dishes used milk or other dairy products as ingredients together with meat. The historian Donna Gabaccia pointed out: "Most of the food consumed by Jewish diners in Chinese restaurants was probably not strictly kosher. But since Chinese chefs chopped the forbidden pork and shellfish very finely, offered a wide range of poultry dishes, never used milk (which kashruth laws forbade in meat dishes), and served tea (also popular with Russian Jews), a chop suey meal offered Jewish New Yorkers a so called 'safe treyf,' a combination of the familiar and the forbidden."[14]

In truth, Chinese food as "safe treyf" was more imagined than real. What brought the two groups together was the social context in which they lived. Both were ethnic minority and immigrant groups facing racial bigotry and discrimination, feeling pressure to assimilate into mainstream American society. Both groups brought with them their old and rich cultural traditions upon arrival and had to decide how to adapt to American culture. The Chinese community was not influenced by prejudice against Jewish people. Chinese restaurants did not have any religious decorations that made Jewish people uncomfortable, as some of the Italian restaurants did. Moreover, chop suey houses became part of the metropolitan New York life that Jewish immigrants wanted to belong to. Chinese food was not only tasty but also American enough to attract Jewish customers.

What attracted Jewish immigrants was not Chinese cuisine in its original form but Americanized Chinese dishes like chop suey, chow mein, and egg foo yong. On the menus of Chinese restaurants in the 1890s, Beck noticed expensive dishes like shark's fin, bird's nest, or sturgeon head, and each cost $2 per dish. Meanwhile, there were also dishes between 35 to 75 cents like "Chow Mein (Fried Noodles), Foo Yong Dan (Ham and Egg Omelet), or Chop Suey."[15] Beginning in the early 1900s, chop suey houses spread all over New York and catered to mainly American customers. Dishes like shark's fin or bird's nest soup disappeared as they were only attractive to Chinese customers. Animal intestines were rarely used. Sliced meats, chopped celery, onions, and bean sprouts were standard ingredients. The menu began with hot tea as a free drink. Soup was served at the beginning rather than at the end of the meal. A typical entrée would be chicken chop suey, beef chop suey, or chow mein. When appearing as "safe treyf" for Jewish customers, Chinese food had already transformed itself into a popular American ethnic cuisine.

CHOW MEIN FOR CHRISTMAS

As the two largest non-Christian ethnic groups, neither Chinese nor Jewish immigrants celebrated Christmas. Both had to learn how to adapt to this important public holiday in the United States. On Christmas Day, Chinese restaurants remained open. They operated their businesses seven days a week and twelve hours a day. Chinese waiters and cooks might take turns to have a couple of days off during the Chinese Lunar New Year, but they worked during the Christmas season. In Jewish culture, a major holiday was Chanukah (Hanukkah), an eight-day Jewish holiday known as the Festival of Lights, which could take place from late November to late December based on the Hebrew calendar. According to several surveys among Jewish people in the late 1950s, in 1962, and in 1981,

Chanukah was their most celebrated ethnic holiday because it was an alternative to Christmas. Passover ranked second.[16] While the Chinese found Jews to be
their most loyal patrons for the Christmas restaurant business, American Jews
made eating Chinese food their Christmas tradition.

On Christmas Day of 1935, Eng Shee Chuck, a Chinese restaurant owner,
summoned his relatives and employees to prepare eighty chow mein dinners
and eighty toys tied with red ribbons for the orphans at the Jewish Children's
Home in Newark, New Jersey. As the warm chow mein replaced the regular
dinner and the toys were passed among the eager youngsters, the children sang
songs to express their gratitude. In exchange, Chuck told them ancient Chinese
fairy tales. He said that it was a wonderful Christmas around eighty toys. Chow
mein fit the Jewish feeling for Christmas culturally.[17] As non-Christians, American Jews did not prepare Christmas food and celebrate the holiday. But it was
almost impossible not to have any social gathering or celebration during this
most important public holiday in America. Still open on Christmas, Chinese
restaurants properly filled a special need for Jewish people. Moreover, different
from roast turkey for Thanksgiving or pumpkin pie for Christmas, chow mein
was not a culinary tool for assimilation. In addition to Chuck's charitable spirit,
the story also showed that by the 1930s, eating Chinese food on Christmas Day
had already become a tradition for American Jews.

Chow mein was obviously a favorite food item for many Jewish children, as
Chuck selected it for their Christmas dinner. Roger Nash, former president of
the League of Canadian Poets, once published a poetry collection entitled *In the
Kosher Chow Mein Restaurant*, which won the Canadian Jewish Book Award for
Poetry for 1997.[18] Chow mein, chop suey, kung pao chicken, and moo shu pork
were some of the most popular dishes with American Jews. Unlike many American children, who preferred chicken noodle soup when they were sick, Jewish
children wanted some Chinese meals for comfort food. The Jewish humorist
Molly Katz once wrote: "Never mind chicken soup; when Jews need comfort,
solace, or medicinal nourishment, we dive for Moo Shu Pork."[19] Chuck's story
was a meaningful episode showing how the two groups embraced each other's
culture. The Chinese and American Jews viewed each other simultaneously as
Americans and foreigners, and affirmed prospective traditional values while
accepting new ones. When Jewish orphans sang, their songs were not "Jingle
Bells." Chuck told the Jewish children Chinese fairy tales that were a thousand
years old. America was a meeting ground of different ethnic cultures rather than
a melting pot of assimilation in this touching story.

Jewish immigrants found certain similarities between some Chinese dishes
and their own food. For example, wonton, a favorite dish of many Jewish
patrons, looked like kreplach in appearance and tasted good. Kreplach are triangular or square flour dumplings containing chopped meat, mashed potatoes, or

other fillings usually boiled in chicken soup. It was a popular eastern European Jewish delicacy and was often served as a pre-fast meal before Yom Kippur and on Rosh Hashana (Hoshana Raba). Wontons were Chinese miniature dumplings filled with finely minced pork mixed with green onions, ginger, and other ingredients and sauces. They were also often boiled in chicken soup. Sometimes Cantonese immigrants deep-fried them and served the dish as a snack. Chinese meatballs reminded Jewish immigrants of their matzo ball soup. Cantonese noodles, known as lo mein, were similar to luckshen, the Jewish noodles. Donald Siegel, a science professor and a longtime fan of Chinese cuisine, authored a hybrid recipe book entitled *From Lokshen to Lo Mein: The Jewish Love Affair with Chinese Food.*[20]

The Christmas season can still be boring for many American Jews today. On Christmas eve of 1994, the *New York Times* carried an article about the dilemma of Jews in the San Francisco Bay Area. It stated: "They can't watch television, because it is filled with Christmas specials. They can't go shopping, because everything is closed. They can't visit their Christian friends, who are sitting with their nearest and dearest around Christmas trees. They can't go to church and, at least in many parts of the country, it's too cold to go outside."[21] Traditionally, American Jews took refuge in movie theaters or, better still, in Chinese restaurants, where family dinners, friends' reunions, or social gatherings took place. For generations, Chinese food was their Christmas dinner. The busiest Chinese restaurants on Christmas Day were always those located in or close to Jewish communities. Entitled "For Some, It Was a Very Moo Shu Christmas," a *New York Times* article in 2003 reported that Christmas was usually the busiest day for Shun Lee West and its adjoining Shun Lee Café on the Upper West Side of Manhattan. From noon until 11 P.M., they would receive 900 diners and make 800 deliveries.[22] Most of the patrons were Jews who had nothing to celebrate at home and nowhere to go but to come out to eat in Chinese restaurants after watching a movie.

Different from other American customers, American Jews became collective fans of Chinese cuisine. Their interest in Chinese food was not a personal or individual curiosity or the adventure of a few Jewish immigrants into an exotic cuisine. It was a collective affection by almost the entire Jewish community in New York City. Eating Chinese food became a tradition of American Jews that was passed down from one generation to another. In her book on Chinese restaurants in America published in 2008, *New York Times* journalist Jennifer Lee wrote: "The average American Reform Jew is more likely to know how to use chopsticks than how to write the Hebrew alphabet. Chinese food on Christmas Day is as much an American Jewish ritual as the Seder on Passover (maybe even more so, once you take into account non-observant Jews). When my friend Orli Bahcall was growing up, her family even had take-out Chinese food for family

Shabbat dinner."²³ Though extreme, the example shows that eating Chinese food has been a tradition of American Jews for generations.

However, some third-generation American Jews wanted to go beyond merely eating Chinese food for Christmas. A 1994 *New York Times* article reported that "this Christmas Eve 800 Jews in the Bay Area will do even better. Half of them would dine on an eight-course Chinese meal, complete with Yiddish fortune cookies. Then all of them would indulge in a six-course feast of Jewish humor. The show was called 'Kung Pao Kosher Comedy,' but the Kosher referred to the jokes, not the cuisine."²⁴ Kung pao chicken or beef became food for thoughts when Lisa Geduldig decided to found a comedy event in a Chinese restaurant for Jews in San Francisco during Christmas of 1993. The show became an annual tradition and drew an increasing number of patrons. In 1997, 3,000 people flocked to the show when comedian Henny Youngman came to perform.²⁵ Today, a live performance in a Chinese restaurant during Christmas time has become a Jewish tradition in all major cities in America.²⁶ For American Jews, a Chinese restaurant is not just an eating place but a meeting hall for a new ethnic tradition. Chinese food has been more than a dietary influence for American Jews. As their designated Christmas dinner for generations, it has become an expressive form of their American identity.

CHINESE RESTAURANTS IN JEWISH COMMUNITIES

Chop suey houses appeared wherever there was a sizable Jewish population. As Chinese proprietors timely recognized Jewish affection for their food, they were motivated to establish restaurants in Jewish communities and catered to their specialized needs. In the 1920s, the Chinese restaurant business became a durable fixture in most Jewish neighborhoods, almost as commonplace as a kosher butcher shop. Jewish patrons supported nearly thirty chop suey houses within walking distance of Ratner's, the mainstay kosher dairy on Delancey and Essex Streets in New York. Children institutionalized it as parents took home Chinese food every Sunday night.²⁷ Many Jewish families faithfully visited their favorite Chinese restaurant every Sunday night. At a Chinese food history exhibition in New York, there were menus selected from Glatt Wok, Kosher Chinese Restaurants, and Takeout in Monsey, New York, and Wok Tov in Cedarhurst, New York.²⁸ Describing this 1930s phenomenon, Mimi Sheraton, a food column writer and reporter for the *New York Times*, wrote in 1980: "Even 50 years ago, in the otherwise gastronomically homogeneous neighborhoods of Brooklyn, Queens, and the Bronx, Chinese restaurants flourished, all Cantonese, but with far blander and more limited menus than one today. . . . Cantonese dishes such as egg roll, chicken chow mein, moo goo gai pan, and wonton are standards in the repertory of kosher caterers for weddings and bar mitzvahs. Those same dishes appear as a once-a-week treat in the faculty and student cafeteria of the Jewish Theological Seminary."[29] By the 1950s, many Jewish families in the United States made visits to their favorite local Chinese restaurants a weekly routine.

Some Jewish families learned to cook their own Chinese food. In another article, Mimi Sheraton recalled how her mother cooked Chinese meals. "My cross-culinary experiences began in Brooklyn in the late 1930s and early 40s, when my mother would try to duplicate the dishes we favored in local Chinese restaurants. Her favorite recipes included Egg-roll Blintz, shrimp with lobster sauce, Subgum Chicken or shrimp chow mein."[30] Women were typically gatekeepers of their own ethnic culture. Many Jewish women were familiar with kashruth rules, and some were even involved in animal slaughtering in order to prepare Jewish traditional food properly. When Sheraton's mother learned how to cook Chinese dishes for lunches or late-supper parties or named her own kreplach wontons, it showed how deeply Chinese food entered into Jewish life in America.

In the 1930s and 1940s, different from those fancy Chinese restaurants like Ruby Foo and Lum Fong's in Manhattan, chop suey houses in Jewish neighborhoods were small, often on the second floor above shops, and always decorated in red lacquer with pagoda motifs and red, gold, and black tassels. Their prices were cheap, especially for lunch. A child's meal cost only 25 cents, although it included a soup or tomato juice, a main course with rice and fried noodles, and canned pineapple or rice cream for dessert. Tea was always free. Adult patrons paid 40 cents for larger portions of the same choices.[31] Modest prices in Chinese restaurants enabled many poor Jewish families to eat out from time to time. Sheraton observed that Chinese restaurant operators sometimes followed the Jewish communities, and "one of the better known facts of restaurant life is that Chinese restaurants are more likely to do well where they are in easy reach of a Jewish clientele, more especially if the food they serve is Cantonese."[32] Cantonese cuisine was mild in flavor. When it became Americanized, it easily fit the Jewish appetite.

Jimmy Eng came from Taishan, Guangdong Province, in 1936. He worked in laundries and restaurants in New York City for a long time and was often disappointed that his father did not have money to send him to school. When he noticed the Jewish affection for Chinese food, he developed a vision to build a restaurant career with American Jews as his potential clients. In 1953, he purchased a small Chinese restaurant called King Yum in Queens, New York. The price was $8,000, a huge sum for him, but Eng had noticed that Jewish families were moving from the city's core to its peripheries. Though the neighborhood of this restaurant had little sign of human activities at that time, he was hopeful of a change. Soon more and more Jewish families moved in. Eng was able to transform his tiny storefront into a massive red-walled banquet hall with Chinese lanterns swinging from the ceiling.[33]

In the 1980s, Queens witnessed a rapid growth in the number of Chinese restaurants following the arrival of new immigrants from Taiwan and mainland China. When Hunan, Sichuan, or other Chinese regional-flavored restaurants replaced traditional chop suey houses, King Yum was still able to maintain its Americanized Chinese food and served egg foo yong and chicken chop suey, a specialty of the house. According to a *New York Sun* article, "King Yum has been around since the 1940s, and it long ago perfected its shtick. When you open the door, you're greeted by a glassed-in waterfall, and things just get better from there. The bar has a thatched 'roof,' and the dining room is full of bamboo accents. Octogenarian owner James K. Eng, a Queens legend, diligently hob-nobs his way from table to table, making sure everyone's having a good time."[34] Faithful Jewish customers helped King Yum survive the fierce competition in the Chinese restaurant business.

The baby boomer generation of American Jews often recalled how their fami-lies routinely visited Chinese restaurants. According to one man's recollection of his "bubbe": "She was boiling up chicken feet in her soup years and years ago when the menu in the three or four Chinese restaurants in America could be printed on a fortune cookie note. 'Chop Suey.' It said. And, on weekends, they added 'Chow Mein.'"[35] Another man recollected, "Growing up Jewish in Brooklyn, Chinese food is a birthright, and I was weaned on chicken chow mein, the quintessential Chinese-American dish."[36] When I mentioned my research to a Jewish colleague, she replied that her generation has expanded this habit to include Thai, Japanese, Vietnamese, and Korean food.[37] Eating Chinese food as a tradition has enabled many American Jews to be open and receptive to the Asian food culture.

Today there are many fine kosher Chinese restaurants in New York, New Jer-sey, Philadelphia, and other areas where Jews have congregated. Cooking kosher chow mein or other Chinese dishes has become a lifelong career for some con-temporary immigrant Chinese. Chao Lin, owner of Lin's Kosher Chinese Kitchen in Manville, New Jersey, for example, invited the Chabad House of Somerset County, a Jewish cultural and community organization, to park its mobile suk-kah outside his restaurant for several evenings during the Jewish holiday of Suk-kot in 2003. Lin had worked in kosher Chinese restaurants throughout New Jersey for ten years before he owned his own kosher-certified restaurant.[38]

Globalization in food production has also impacted Jewish food culture. The making of kosher food began to be outsourced in China. While the United States is the largest kosher food market, China has become "the world's fastest-growing producer of kosher-certified food. By 2008, more than 500 Chinese factories produced the approved products."[39] Meanwhile, familiarity with Chinese food enabled a number of Jewish entrepreneurs to build their careers and fortunes on their connection with the Chinese cuisine. Eddie Scher, a businessman who lived in Felton, California, developed a popular brand of Asian-themed sauces widely sold in Trader Joe's, Whole Foods, and Dean & DeLuca. He drove around with the company name on his vanity license plate: "soy vay." Kari-Out, the largest distributor of soy sauce packets in the country, was owned by a Jewish family, the Epsteins of Westchester, New York.[40]

AMERICAN IDENTITY THROUGH CHINESE FOOD

For many Jewish immigrants and their families, eating in chop suey houses was their first American restaurant experience. Different from other European immigrant groups who started their American experience as farmers, miners, or railroad workers, most Jewish immigrants began their American journey as city dwellers. The first city in which they congregated was New York. Dining out allowed them to explore and satisfy their curiosity about urban American life, and to develop a new taste, as well as a new perspective on food culture. Chinese food was not the only option. Jewish, French, Italian, German, Greek, Russian, and other ethnic cuisines were also available. New York had more varieties of restaurants than any other city in the world. When eating out in Chinese restaurants, Jewish immigrants realized that food consumers in America had more opportunities than people elsewhere to be able to constantly try different ethnic foods brought in by different waves of immigrants. Eating different ethnic foods was a lifestyle in metropolitan New York City.

American Jews, of course, had their own restaurant businesses. In 1899, the Jewish community of the Lower East Side in New York City boasted 140 groceries, 131 kosher butchers, 36 bakeries, 9 bread stands, and 10 delicatessens.[41] By the 1930s, Jewish restaurants did about $292 million in annual trade. But most of the early Jewish restaurants were simple and undecorated, serving only kosher food and catering mostly to Jewish clients. Many of the restaurants were places for Jewish social gatherings.[42] The flavor and cooking could be different, as Jewish immigrants came from different countries. There was no standard traditional Jewish food for everyone. New York also claimed roughly 10,000 Italian restaurants in the 1930s. Every district, city, and province of Italy was allegedly represented in New York by its restaurants.[43] Ethnic flavor was a cultural capital to attract patrons from the same home region. Functioning as a meeting place of social gathering for fellow townsmen and women, those Italian, Jewish, and other ethnic restaurants often only served their own ethnic customers.

Chop suey houses in New York were different from Jewish or Italian restaurants from the very beginning. They served mainly non-Chinese patrons. Chinese proprietors modified their food more than Jewish or other ethnic restaurant operators did. Chop suey, chow mein, and wontons were reinvented American versions of Chinese dishes, which contemporary Chinese immigrants would shy away from. However, Chinese proprietors did more than modify cookery and change ingredients. With modest prices, Chinese identity, and warm and palatable food, chop suey houses satisfied New Yorkers' cultural expectations for an ethnic restaurant. They were attractive to Jewish patrons because they appeared simultaneously American and foreign. In the eyes of American Jews, chop suey houses were an integral part of the unique and intriguing life of New York City.

As portrayed in American artist Edward Hopper's painting, a polished chop suey house was not necessarily a cheap food joint in Chinatown but could be a trendy place for middle-class New Yorkers to eat out.[44] Though many chop suey houses were not as trendy as the one in Hopper's art, they were still popular eateries that embodied the city's metropolitan spirit. That made chop suey houses different from other ethnic restaurants. Reflecting his Chinese restaurant experience, a Jewish man said: "I felt about Chinese restaurants the same way I did about the Metropolitan Museum of Art—they were the two most strange and fascinating places my parents took me to, and I loved them both."[45] Through Chinese food, American Jews became more metropolitan, became more adapted to American urban life, and gradually broke away from their dietary rules, which were religious, restrictive, and symbolic of the old world from which they had come. Their attachment to Chinese food was part of their American identity formation process. As the food historian Anna Miller pointed out, "Eating Chinese was cosmopolitan, sophisticated, and secular."[46]

In the 1920s, the rapid growth of the middle- and lower-middle-class city population created a booming restaurant market in New York. "New York City, large and cosmopolitan, shared in all the new trends in eating out. Great wealth supported luxurious restaurants; immigrants from many countries promoted variety; and the heavy concentration of people in Manhattan made the city a laboratory for space-saving and labor-saving techniques in food service."[47] Chop suey houses often displayed a flair for creativeness and adventure that aided their survival and success. While known for free tea, some Chinese restaurants also served self-made liquor for demanding diners despite the Volstead Act (the Prohibition law) during the 1920s. *The Tea That Burns* by Edward Hall was a book about the history of a four-generation Chinese family in New York.[48] The title was an obvious allusion on how Chinese restaurants sold self-made liquor during that period. In the 1930s, the Great Depression made dining out in an ethnic neighborhood or ethnic restaurants such as a chop suey house a common experience for urban Americans. New York residents and tourists flocked to Harlem, Little Italy, and Chinatown for food. In those years, as more and more American Jews dined out, they became regular patrons of Chinese restaurants.

In the 1930s, Jewish food culture was also changing. In fact, American Jews made many significant contributions to American food culture. Haagen-Dazs Ice Cream, though sounding like a Danish name, was invented by Reuben

Mattus, the son of a Jewish immigrant. Sara Lee and its famous cheesecake were created by Charles Lubin, an American Jew, in 1926. Arnold Reuben took the lead in reaching out to wider groups of multiethnic patrons in New York with his famous sandwiches, cheesecakes, and apple pancakes. Reuben's Restaurant and other Jewish delis became full-fledged restaurants through their oversized portions, friendly waiters, and twenty-four-hour service. His "Jewish" sandwiches, however, were not only stuffed with ham but also included Swiss cheese. Moreover, chow mein was one of the few "safe treyf" items on the restaurant's menu. Many of them were no longer kosher. Eventually, Jewish delis became synonymous with good sandwich stores across the country and served all American customers. Nevertheless, chow mein was still part of Reuben's menu, while Jewish restaurants broke away from their orthodox food restrictions.

In the Jewish Diaspora, eating Chinese food is only an American phenomenon. The Jewish community in China, especially in Shanghai, was a well-known part of the Jewish Diaspora history. However, they did not develop the same kind of affection for Chinese food as did American Jews. As a consequence of the Russian Revolution in 1918, about 40,000 Russians and Russian Jews traveled through Siberia to Harbin in northeast China. By 1922, there were at least 11,000 Jewish people in the city.[49] Many later moved to Shanghai. From 1938 on, between 15,000 and 20,000 Jewish refugees from Germany and Austria escaped to Shanghai during the Nazi regime. During 1939 and 1940, approximately 1,000 Polish Jews also escaped to Shanghai.[50] Though smaller in number, they shared an important similarity with Jewish people in New York. They came from a variety of different countries and brought with them different lifestyles or cultural traditions, including eating habits. Shanghai was an international city where tens of thousands of foreigners lived. Jewish people were just one of the many Western communities. There was no pressure for Jewish people in Shanghai to assimilate into Chinese society. Jewish people obviously also ate Chinese food there, but they never made Chinese cuisine an integral part of their diet or ethnic identity as New York Jews did.

CONCLUSION

By historical chance, the Chinese and American Jews, as two minority groups, met and shared residential proximity in New York City at the turn of the twentieth century. The enterprising Chinese immigrants deliberately changed their cooking and restaurant food to cater to American tastes. Though little known in China, chop suey, chow mein, and egg foo yong were famous American versions of Chinese dishes popular with many local residents. Chop suey houses in New York embodied not only Chinese ethnicity but also metropolitan Americanness. Partly based on this cultural reinterpretation process, the Chinese restaurants prospered and won unlikely customers among the Jews. As the food historian Anna Miller pointed out, eating Chinese food "has become a meaningful symbol of American Judaism, with all its quirks and ceremonial selectivity, for in eating Chinese food, the Jews found a modern means of expressing their traditional cultural values. The savoring of Chinese food is now a ritualized celebration of immigration, education, family, community, and continuity."[51] Eating Chinese food has become an integral part of Jewish culture in America.

It is a rare but significant case that the food of one ethnic group became an expressive form of another group's identity. Jewish affection for Chinese food is a meaningful episode in both Jewish and Chinese American history. The evolution of both Chinese food and American Jews' eating habits was taking place almost simultaneously. The dynamic interaction between the two cultures reflected the complexity of the American ethnic identity formation process. Innovation of their food traditions and deliberate efforts to enter the American restaurant market by Chinese Americans and the longing for a new cultural identity by American Jews have made this episode of American ethnic history possible.

6 · GENERAL TSO'S CHICKEN MADE IN TAIWAN

In 1974, the ABC station in New York featured a segment on Peng Garden Restaurant. Reporter Bob Lape visited Chef Peng in the kitchen and taped how he cooked General Tso's chicken, the most famous dish in Hunan cuisine in Taiwan. After the segment ran, about 1,500 people wrote in and asked for the recipe.[1] New Yorkers' enthusiasm for Chef Peng's cooking reflected a new trend in the Chinese restaurant business in America. Americanized Chinese food lost its historical appeal. Authentic Chinese cuisine began to attract American customers. Chinese restaurant owners no longer labeled their businesses "chop suey houses" but Hunan, Sichuan, Mandarin, or Shanghai restaurants. American customers gradually realized that authentic Chinese food was very different from chop suey meals and much richer in its culinary content. When New York consumers wanted to eat out in a Chinese restaurant, they needed to decide which regional flavor to choose. Among those flavors, Hunan cuisine was the most famous and popular one in the 1970s and 1980s.

However, few American customers knew that those Hunan, Sichuan, Mandarin, or Shanghai restaurants were operated by immigrants from Taiwan rather than from mainland China, which did not have diplomatic relations with the United States and could not send immigrants until after 1979. When the Immigration and Nationality Act of 1965 became law, the first groups of Chinese immigrants came mainly from Taiwan and Hong Kong. Their arrival initiated changes in the Chinese restaurant business in America and made it more diverse in culinary flavors. In his book *Taiwanese Americans*, the anthropologist Franklin Ng pointed out,

Chinese food has many regional cuisines, and most Americans were previously most familiar with the Cantonese variety. But other regional cuisines from other parts of China have now been introduced into the United States to the delight of those who appreciate Chinese food and the idea that variety is the spice of life. Chinese restaurants now feature those that specialized in dishes from Sichuan, Beijing, Hunan, and Shandong. There are also restaurants that offer the Chaozhou (Teochew or Chiuchow) and Hakka types of cuisine. In bringing these regional cuisines to this country, the Taiwanese have served as brokers or midwives in helping to educate [the] American palate.[2]

What Ng observed is more than a food phenomenon. The development of the restaurant business in Taiwan and how Chinese regional cuisines were transplanted from Taiwan to America reflects issues in Chinese political history, the relationship between food and identity, and change and resilience in cultural traditions. After the Nationalists escaped to Taiwan in 1949 when they were defeated by the Communists, there had been no cultural or any other types of exchange or communication between Taiwan and mainland China until the 1980s. For half a century, regional Chinese cuisines in Taiwan were made and developed according to the collective memory of the Nationalists and their followers. Nevertheless, the translocal Chinese restaurant market in Taiwan was growing into a thriving business. Taipei became a capital of Chinese cuisine with numerous regional-flavored restaurants—far more numerous than in any city in mainland China. When immigrants from Taiwan came to the United States, Chinese regional cuisines followed them again and spread into American society.

Food is an integral part of human life. A key factor responsible for the growth of Chinese regional-flavored restaurants in Taiwan was the arrival of the Nationalists and their families, who were often referred as mainlanders, or *Waisheng ren* in Taiwan. Being away from mainland China made them increasingly sensitive about their Chinese identity. As they often felt nostalgic or even sentimental about their native origins, they were consciously or sometimes unconsciously acting as much Chinese as possible in their way of thinking, lifestyle, speech, and, of course, eating habits. Food was an expressive form of their political identity and cultural behavior. The long separation between Taiwan and mainland China actually fostered a thriving Chinese translocal restaurant business on the island. It shows how deeply food as a tradition could exist in human memory and how intimately food relates to human identity. Underlying this food phenomenon is the theme that culinary identity is essentially a human identity.

THE CHINESE TRANSLOCAL RESTAURANT BUSINESS

In China as in many other countries, there is no such a thing as national cuisine. Chinese culinary culture in fact consists of a variety of regional cuisines.[3] As a country, China has a very diverse geographical landscape. Different climates, soil conditions, water resources, and local cultures in China led to the development of many different regional food traditions. Each regional cuisine has its own unique flavor and representative dishes. Some regional dishes are recognized as national delicacies. Experienced Chinese restaurant customers usually know that "shi zi tou" (boiled meatballs) is a Yangzhou specialty; "xiao long bao" (steamed dumplings), a Shanghai delicacy; "mapo toufu" (stir-fried spicy bean curd), a famous Sichuan dish; "guoqiao mixian" (rice noodles cooked in hot chicken soup), a Yunnan treat; and "Dongan zi ji" (Dongan baby chicken), a traditional Hunan dish. These dishes frequently function as a label for a restaurant's culinary specialty and identity. Food markets in China are often a congregation of specialized restaurants serving a variety of regional flavors. The translocal restaurant business exists not only in big cities but also in many medium-size and small cities. In metropolitan cities like Shanghai, Hangzhou, Nanjing in East China, Guangzhou in the South, and Beijing, Tianjin, and Qingdao in the North, the most frequented restaurants are not necessarily the ones that serve local flavors but those that have the best quality of food.

The translocal restaurant market has a long history in China. As the French scholar Jacques Gernet pointed out, Hangzhou (Hangchow), the capital city of South Song (1127–1279), had many restaurants that specialized in various regional cuisines, such as Sichuan, Shandong, and Hebei, and some restaurants even featured Muslim food.[4] Geographically, Sichuan in southwest China or Shandong in North China is far away from Hangzhou, which is located in East China. If Hangzhou had restaurants featuring flavors from those areas as early as the twelfth century, it shows that regionalism has long characterized Chinese food culture. According to the historian Jonathan Spence, a good Cantonese restaurant could have a thriving business in Beijing in the nineteenth century. In addition to many take-out orders, wealthy families would request chefs from such restaurants to cook in their homes from time to time. As Spence put it, "a cook in Beijing, after serving his apprenticeship in Canton, could rise to own his own restaurant, employing a dozen porters to handle take-out orders, with an extra four chefs on his own staff just to rent to wealthy families."[5] According to another historian, restaurants in Shanghai in the 1910s were "divided into Beijing restaurants, Nanjing restaurants, Suzhou restaurants, Zhenjiang-Yangzhou restaurants, Anhui restaurants, Ningbo restaurants, Guangdong restaurants, Fujian restaurants, Sichuan restaurants, and Sectarian (Jiaomen or Muslim) restaurants. For fresh seafood, the most frequented are Fujian, Guangdong, and Ningbo restaurants. In terms of price, Sichuan and Fujian restaurants are the most expensive."[6]

In the 1950s and 1960s, Beijing had several dozens of famous regional-flavored restaurants featuring Shanghai, Shanxi, Sichuan, Shandong, Hunan, and Muslim cuisines. Among the most famous ones, Hongbin House (Hong bin lou) and Barbecue Garden (Kao rou wan) were Muslim-style restaurants. Jinyang Restaurant (Jinyang fan zhuang) served Shanxi cuisine. Fengze Garden (Feng ze yuan) featured Shandong flavors. Donglai Shun Restaurant (Dong lai shun) was famous for its mutton pot dish. Quanjude Restaurant (Quan ju de) was well known for its Peking duck. The two most established Hunan restaurants were Qu Yuan Restaurant (Qu yuan) and Ma Kai Restaurant (Ma kai).[7] However, the number of restaurants in Beijing was modest compared with what Taipei had in those decades.

According to a *New York Times* article in 1968, Taipei was, almost without question, the finest source for Chinese food outside of mainland China. "It is fantastic, whether the food be Peking, Shanghai, Hunan, Szechuan, Cantonese, or whatever city or province you name." There were also dishes with a wide range of prices. In a hotel restaurant located at 16 Nanking East Road, prices ranged from 28 to 320 Taiwan dollars, or 70 cents to U.S.$8.[8] Since the Nationalist government retreated in Taiwan, numerous regional-flavored restaurants and food stores appeared in Taipei. Every street corner of the city had one or more than one regional cuisine restaurant. They coexisted and competed with each other for local customers. In the 1970s and 1980s, many Western tourists observed that when visiting mainland China, their experience with Chinese food was often limited to the particular regions they toured, and that the restaurant business was not as prosperous and diverse as it was in Taiwan. Their impression was accurate. During those decades, no cities in mainland China could be compared with Taipei in terms of the restaurant business. What Western tourists were exposed to in Taipei was not one kind of Chinese food but a variety of Chinese regional flavors. With numerous regional-flavored restaurants in Taipei, the translocal restaurant business reached an unprecedented level in Chinese food history. It was against this background that immigrants from Taiwan brought various Chinese regional food traditions to the United States.

TAIWANESE IMMIGRANTS

Students from Taiwan began to study in American universities as early as the 1950s. American aid to the Nationalist government also significantly improved education in Taiwan. In 1950, there were 1,504 schools serving 1,054,923 students. By 1961, the figures doubled, with 3,095 schools serving 2,540,665 students. In 1977, there were 4,698 schools with 4,522,037 students.[9] The number of higher education institutions jumped from four in 1952 to fifteen in 1960.[10] By the late 1960s and early 1970s, about 2,000 students were leaving Taiwan each year to pursue graduate study in America.[11] According to one source, from 1950 to 1974 a total of 30,765 students from Taiwan came to American colleges and universities.[12] According to another source, Taiwan sent 120,000 students to the United

States between 1950 and 1993, and fewer than 27,000 of them returned home after graduation.[13]

The Immigration and Nationality Act of 1965 was another turning point in Chinese migration to the United States. When the law was passed, the annual immigration quota for the Chinese jumped from 105 to 20,000. The law provided an equal quota to every nation-state and removed racial criteria from immigration policy for the first time in U.S. history. In the next fifteen years, approximately a quarter of a million Chinese entered the United States.[14] They mainly came from Taiwan and Hong Kong since the People's Republic of China did not have diplomatic relations with the United States until 1979.

The Immigration and Nationality Act of 1965 allowed many students from Taiwan to change their student status. After they earned their master's or doctorate degree from a university, students from Taiwan could become lawful permanent residents either through work or marriage. After five years of permanent residency, they could apply for citizenship and then bring in not only quota-exempt parents but also brothers and sisters under the fifth category of the 1965 act. Their siblings, most of them adult immigrants, could in turn petition for their spouses and children after they received their permanent residency or citizenship. The late historian Ronald Takaki quoted a typical immigrant of this kind: "My brother-in-law left his wife in Taiwan and came here as a student to get his Ph.D. in engineering. After he received his degree, he got a job in San Jose. Then he brought in a sister and his wife, who brought over one of her brothers and me. And my brother's wife then came."[15] Following a chain-migration pattern, the immigrant population from Taiwan grew rapidly in the United States. When Monterey Park was dubbed "Little Taipei," it implied that most of the newly arrived immigrants came from Taiwan. From Monterey Park, many Taiwan immigrants later spread into other San Gabriel Valley cities. This dispersion was referred to by some scholars as the "Taiwan Syndrome."[16]

"Little Taipei" was different from "Little Canton," which was how Chinatown was referred to in the late nineteenth century. Early Chinese immigrants mostly came from Guangdong Province and shared many similar cultural traditions, including food. Contemporary immigrants from Taiwan belonged to a very heterogeneous group. On the surface, "Taiwanese American" refers to those immigrants and their descendants from Taiwan. In reality, the term includes "three different groups of Chinese: the Fujianese, the Hakka, and the mainlanders. The Fujianese were people from southern Fujian Province who migrated to Taiwan from the sixteenth century onward and were now the majority on the island. The Hakka were a group who moved from Guangdong Province to Taiwan. Finally, the mainlanders were refugees from the Chinese civil war in mainland China after World War II."[17] Their influx took place within a few months after the Communist troops won several decisive battles across the country in the late 1940s.[18]

From late 1948 to early 1949, 4,000 to 5,000 refugees arrived in Taiwan every day. Nearly two million people fled mainland China to join an estimated six million Taiwanese already there.[19] It was probably the largest human migration in Chinese history.

In identity politics in Taiwan, southern Fujianese and Hakka were usually perceived as more native than the mainlanders, as many of them had been there for more than two or three generations. Moreover, the Nationalists and their families retreated to Taiwan from all kinds of geographical locations in mainland China. They were diverse in their regional cultural background. They were natives of Hunan, Hubei, Sichuan, Zhejiang, Jiangsu, Fujian, Guangdong, Guangxi, Henan, Shandong, and other provinces. The arrival of mainlanders greatly changed the social landscape of Taiwan, including the food market. Local southern Fujian cuisine was quickly overwhelmed by all kinds of restaurants that featured all kinds of Chinese regional flavors. When Taiwanese immigrants entered the United States after the Immigration and Nationality Act of 1965, Chinese regional cuisines followed them again. The Chinese translocal restaurant business became a transnational food business.

TAIPEI AS THE CHINESE FOOD CAPITAL

The rapid growth of Chinese translocal restaurants in Taiwan was a by-product of the Nationalists' retreat in 1949. Among the Nationalists who escaped to Taiwan, there were senior government officials, military generals, wealthy businessmen, and some famous scholars. There were also many military officers of middle or low rank and ordinary soldiers, government clerks, merchants, professionals, or any person who trusted the Nationalists more than the Communists. In the following decades, those mainlanders dominated the government, senior military positions, and the economic, educational, and cultural leadership positions in Taiwan. Though their regional background did not directly relate to their social-class background, generally speaking, most ordinary soldiers came from Sichuan Province in southwest China or Shandong Province in North China, while many senior military officers were Hunan natives, and high-ranking government officials were Zhejiang and Jiangsu natives. Among the Nationalist followers, there were also wealthy businesspeople from big cities like Shanghai, Beijing, Tianjin, and Guangzhou (Canton).

Not all mainlanders, however, belonged to the privileged class. In fact, most of them were struggling to make a decent living in the 1950s. Some wealthy people lost many of their possessions as they escaped from mainland China. Many ordinary people could not find jobs when they arrived in Taiwan. Moreover, mainlanders came from areas that had different climates and cultural traditions from Taiwan. They had to adapt to the new environment. As 50 percent of the

mainlanders were military personnel and their families, the government established about 700 to 800 Juancun (military home quarters) in cities and counties
like Taipei, Taoyuan, Xinzhu, Taizhong, Gaoxiong, Taidong, and others. Except
for senior military officers, houses in such military home quarters were modest
or even shabby. Many families shared one public bathroom, and had no refrig-
erators, air conditioning, or modern kitchens. The quarters were separated from
the outside only by bamboo fences. Though life was not easy, Juancun gave the
mainlander Chinese a sense of belonging and functioned as a home away from
home.

More significant, each Juancun was like a Chinese cultural village. Mainlander families communicated to each other in a variety of different Chinese
dialects; held all kinds of cultural activities like movies, local operas, and dance
parties; and of course shared different food traditions. Wives, mothers, or other
family members often exchanged recipes, tasted each other's food, and invited
each other to dinners. Consequently, regional cuisine traditions spread and
circulated both in and out of the military home quarters. Steamed bread from
Shandong was no longer a strange food to a Sichuan family. Spicy beef noodles
from Sichuan became a popular dish to many Juancun villagers who were not
Sichuan natives. Life and culture in Juancun communities were themes and
subjects by many contemporary Taiwanese writers like Bai Xianyong (Hsien-
yung Pei), Zhu Tianwan, Zhu Tianxin, and Su Zhiwei.[20] Mainlanders' collective
memory about China, efforts to maintain their hometown cultural traditions
such as food, and affiliation with the Nationalist government formed a tangible
Diaspora Chinese community and a visible Chinese national consciousness in
Taiwan.

When the Nationalist government took Taipei as the nation's capital city,
mainlanders and their families became a dominant population in the city. To
make it look like a Chinese political center, the government maintained many
of its institutions and organizations it used to have in mainland China. Its basic
structure, such as Legislative Yuan ("Yuan" means branch), Executive Yuan,
Judicial Yuan, Examination Yuan, and Control Yuan, remained the same. In city
construction, the government expanded the old streets, built new ones, and
named many of them after the cities or provinces in the mainland. There were
street names like East Nanjing Road, North Chongqing Road, Xiamen Avenue,
Hengyang Avenue, Guilin Avenue, and Kunming Avenue. Even more interesting, if one takes a close look at the city map of Taipei, it is not difficult to discover
that the positions of those streets correspond roughly to the geographical locations of the cities and provinces in China that they were named after. For example, Dihua is a city in Xinjiang Province, and therefore Dihua Street is located in
northwest Taipei City. Changchun is a city in northeast China, and Changchun
Road is accordingly located in northeast Taipei.[21]

A political motivation was obviously behind the positioning and naming of these streets. An even more visible anti-Communist element was seen in the names of three east-west thoroughfares called Minzu (Nationality), Minquan (Human Rights), and Minsheng (Livelihood), and close to them were other avenues—Zhongxiao (Loyalty and Filialness), Renai (Kindness), Xinyi (Trust), and Heping (Peace). There were also north-south avenues called Guangfu (Regain) and Fuxing (Restoration). Through street names, the government was building a public memory about their past domination in mainland China. Public memory, as John Bodnar pointed out, is a body of beliefs and ideas about the past that help a public or society understand its past, its present, and, by implication, its future.[22] Street names became cultural symbols that constantly reminded ordinary people in Taiwan about the political agenda of the Nationalist government and its legitimacy to represent China. The government tried every way possible to build a protocol Chinese nation-state and strengthen a Chinese national identity among people in Taiwan.

With the arrival of mainland Chinese, Taipei was quickly growing into a metropolitan city. It housed all major government institutions, several universities, museums, theaters, and luxury hotels. Meanwhile, the Nationalist government realized that its stay in Taiwan was no longer a temporary retreat. To consolidate its power, the government introduced land reform, developed light industries for export, and invested in petrochemicals, steel, and other heavy industries. The government also established and enforced its conscription law, improved the public transportation system, and built more schools and universities. More important, it made Mandarin, spoken mainly by residents in Beijing, the official dialect used in schools, in radio and television broadcasts, and on public occasions. The Nationalist government referred it as Guoyu (national dialect), which was another cultural symbol of Taiwan's Chineseness.

American aid played an important role in developing the Taiwan economy. When the Korean War broke out in 1950, the United States deployed its Seventh Fleet in the Taiwan Strait, established the U.S. Military Assistance and Advisory Group in Taiwan in 1951, and offered $1.5 billion in nonmilitary aid to the Nationalist government.[23] From this time to 1964, the United States injected an average of $100 million a year into the Taiwanese economy. By 1978, Taiwan-U.S. trade was $7.39 billion.[24] To further help build the Taiwan economy, the United States opened its domestic market for merchandise produced in Taiwan. "During the 1950s and 1960s American aid provided about 40 percent of Taiwan's income."[25] While maintaining the Martial Law of 1947 for decades, the Nationalist government rapidly transformed the Taiwan economy. "Between 1960 and 1970, the average annual growth rate of the gross national product (GNP) in Taiwan was 9.7 while that per capital income was 6.6 percent."[26] Its economic boom in the 1970s made Taiwan one of the "four little dragons" in Asia. In the 1980s and 1990s, "millions of Taiwanese also migrated out of the countryside and small towns and moved to cities like Taipei, Kaohsiung, or Taichung, and others, in response to rapid increase in job opportunities."[27]

While the Nationalist government used its political agenda, street names, or language to construct a public memory about the people's past, ordinary mainlander Chinese learned how to readjust themselves and started a new life in Taiwan. To make a living, many mainlanders entered the restaurant business. Different regional-flavored restaurants and food stores featuring regional dried fruits, cookies, snacks, and other food items quickly spread in Taipei. The Xi-Men-Ting area, for example, was filled with restaurants owned by those new-comers since the 1950s and has become one of the most famous shopping plazas in the city. Meanwhile, prosperous food markets also appeared in Yuan Huan district, North Chongqing Road, Taipei Railroad Station, and Yonghe district.[28] To the west of the Zhonghua Road were many regional-flavored restaurants such as Beiping Du-Yi-Chu (Beijing Corner), Yi-Tiao-Long (One Dragon), and Xiao Chengdu (Little Chengdu). To the east were Da Li (Big Profit), San-Liu-Jiu (Three Six Nine), Lu Yuan (Green Garden), Fuxing Yuan (Restoration Garden), and Jufeng Yuan (Jufeng Garden).[29] Some of the restaurants, like San-Liu-Jiu, were relocated from Shanghai to Taipei following the Nationalists' retreat. Different from the street names, which reflected the government's political efforts to build a "virtual" little China in Taiwan, the regional-flavored restaurant business was mainly a survival strategy of those ordinary mainlanders who simply used their places of origin as cultural capital in a small business.

While the government attempted to reclaim what it lost politically; ordinary people tried to regain what they lost culturally. The anthropologist David Wu recalled: "During the 1960s and 1970s, the city was renowned as the repository of the great cuisines of mainland China; I still recall, with a pleasure difficult to describe, the culinary wonders of the Peking, Shandong, Zhejiang, Jiangsu, Hunan, Sichuan, and Yunnan restaurants (to mention only the most obvious), with one or more of them, it seems, on nearly every street corner. Established by refugees from the Chinese mainland in the 1950s, these restaurants were known for their 'authentic' regional Chinese cuisines. Their chefs made every effort to maintain the taste and special characteristics of the foods of their native provinces."[30] In Chinese food culture, authenticity matters because each regional cuisine has its own unique flavor, representative dishes, and local food ingredients. Taipei's colorful translocal restaurant world in Wu's description also reflects the diverse regional backgrounds from which mainlander Chinese came. Regional culture is an important component of Chinese identity.

Restaurants spread food culture. In no other place were people exposed so much to so many different Chinese regional-flavored cuisines as were residents in Taipei. In no other time in Chinese history were there so many different regional-flavored restaurants existing and competing for customers in one city. In Taipei, customers could find Sichuan spicy beef noodles, Hunan stir-fried chicken, Shandong steamed buns, Shanxi's hand-sliced noodles, Beijing boiled dumplings or hotpot, Shanghai steamed dumplings, Mongolian roasted mutton, or Yunnan's rice noodles soaked in burning hot chicken soup, called "bridge-crossing." The rapidly growing translocal restaurant business quickly made Taipei a famous tourist destination. Compared with the Nationalist government's political agenda, the thriving translocal restaurant business was much more real and substantial in sustaining and promoting Chinese culture in Taiwan. Food has played an important role in making Taipei a metropolitan city and a Diaspora Chinese cultural center.

Food evoked memories of one's hometown through familiar dishes and their flavors. Though serving all local customers, many Hunan, Sichuan, Shanghai, Jiangsu, Zhejing, Shandong, and other regional-flavored restaurants had for decades a critical mass of their own loyal clients who were natives of those areas. It is important to note that translocal restaurants in Taiwan were different from their counterparts in mainland China in their customer base. In a Chinese city, regional-flavored restaurants served mostly local customers who were there to taste a different flavor of food from that which they routinely ate. They went to such restaurants to eat some nationally famous dishes from another region. In contrast, loyal costumers in a regional-flavored restaurant in Taiwan were often those mainlander Chinese who missed their native food while being away from home. In his short story "Huaqiao Rong Ji" (Huaqiao Rong Family Restaurant), Bai Xianyong described how a restaurant, owned by a widow of military officer, was transplanted from her hometown in Guangxi Province and relocated on the Changchun Road in Taipei.[31] Many of its regular patrons were poor and homesick veteran soldiers from Guangxi.[32] When they were separated from their families in mainland China, hometown cuisine became one of the few cultural comforts in their life in Taiwan.

The Chinese translocal restaurant market in Taiwan was thriving because mainlanders were both consumers and proprietors. An American journalist recalled what a Taiwan professor told him in the 1960s about the restaurant business in Taiwan. When the Nationalists retreated to Taiwan, many military generals, government officials, and wealthy merchants brought their cooks with them. "Even more fortunately, many of these chefs were from Sichuan, the normally isolated province in Southwest China that the Nationalists had made their head-quarters in World War II. These accidents of history, combined with Taiwan's sudden affluence, have led to an explosion of new restaurants." According to the journalist, Taipei probably had "over 300 eating establishments serving the peppery cuisine of Sichuan alone by 1984." No city in mainland China would ever have 300 Sichuan restaurants. The journalist further wrote: "Most Chinese and foreigners I know think the restaurants in Taiwan are better than those in China. With its superior transportation system, Taiwan offers fresher ingredients, and socialist cooks on the mainland have less economic incentive to delight their customers."[33] His observation was not biased. In the mid-1980s, the restaurant business in mainland China was just beginning to prosper after the government implemented the reform policy in the late 1970s. But the restaurant business did not thrive until most restaurants became privately owned businesses in the 1990s. In comparison, Taipei had numerous regional-flavored restaurants as early as the 1960s.

Settling down in Taiwan, mainlander Chinese were not socially isolated individuals but congregated in residential communities. They had a collective memory about their past and a group identity that reflected from where they originally came. On the one hand, food tradition functioned as cultural capital for some of them to survive economically in a new environment. On the other, food tradition was a real, tangible cultural demarcation about their native origin. Long after their arrival, many mainlander Chinese in Taiwan kept their local accent, food habits, and fond memories of their native regional culture. In their studies on the global phenomenon of Chinese food, the anthropologists David Wu and Sidney Cheung pointed out: "When Chinese meet fellow Chinese overseas, consciousness of regional cultural, linguistic, and social distinctions among fellow Chinese are pronounced."[34] A person's native origin is often the first component of that person's Chinese identity. In social conversation, Chinese people commonly ask each other's place of origin. Mainlander Chinese in Taiwan were even more conscious of their Chinese identity as they originated from China, and the Nationalist government claimed itself as the only legitimate Chinese government.

Being Chinese often means originating from a specific region. In discussing Chinese identity, the anthropologist Myron L. Cohen wrote: "In general, there was, among the Chinese, a deep and sentimental attachment towards localism—be the customs, food or 'local products'—of their home communities. . . . One dimension of being Chinese was to have a place of origin somewhere in China."[35] Regional-flavored restaurants and many food products in Taiwan were meaningful examples of Chinese localism. Shopping in their grocery stores, customers in Taiwan could easily find Zhenjiang vinegar, Shaoxing cooking wine, or Longkou rice noodles. These products were not imported from mainland China but were made in Taiwan. Due to differences in climates and physical landscapes, food products in China reflected regional character and flavor. Vinegar in Zhenjiang, Jiangsu Province, and cooking wine in Shaoxing, Zhejiang Province, were cases in point. They had long been famous food products in China. Some food companies in Taiwan simply labeled their products as if they were made from the native regions in China. Whether these companies meant to maintain a sense of authenticity or to promote sales, they were obviously aware that regional identity, historical reputation, and unique flavor characterized many Chinese food products.

As mentioned previously, the translocal restaurant business reached an unprecedented level in the Chinese food history in Taiwan. Chinese regional cuisines became popular and rooted in Taiwan, with translocal restaurants as an effective channel. Though there was no social contact between Taiwan and mainland China for a long time, food customers in Taipei were familiar with many classic Chinese dishes. In Chinese food culture, each and every regional cuisine was characterized by its unique flavor and cookery. Most regional-flavored restaurants in Taiwan attempted to be original in flavor, as authenticity was always a selling point. Proprietors did not want their food to appear less original. Customers in Taiwan had more choices in regional-flavored restaurants than did people in any city in mainland China.

The movie *Eat Drink Man Woman*, directed by Ang Lee, a renowned Taiwanese immigrant director in America, was a vivid showcase of Chinese translocal food culture in Taiwan. In the movie, audiences could find familiar dishes like Shanghai steamed dumplings, Wuxi spareribs, or Sichuan water-boiled beef.[36] According to one source, over 100 different recipes were used in the movie. Each dish was authentically prepared for its presentation on the screen. Lee was demanding and meticulous about the dishes served in his movie. To ensure the quality and authenticity of the recipes used in the movie, Lee hired food consultant Lin Huei-yi to make a recipe selection. In addition, Lee also asked Lin to coach the actors on the physical preparation of the dishes that would be cooked by their characters on camera.[37] Dishes used in the movie were not native Taiwanese food but several dozens of classic Chinese dishes representing different regional cuisines. They were the most famous dishes in Chinese culinary culture. Lin Huei-yi later published a book entitled *Recipes of Eat Drink Man Woman*.[38]

Ang Lee belonged to the same generation of David Wu and, growing up, witnessed the prosperous translocal restaurant market in Taipei. Food is an important theme in his movies about Chinese and Chinese American life. When Lee was a graduate student studying film at New York University, he produced a short movie entitled *I Love Chinese Food*. In an interview, he characterized some of his best movies as Chinese regional cuisines. He metaphorically described *Wedding Banquet* as a sizzling spicy Sichuan dish and *Eat Drink Man Woman* as a tasteful Zhejiang delicacy.[39] With a young gay character living in New York, the first movie could touch the nerves of many Chinese parents. In the second movie, the major character was Mr. Chu, a master chef of a luxury hotel. Though retired, he was a highly respected chef and was often invited back to work in emergency situations. Food was a recurring theme to reflect Mr. Chu's pride as a master chef and his stubbornness as a father. As a family routine, he prepared a sumptuous dinner every Sunday for his three adult daughters, who often reacted toward this unique fatherly love with mixed feelings. Embodied in Chef Chu's gourmet food for his daughters was not only a generation gap in a Chinese family but also the rich culinary culture transplanted from mainland China to Taiwan.

HUNAN CUISINE MADE IN TAIWAN

When the Nationalists retreated to Taiwan, it was common that senior government officials, military generals, and wealthy families brought cooks with them. Many cooks later on opened their own restaurants. During the 1950s, the more popular restaurants were those that featured Hunan, Jiangsu, Zhejiang, and Shanghai cuisines. The popularity of those restaurants owned a great deal to their elite clients. Many of them were natives of those areas. The Nationalist leader Chiang Kai-shek was a native of Zhejiang and had a Shanghai power base.[40]

Among those flavors, Hunan cuisine deserves special attention because hundreds of Hunan restaurants appeared in New York and its surrounding area in the 1970s and 1980s. General Tso's chicken became the most famous Chinese dish and Hunan cuisine the most famous Chinese flavor to American customers at that time. The popularity of Hunan cuisine in Taiwan led to its spread in the United States.

One of the chefs who followed the Nationalist government was Peng Chang-gui. When Peng was young, he learned cooking skills from Cao Jinchen (曹荩臣), better known as "Cao Si" (曹 四). Cao was the family chef of Tan Yankai (谭 延 闿), the prime minister of the Nationalist government from 1926 to 1928. A Hunan native, Tan was from an elite family. Both his father and grandfather were senior government officials during the late Qing Dynasty. Tan loved gourmet food and often discussed with Cao how to cook. His interest in food was similar to Yuan Mei's. A Qing scholar and official famous for his passion for gourmet food, Yuan wrote a book that had a collection of more than 300 recipes from Chinese regional cuisines. He often talked to his chef, Wang, about cooking. Like Yuan's chef, Cao was a creative cook. Though shark's fin was not a traditional Hunan food, he invented several shark's fin dishes in Hunan flavor. Tan's family banquets always attracted other government officials and business elites. When Cao and other celebrated chefs opened Hunan restaurants, they all used Tan family recipes. Today, the Tan family recipe still has a high reputation in the Chinese culinary world. There are high-end restaurants in Beijing and other metropolitan cities in China that claim to be authentic Tan family restaurants. Although Peng Chang-gui once worked under Cao, he was not an ordinary cook but a master chef specializing in Hunan cuisine. After he arrived in Taiwan, Peng had allegedly cooked for Chiang Kai-shek, the former president of the Nationalist government in Taiwan. It was not surprising that Peng Garden became the most famous Hunan restaurant in Taiwan.

In Chinese society, what one eats often reveals one's place of origin, social status, and relationship with others. Among the loyal customers of Hunan restaurants in Taiwan, many were military officers from Hunan. As they became a critical mass of patrons of Peng Garden and other Hunan restaurants, Hunan cuisine was sometimes referred to as *"jun fan"* ("military food"). Eating Hunan food reminded these officers of their native origin and mainland China. From the late Qing Dynasty to the early Republic era, many Hunan youth went into the military. As an old local saying goes: there would be no army without Hunanese (*Wu xiang bu cheng jun*). In the 1920s and 1930s, the most prestigious military school in China was the Huangpu Military Academy. Chiang Kai-shek used to be the president of the academy. Zhou Enlai, premier of China until his death in 1976, was the director the academy's Political Department. Some graduates of the academy became the Communists. Many joined the Nationalists. A considerable number of the high-ranking officers in the Nationalist Party were Hunan natives. The father of the present president of Taiwan, Ma Yingjiu, was, for example, a Hunan native and a former senior government official. The father of former Nationalist Taiwan provincial governor Song Chuyu (James Soong) was also a Hunan native and a retired military general.

Peng and owners of other Hunan restaurants made their food as original as possible in flavor. They knew whom they served and understood that native place meant so much to those generals and officers. Chef Peng must have had a sense of history in entertaining his military clients. While cooking traditional Hunan dishes, Peng invented new dishes such as sautéed tofu (Pengjia doufu) or Fugui kao shuangfang, which was cooked honey ham and a crispy vegetable cracker wrapped in thin toast. But his most famous invention was General Tso's chicken. Several sources indicated that he created the dish in 1955.[41] Peng himself claimed that he did so in 1952 when the navy commander of the Nationalists asked him to be the chief chef for a banquet to entertain the commander of the U.S. Navy Seventh Fleet.[42] His recipe was simple: deep-fry seven or eight small pieces of starch-coated chicken until they become crispy, let them drain of oil, and then stir-fry them with red pepper and soy sauce. With a typical Hunanese spicy flavor, the dish was tasty but not a highly priced delicacy. It became one of the most popular dishes in Peng Garden and attracted many customers. Following Peng Garden, many more Hunan restaurants appeared in Taipei. They all offered General Tso's chicken as an authentic Hunan dish. Gradually, General Tso's chicken evolved into a culinary icon of Hunan cuisine in Taiwan.

General Tso's chicken is a very symbolic dish. Peng named it after Zuo Zongtang, a famous late Qing Dynasty general or governor who defeated several Western imperialist invasions against China and successfully recovered territories occupied by foreign military forces. The general was a Hunan native. "Tso" is the old spelling of Zuo. The province produced other famous Qing generals, such as Zeng Guofun, whom Chiang Kai-shek and other senior Nationalist generals admired. In their political agenda, Chiang and his generals never gave up their dream of regaining mainland China from the Communists. With its symbolic name, General Tso's chicken reflected the political culture in Taiwan in those decades. It became an authentic Chinese dish more for its cultural implications than its culinary quality. Food is a cultural tradition. A tradition needs stories that make it look ancient and timeless. By its name, General Tso's chicken invoked the collective memory of those Hunanese Nationalists about the heroes of their native place. It could even imply that it was a favorite dish for General Zuo in his military career. The popularity of General Tso's chicken illustrates what China studies scholar Wang Gongwu once said: being away from China "can mean the effort to reproduce what is remembered of Chinese ways and then transmitting them, however imperfectly, to descendants."[43] Chef Peng himself probably did not expect that his creation would become one of the most famous Chinese dishes in Taiwan and later in the United States.[44] When it did, General Tso's chicken demonstrated how Chinese regional-flavored cuisines became rooted in Taiwan.

Understandably, General Tso's chicken remained largely unknown in mainland China. Hunan cuisine was one of the oldest cooking traditions in China. Characterized by a rural style and local ingredients, its flavor was heavy and spicy.[45] In the 1950s and 1960s, the most famous chef of Hunan cuisine in mainland China was Shi Yinxiang, who died in April 2008. Shi was officially recognized and named as a master Hunan cuisine chef by the Hunan provincial government in 1984. By then, Shi had been a chef for over sixty years and had cooked many times for Mao Tse-tung (Zedong), the late leader of China, when he toured Hunan in the 1950s and 1960s. Mao was also a Hunan native and loved his hometown food. He obviously had never heard of General Tso's chicken. Shi published a cookbook entitled *A Collection of Hunan Recipes* (Xiang cai jin ji) in 1983, which included 500 recipes of Hunan cuisine.[46] General Tso's chicken was not listed in Shi's book.

In fact, many Chinese regional dishes in Taiwan were different from those in mainland China. Some bore similar names but tasted slightly or considerably different from their counterparts in mainland China because flavor, ingredients, and cookery were changed in order to adapt to the food supply market. For example, many traditional Hunan dishes like Dongan baby chicken (Dongan zi ji) and Junshan tea-leaf chicken (Jun shan yin zhen ji pian) were not available in Hunan restaurants in Taiwan. As a famous Hunan dish, the Dongan baby chicken recipe was included in Barbara Tropp's internationally renowned cookbook *The Modern Art of Chinese Cooking Techniques and Recipes*, published in 1982.[47] Dongan was the name of a county, while Junshan was the name of a mountain. Dongan chicken used young chickens raised in the county. Boiled first and then stir-fried with red pepper, onion, and ginger, the dish tasted spicy, rustic, and also delicious. To stir-fry thinly sliced Junshan chickens, tea leaves of the Jun Mountain were needed.[48] As those ingredients were not available in Taiwan, the two dishes were lost on the menus of Hunan restaurants in Taipei. Cookery and content of some Hunan dishes in Taiwan could also be different from their counterparts in mainland China. Cultural preservation and reproduction was often a process of cultural reinvention. General Tso's chicken by Peng essentially produced a new dish based on an old tradition. Though the dish was unknown in mainland China, its very name gave it a solid Chinese identity. This contradictory character of General Tso's chicken or other Hunan dishes made in Taiwan helps us understand the nature of Diaspora Chineseness. Chinese food does not exist in a social vacuum. Authenticity in food culture is often a flexible concept.

HUNAN RESTAURANTS IN NEW YORK

In Ang Lee's film *Wedding Banquet*, the scene was in New York rather than in Taiwan. The movie was about how a young gay Taiwanese immigrant in New York planned a fake marriage to placate his parents. While the plot depicted family relationships, the movie also reflected how Chinese food followed Taiwan immigrants to the United States. When the parents arrive in New York, the family eats in a Chinese restaurant, which is coincidentally owned by a former subordinate of the father, who is a retired senior military officer. The restaurant is not a cheap chop suey house in Chinatown but a trendy, upper-scale, full-service Hunan cuisine restaurant located in Manhattan. The restaurant owner, of course, waives the charge and adds two more dishes, one of which is General Tso's chicken, the most famous dish in Hunan cuisine in Taiwan, though the owner speaks in an obvious Shandong accent, a northern provincial dialect. The dish also figured prominently in another Lee film, *Pushing Hands*.[49] In his book *Chinese Food: An Introduction to One of the World's Great Cuisines*, the food historian Kenneth Lo listed several dozens of basic Chinese dishes provided by Chinese restaurants overseas before the early 1970s. While chop suey and chow main were the very first two items, General Tso's chicken was not on the list.[50] In Lee's movie, however, General Tso's chicken was a must dish that the restaurant owner wanted to serve to treat his former boss from Taiwan. The episode reflected changes in Chinese restaurants in New York in the 1970s. Authentic Chinese restaurants began to replace chop suey houses after the arrival of Taiwanese immigrants. Among various regional flavors, Hunan cuisine was the most visible and popular one, with General Tso's chicken as its representative dish. It was listed on the menu of every Hunan restaurant in New York City.

No doubt the popularity of Hunan cuisine in Taiwan led to its spread to the United States. Jennifer Lee attributed the spread of Hunan cuisine in New York to three chefs who migrated to America and opened restaurants in New York in the late 1960s and early 1970s. "Chef Peng opened Peng Yuan on the East Side. Chef T. T. Wang opened Hunan and the different Shun Lees. Wen Dah Tai, also known as Uncle Tai, joined forces with David Keh and opened Uncle Tai's Hunan Yuan on Third Avenue and Sixty-second Street."[51] Tsung Ting Wang was not a Hunan native. As a child, he worked in a Shanghai kitchen with his father and then as a cook in restaurants in Chongqing, Sichuan Province, then in Hong Kong, and finally in Tokyo, where he was hired by the Taiwanese ambassador, Harrington Tung, there. When the ambassador was transferred to Washington, D.C., he brought Wang with him. When Tung returned to Taiwan, Wang decided to stay and cofounded Shun Lee Dynasty restaurant in New York. While featuring Hunan cuisine, the restaurant offered other flavored dishes as well. Then Chef Wang set up a new restaurant, the Hunan at 845 Second Avenue, by taking over a defunct Chinese restaurant there and bringing in two chefs from Asia.[52]

Chef Peng arrived in New York in 1974. As a famous Hunan cuisine chef, his decision to open a restaurant in America was widely reported in the Taiwan media. While Uncle Tai's restaurant was located at 1059 Third Avenue, Peng Garden Restaurant was located at 219 East Forty-Fourth Street and under "the supervision of Uncle Peng, China's foremost master chef," as the *New York Times* ad read.[53] Taiwan's president, Ma Yingjiu, and his wife, Zhou Meiqing, were allegedly married in Peng Garden Restaurant in August 1977 when they were exchange students in the United States. Apparently Ma chose to marry there because Peng Garden Restaurant was a famous restaurant in Taiwan transplanted to New York. Moreover, born in a Hunan native family, Hunan cuisine was Ma's favorite food.

In her book on Chinese Diaspora culture and communities, Lynn Pan noted that many Hunan restaurants appeared in New York and its surrounding areas in the early 1970s, and they were operated by immigrants from Taiwan. "The specialization of restaurants in regional styles of cooking reflects not just the sharpening of collective American palates but also the diversity of Chinese immigration: there would have been fewer good Hunanese restaurants if there had been fewer immigrants from Taiwan, and there would certainly have been no Cuban-Chinese restaurants at all if there hadn't been a wave of migration of Chinese from Cuba."[54] The number of Chinese Cuban restaurants was also growing in New York when thousands of Cubans of Chinese descent came to the city after Fidel Castro's rise to power in the 1960s. *New York Times* food critic Mimi Sheraton concluded in 1977: "For the last several years one of our very best Chinese restaurants has been Hunan, featuring the hot, spicy, and gingery cuisine of the province for which it is named."[55] When the

Chinese American Museum in New York held an exhibition of Chinese restaurant menus in 2004, Michael Luo recollected about the significance of Hunan cuisine in the 1970s: "Hunan and Sichuan restaurants in New York influenced the taste of the whole country. Dishes like General Tso's chicken and crispy orange beef caught on everywhere."[56]

In 1972, President Richard Nixon made his historic visit to China after decades of hostility between the two countries. A by-product of this political event was another strong push for authentic Chinese food in America. After millions of Americans watched the president and his wife use chopsticks at the banquet hosted by Premier Zhou Enlai in the Great Hall of the People in Beijing, many rushed to Chinese restaurants and asked about Peking duck. Though Taiwanese restaurant owners had never tasted Peking duck like their American customers, it did not stop them from serving this famous dish in their restaurants. As Nixon's visit greatly aroused American public interest in Chinese food, Chinese restaurant owners in New York, Washington, D.C., Chicago, and other cities were eager to cash in on the enthusiasm. Many quickly put together a nine-course menu that supposedly replicated Zhou Enlai's banquet for Nixon, which further accelerated the growth in the number of customers at Chinese restaurants. "When we opened," said Susan Sih, co-owner of Chicago's Dragon Inn, "I couldn't give away a Peking duck. And then President Nixon went to China. He's been the greatest salesman for Peking duck. Now many people want it. . . . The Flower Drum Restaurant now serves Nixon-Chou banquets at $10 a head."[57] In fact, many Chinese restaurants charged more than $50 or even $100 per person for such a meal.

In response to Nixon's visit, the Taiwan government flew in a team of chefs to show that they were "the true guardians of Chinese culinary tradition."[58] This political effort did not help the Taiwan government much diplomatically, but it made Taiwanese immigrants even more anxious to open restaurants. They realized that authentic Chinese food had a great potential in American society. The number of Chinese restaurants was growing rapidly in the 1970s. According a *New York Times* article in 1972, there were up to 1,200 Chinese restaurants in the city and adjacent Long Island, with another 500 to 600 in New Jersey and Connecticut combined. Furthermore, the article claimed that in the past five years, "the number has grown by about 300—or an average of about one opening a week—and the current rate is now put at 100 openings a year."[59] Most of the newly established Chinese restaurants served Hunan cuisine. However, not all restaurant operators were Hunan natives, and the popularity of Hunan cuisine was more than a culinary success. Its flavor and cookery were indeed unique. But all Chinese regional cuisines were unique. Immigrants from Taiwan chose to open Hunan restaurants because Peng Garden Restaurant had been successful in New York. They had a role model to follow. Furthermore, there were so many Hunan restaurants in Taiwan, and they had probably tasted General Tso's chicken many times. Some of them might have even worked in a Hunan restaurant in Taiwan and cooked the dish themselves. When restaurant operation was a survival strategy and Hunan cuisine was trendy in America, they did not hesitate to claim that their food business was a Hunan restaurant.

It was not unusual that food tradition spread out of its native place following human migration. But many Taiwanese immigrants or their parents were originally from mainland China. The Chinese regional cuisines they brought with them were similarly retransplanted to America through Taiwan. As Jack Williams pointed out, Taiwan played a special role in the Chinese Diaspora, serving both as a receiver of immigrants from the Chinese mainland and a sender of emigrants abroad.[60] The explosive growth of Chinese regional-flavored restaurants in Taiwan enabled immigrants from there to play an important role in spreading Chinese food into American society when there was no diplomatic relationship between China and the United States.

In 1977, arranged by the then secretary of state Cyrus Vance, the Chinese national soccer team came to play in New York. After the game, Chinese players were taken to a Hunan restaurant close to the Biltmore Hotel.[61] Obviously, the American hosts viewed Hunan cuisine as a trendy and more authentic Chinese food since they did not take their guests to a chop suey house. But that restaurant was very likely owned by a Taiwanese immigrant. A *New York Times* article reported in 1977 that "the newest Hunan restaurant is Hunan Garden. It opened just over two months ago in Westport. It is the same ownership as the Hunan Garden in Riverside, but is much better. In fact, it is probably the best example of this style of cooking in the area. . . . Like its counterparts elsewhere in the state, Hunan Garden is not just Hunan. Its menu has Sichuan, Peking, even a few Cantonese dishes as well."[62] Another *New York Times* article reported in November 1980: "In the last year, more than a half-dozen Chinese restaurants have opened in southern Westchester, and every one has to be commendable in one way or another."[63] Still another article concluded in July 1981: "As recently as three years ago, there were few, if any, Hunan-style Chinese restaurants in Connecticut. Since then, at least three or four have sprung up in Fairfield County alone. This peppery and oily style of Chinese cooking has caught on, as has its near neighbor Sichuan. The newest Hunan restaurant is Hunan Garden."[64] During the 1970s and 1980s, numerous Hunan restaurants appeared in New York and other American cities. Hunan cuisine became the most visible Chinese regional food in the United States.

Beginning in the late 1980s, pushed by Hong Kong immigrant entrepreneurs, Cantonese-flavored restaurants started to regain their popularity with dim sum food. Many immigrants from mainland China began to operate restaurants that featured northern cuisines such as Shangxi pan cakes, baked bread, or hand-made noodles. The number of other Chinese-flavored restaurants began to catch up. Hunan cuisine gradually lost its momentum in the growth of Chinese restaurants. A *New York Times* article in 1986 reported:

> Although restaurants offering Chinese cuisines continue to open in the county with a regularity for which, no doubt, all are grateful, places offering distinctive cooking have become increasingly rare. When more than a dozens years ago, those restaurants starring Hunan-Sichuan cuisine entered the country, they generated a store of interest. The earthy dishes, many lively with spicy heat, brought to the dining table excitement . . . [which was] lacking in the prevalent and bastardized Cantonese fare. Since then, Hunan-Sichuan places have overloaded the county's dining-out resources, and while lean pickings once made every opening a major culinary same thing, and mediocre renderings of this popular cuisine have left many palates jaded and ready for the next culinary wave. While few would reject a Mongolian fire-pot or a bowl of shredded swallow-skin soup, at this point, most would settle for an assortment of juicy dim sum, long overdue in the past.[65]

However, Hunan restaurants are still popular in many American cities.

While Hunan restaurants in America remained popular and General Tso's chicken became increasingly famous, Chef Peng returned to Taiwan in the early 1980s. When Jennifer Lee interviewed him in 2006, Peng was shocked to hear that General Tso's chicken in New York had begun to taste sweet. As a Hunan cuisine chef, he knew that a Hunan dish should never taste sweet. He was even more surprised when he saw broccoli in the dish from Lee's photos. Hunan did not produce broccoli; neither did his original version of General Tso's chicken use this popular American vegetable. However, he should be satisfied about his invention as Lee informed him that the dish, though appearing and tasting increasingly different from his original version, spread to Korea, the Philippines, and the Dominican Republic.[66] His own restaurant, Peng Garden, has also expanded into a prominent chain business in Taiwan.

Ironically, according to some of his loyal customers—including the mother of the then Taipei mayor Ma Yingjiu, the flavor of Peng Garden's food tasted less and less Hunanese. One day in August 2006, Madam Ma requested a chef from Peng Garden for a family meal and complained again after the service. Coincidently, a woman kitchen worker of the restaurant was a Hunan native who recently arrived in Taipei through her marriage with a Taiwanese resident. She had learned cooking in mainland China and offered to help. With the manager's permission, Ji Liyuan, the worker, went to Ma's house and cooked a meal that delighted Ma. Overnight Ji became famous for her authentic Hunan dishes and was soon invited to cook for numerous elite and ordinary Taipei families. Blessed by President Ma Yingjiu personally, Ji opened her own Hunan restaurant in Taipei on February 12, 2008.[67] The flavor of Hunan cuisine in Taiwan will probably take a new turn after Ji's restaurant and the numerous other social and cultural exchanges between Taiwan and mainland China that started in the 1990s.

Though not all immigrant restaurant operators from Taiwan were celebrated chefs like Peng Changgui, their entrepreneurship made Chinese food a thriving ethnic cuisine in America in the 1970s and 1980s. According to the sociologist Min Zhou, the number of restaurants run by the Chinese in New York City grew from 304 in 1958 to nearly 800 in 1988, employing at least 15,000 immigrant workers.[68] The restaurant business has become a cornerstone in the Chinese American economy again after the new immigrants arrived. A report in 2007 indicated that about 70 to 80 percent of American clients who frequented Chinese restaurants became familiar with Hunan, Mandarin, Sichuan (Szechwan), and Shanghai cuisines.[69] The food historian Harvey Levenstein also observed that "with self-assured but competitive New Yorkers in the lead, the plunge into foreign cuisines became quite frenetic. This was first apparent in the restaurant industry. Northern Italian, Shanghai, Szechuan, Hunan, and even-more obscure forms of Chinese food came to the fore, followed closely by Greek, Indian, Middle Eastern, Indochinese, and even Afghan and Ethiopian cuisines."[70] With the arrival of new immigrants, American customers have gradually realized that Chinese cuisine consists of many different regional flavors. After more than 150 years in America, the Chinese restaurant business has finally become translocal in flavor and transnational in identity.

7 · THE SAN GABRIEL VALLEY AS A CAPITAL OF CHINESE FOOD

On a Thursday afternoon in November 1985, General Lee's, the oldest restaurant in Los Angeles's Chinatown, was permanently closed. Originally called Man Jen Low (Ten Thousand Treasure House), the restaurant dated back to 1878 and had hosted many Hollywood celebrities and California dignities in its peak days.[1] Together with Soochow, Tuey Far Low, Grand East, and Grand View, Man Jen Low was an anchor restaurant in Los Angeles's Chinatown for years. The closing of this landmark restaurant marked visible changes in Chinese American communities since the 1965 immigration reform. When a new wave of Chinese immigrants arrived, they brought new tastes, created new businesses, and built new communities. Suburban Chinese neighborhoods emerged in Monterey Park and a host of San Gabriel Valley cities, where thousands of Chinese restaurants, food stores, and groceries have congregated. Cookery and menus of those contemporary Chinese restaurants followed the culinary trends in Asia. They served authentic Chinese food rather than chop suey meals. Riding the immigrant boom, the Southern California Chinese restaurant business began a new chapter in Chinese American history.

Food is a meaningful aspect of the contemporary Chinese American experience. The restaurant business reflects the social background, lifestyle, and ethnic identity of the post-1965 Chinese immigrants. In food and restaurant experience, we see how transnational culture is deeply ingrained in the contemporary Chinese American community. Instead of wholesale assimilation, post-1965 Chinese immigrants have selectively maintained some of their native cultural traditions, such as food. With restaurants, grocery stores, and ethnic strip malls visibly congregated and rooted in the San Gabriel Valley, the transnational and multicultural identity of Chinese Americans is no longer an abstract idea but a solid and tangible reality.

Food culture of contemporary Chinese Americans brings out a seemingly paradoxical outcome of immigrant adaptation. It is not only possible but also increasingly preferred for many immigrants to maintain their Chinese ethnicity while becoming Americans. Furthermore, the significance of the Chinese restaurant business goes beyond the Chinese American experience. It shows how American food history is not a melting-pot tale of different ethnic groups assimilating into one dominant culture. Instead, it is a story of new immigrants bringing in new tastes and new diets, adding and enriching American culinary culture. It illustrates that multiculturalism has made food choices continually expand in this nation of immigrants.

CHINESE RESTAURANTS BEFORE THE 1970S

In 1900, there were only three or four Chinese restaurants in Los Angeles, frequented almost exclusively by the Chinese themselves. By 1910, there were at least fifteen Chinese restaurants. More and more American customers began to frequent Chinese restaurants as the popularity of chop suey meals spread from the East Coast to the West Coast. Several of these Chinese restaurants were outside of Chinatown, and a few were in downtown Los Angeles.[2] The Los Angeles city directory of 1924 listed twenty-eight Chinese restaurants. By 1941, the same publication listed seventy-three.[3]

From the turn of the twentieth century, the restaurant business became a cornerstone business for Chinese Americans. Living under the shadow of Chinese exclusion laws, Chinese immigrants could form partnerships to start restaurant businesses with relatively little start-up money, and claim merchant status. The exclusion laws permitted only merchant immigrants to enter. Though operating restaurants required long hours and hard labor, it did not pose a direct competition to white laborers. The 1920 census indicates that of the 45,614 Chinese employed in the United States, 26,488 of them worked in restaurants and laundries.[4] In the 1930s, 6 percent of Chinese adult males in California and 20 to 25 percent of them in the East Coast cities worked in restaurant businesses.[5]

According to a 1938 report by the Oriental Division of the U.S. Employment Service in San Francisco, 90 percent of Chinese youth were service workers, mainly in the culinary trades. While the defense industry was in great need of professional employees, Chinese college graduates were passed by. In 1941, 5,000 young Chinese in San Francisco had no future worthy of their education but seemed destined to wash dishes, carry trays, cut meat, and dry fish in Chinatown.[6] By the late 1940s, there were about 4,300 Chinese restaurants in the continental United States. Seven percent of the American population frequented

Chinese restaurants. Ten years later the number of Chinese restaurants grew to 4,500, but even more remarkably now with over 20 percent of Americans as their frequent customers. In 1959, New York City alone had about 750 Chinese restaurants.[7]

By then, Chinese restaurant food had become thoroughly Americanized. Chop suey was a familiar name to the American public. From the late nineteenth century to the 1970s, Chinatowns in New York, Chicago, Los Angeles, and San Francisco always attracted tourists and visitors who were interested in Chinese food. While antique stores, furniture houses, and gift shops drew many tourists, restaurants were the anchor businesses. Food prices were usually cheaper than in restaurants outside of Chinatown. For a long time, the expectation of American customers for Chinese restaurants was cheap Americanized food like chop suey, chow mein, or egg drop soup. More sophisticated Chinese menus would include more expensive dishes like "wu dip har" (butterfly shrimp) or "tim suen yu" (sweet and sour fish).[8] According to Chen Benchang's estimate, there were 9,733 Chinese restaurants across the country in the early 1970s. On the East Coast (Washington, D.C., and thirteen states), there were about 3,755 of them, and New York alone had 1,700. The twelve midwestern states had about 1,900, while the seven states on the West Coast had about 2,250, most of which were located in or close to Los Angeles and San Francisco. The twelve states in the South had about 900, and the six states in the Northwest had 550.[9]

CHINATOWN TURNING CHINESE

When the Immigration and Nationality Act of 1965 ended the former U.S. immigration policy based on race and nationality and established an annual quota of 20,000 immigrants for each country, Chinese immigrants quickly took advantage of the new policy. Similar to the old immigrants, post-1965 Chinese immigrants followed a chain migration pattern. Husband or wife, or both, arrived first and then sponsored their children, parents, and siblings. Soon family networks expanded as relatives, in-laws, and friends followed. Since the new immigration act favored family reunification, the Chinese population grew rapidly. Between 1965 and 1984, an estimated 419,373 Chinese entered the United States—almost as many as the 426,000 Chinese who came between 1849 and 1930.[10] Under the new act, Chinese family networks and social relationships rebounded.

Post-1965 Chinese immigrants were far more diverse in their class and cultural backgrounds than the earlier immigrants. Many were educated professionals, engineers, technicians, or exchange students. Between 1950 and 1993, Taiwan sent 120,000 students to the United States, and fewer than 27,000 of them returned home after graduation.[11] From 1979 to 1989, mainland China sent about 80,000 graduate students and their spouses and children to the United

States, and a majority of them stayed after graduation.[12] Whether they were from mainland China, Taiwan, or Hong Kong, post-1965 Chinese immigrants preferred residence destinations in metropolitan cities like New York, Los Angeles, or San Francisco, where they could find a Chinatown. Homesick immigrants probably missed Chinese food most along with many other familiar commodities available in Chinatown. Food in Chinatown's restaurants connected them to their home culture. To the new immigrants, Chinatown was not only a symbol of Chinese ethnicity but also a place that touched their cultural sensibilities. It gave them a sense of home.

Chinatown, as the sociologist Min Zhou points out, also developed a structure of opportunities that would help channel immigrants into the larger American society.[13] Many newly arrived immigrants found temporary or stable jobs in Chinatown, especially in the restaurant business. Although the racial environment in American society was considerably improved in the 1960s, language barriers and lack of a U.S. college diploma or a professional license were still major obstacles to career success for some entrepreneurial and professional immigrants. The restaurant business continued to be one of the major economic enterprises available and attractive to the Chinese. Many new immigrants turned to the restaurant business for careers and job opportunities. According to Henry Tsai, "Chinese restaurants have gained a slight increase in the percentage of Chinese work force. The 0.8 percent increase between 1960 and 1970 was due mainly to the influx of new immigrants from Hong Kong, who were unable to find employment commensurate with their education, experience, or qualifications."[14] In the late 1960s, there were about 10,000 Chinese restaurants in the continental United States.[15] Restaurant jobs are often the first work experience for many post-1965 Chinese immigrants.

Following the 1965 immigration reform, Chinatowns in San Francisco, Los Angeles, and New York experienced a heavy influx of new immigrants. In the preceding two decades, Chinatowns were declining as more and more American-born Chinese were able to find technical or professional jobs, and many of them moved into the suburbs.[16] In 1966, only one-fifth of the 42,000 Chinese residents in San Francisco actually lived in Chinatown. Thoroughly Americanized fourth-, third-, and second-generation Chinese Americans had dispersed to other sections or suburbs of the city. In contrast, an estimated 7,400 of the annual 20,000 newly arriving Chinese immigrants were expected to settle in San Francisco's Chinatown.[17] The same was true of Los Angeles's Chinatown. In 1959, only a few hundred of the 22,000 Chinese residents in the Los Angeles area lived in Chinatown. The majority had moved to the suburbs.[18] Ten years later, there were 15,000 Chinese residents in Los Angeles's Chinatown. Many were new immigrants who did not speak English.[19] For American-born Chinese, Chinatown was an ethnic ghetto that they tried to move away from when they could. For new immigrants,

Chinatown was a cultural resource channel that they needed in order to adapt to American society. The arrival of new immigrants revitalized Chinatown.

Following the influx of the new immigrants, rent and real estate prices quickly went up, especially after wealthy Chinese merchants from Hong Kong or Taiwan began to invest and purchase housing properties in Los Angeles's Chinatown. When Chinatown was too crowded or too expensive to accommodate the needs of the growing immigrant community, Chinese immigrants began to move out of Chinatown into nearby cities like Monterey Park. However, Chinatown remained an important cultural base for the Chinese until the 1990s. Whenever post-1965 immigrants wanted to see an herbalist doctor for a minor disease, consult a Fengshui master before purchasing a house, or watch the lion dance parade during the Lunar New Year, they would visit Chinatown. Shopping in a Chinese grocery store and having a family meal in a favorite restaurant in Chinatown was a weekend routine for many Chinese families. With banks, grocery markets, bookstores, video shops, and Chinese restaurants, Chinatown continued to serve as a magnet for Chinese immigrants.

With the arrival of the new immigrants, Chinese visitors in Los Angeles's Chinatown gradually outnumbered non-Chinese tourists. In 1977, a businessman in Chinatown observed: "Five years ago, you won't find many Chinese during the weekends. Now 80–90 percent are Chinese."[20] The new immigrants needed to use the banks, grocery stores, and restaurants in Chinatown. Cathay Bank, the first Chinese American bank in Southern California, located in Los Angeles's Chinatown. But the new immigrants brought not only new business but also new tastes to Chinatown. Instead of chop suey, egg foo yong, or paper-wrapped chicken, they preferred genuine Chinese cuisine. Food and menus in Los Angeles's Chinatown's restaurants began to change. Americanized dishes gradually gave way to genuine Chinese food. "At the Golden Palace, non-Chinese were ushered to one side of the restaurant, decorated with plush black banquettes and dim lights, and Chinese to the other side, which has a more authentic décor, full lighting, and simple square tables and chairs."[21] This differential treatment signaled the beginning of change in the Chinese restaurant business. Following the restaurant style in Hong Kong, the Golden Palace was a pioneer in Los Angeles to serve dim sum food by waitresses pushing carts between tables. Catering to the new immigrants, the Golden Palace stayed open all night and was the only restaurant for a long time that could accommodate large banquets.[22]

As the number of Chinese clients was rapidly growing, Chinese restaurants in Chinatown began to make necessary adjustments in their recipes and cookery. Good Chinese chefs were in great demand. In the early 1970s, there was actually a shortage of qualified Chinese chefs. Chinese restaurants in Los Angeles's Chinatown competed with each other in offering higher wages in order to get a good chef. While a beginning cook made about $550 a month, a first-rate chef could earn as much as $1,200. Chinese restaurant owners also worked with the federal Department of Labor's Manpower Training Program to produce more professionally trained chefs. Each paid half of the salary of the intern cooks during the training period.[23] At that time, there were about 550 Chinese restaurants in Los Angeles County.[24] Many chefs were self-made cooks through working as kitchen helpers.

It was also during this period that Cantonese cuisine was no longer the dominant food. Restaurants featuring Shanghai, Sichuan, or Hunan flavor also appeared in Chinatown. Andrew Cherng, a Taiwan exchange student and founder of the Panda Express, opened the Plum Tree Inn in Los Angeles's Chinatown in partnership with his father, Ming Tsai Cherng, and Mark Ting, while operating their Panda Inn restaurant in Pasadena.[25] Both the elder Cherng and Mark Ting were professional chefs from Shanghai who specialized in Jiangsu and Zhejiang regional cuisine. Not far away from the Plum Tree Inn was the All Lucky, a much less elegant and more down-to-earth restaurant owned by P. C. Lee, a professional chef who specialized in Sichuan cuisine. Though only large enough for twenty-four seats, this authentic, spicy Sichuan beef noodle joint used seventy to eighty pounds of noodles every day.[26] Beginning in the 1980s, the arrival of refugee ethnic Chinese immigrants from Vietnam also promoted Chaozhou (Chiu Chow) cuisine, another food tradition in Guangdong Province. By 1997, there were about forty-seven restaurants in Los Angeles's Chinatown.[27]

MONTEREY PARK AS A NEW HOME

Post-1965 Chinese immigrants chose Monterey Park because it was close to Los Angeles's Chinatown. The new immigrants could conveniently fulfill their needs for food, groceries, and banking. This city also had convenient access to Interstate 10 to the north, Interstate 710 to the west, and Interstate 60 to the south. Moreover, the city was one of the most affordable and diverse suburban communities at that time.[28] All these qualities attracted the Chinese. In the late 1970s and early 1980s, dramatic changes were taking place in Monterey Park as Chinese immigrants and their families moved there in increasing numbers. Soon the city was dubbed "Little Taipei" or "New Suburb Chinatown." In 1960, there were only 346 Chinese in Monterey Park.[29] Ten years later the number had increased to 2,202. Between 1980 and 1990, the Chinese population grew from 8,082 to 21,971, representing a change from 14.9 to 36.2 percent of Monterey Park's total population.[30]

Following the immigrant flow, Chinese restaurants, grocery stores, and other businesses appeared. As a *Los Angeles Times* article in 1980 reported, "The first thing Monterey Park residents noticed were the Chinese restaurants that popped up." Then there were "three Chinese shopping centers, Chinese banks, and a theatre that only showed Hong Kong movies."[31] Before 1965, there was only one Chinese restaurant in Monterey Park. By 1983, there were more than forty.[32] The Chinese restaurant business reflected a chain of changes in the city. First came the Chinese real estate agencies, loan offices, and banks, as the new immigrants needed their services. Then Chinese grocery stories, salons, video shops, bookstores, herbal medicine and acupuncture services, gift shops, and mini-supermarkets followed up. Meanwhile more restaurants appeared block by block, up and down the north-south Atlantic Boulevard and the east-west Garvey Avenue, the city's two main thoroughfares. In 1978–79, the city issued 2,700 business licenses. By the mid-1990s, the number had almost doubled to 5,000. The Chinese owned from two-thirds to three-fourths of the city's business enterprises.[33] As a stream of Chinese retail and service businesses revitalized vacant lots, unoccupied office buildings, and desolate shopping plazas, Monterey Park became a prosperous Chinese suburban community.

Some immigrant entrepreneurs foresaw such changes early. Fred Hsie, whose Mandarin Realty played an instrumental role in advertising Monterey Park in Hong Kong and Taiwan as a Chinese Beverly Hills, invited twenty prominent white residents of Monterey Park to dinner in 1977. At the dinner, he told them that "Monterey Park was going to be [the] next Chinatown and that changes were inevitable."[34] On another occasion, Fred Hsie predicted that in five years, Monterey Park would be comparable to Los Angeles's Chinatown and then surpass it. The change actually took place faster than Hsie predicted. "A dozen Chinese-run banks with combined deposits of more than $400 million have opened since 1979. Three Chinese-language newspapers with worldwide circulations are headquartered or have branch offices on a single street in town. The city supports 60 Chinese restaurants and several Chinese-run nightclubs in a 7.7-square-mile area."[35] By the 1980s, Monterey Park replaced Los Angeles's Chinatown as a cultural and economic center for Chinese Americans.

The changes in Monterey Park were fast and overwhelming. Some longtime white, Latino, and American-born Asian residents became confused and uncomfortable. Grocery markets and the restaurant businesses were probably more controversial than any other Chinese commercial activities. Many of the old residents were shocked to discover that "Safeway and Alpha Beta, once anchors for the Anglo and Latino communities, have been replaced with the Hung Hoa supermarket and a two-story Pagoda-roofed Chinese shopping center that stands as the most dominant architectural structure in the city."[36] Jen Shen Wu, an immigrant from Taiwan, opened the first Chinese supermarket in Monterey Park in 1978. Soon Wu's Diho Market became a chain of stores with 400 employees and $30 million in annual sales.[37] Diho was followed by the Hong Kong Supermarket, the Ai Hoa Supermarket, and others.[38] The rapidly growing grocery stores and retail businesses signaled more changes in Southern California that Chinese immigrants would bring.

As many Chinese moved into Monterey Park, the number of Chinese restaurants was growing at an amazing speed. By 1987, the city had over sixty Chinese restaurants, representing 75 percent of the dining business in the city.[39] The restaurant business became the most visible ethnic enterprise of the post-1965 Chinese immigrants. Most Chinese restaurants in Monterey Park were family-owned small businesses. But there were also larger restaurants, investments by wealthy merchants from Hong Kong or Taiwan. Harbor Village and Ocean Star, located on Atlantic Boulevard, became two of the largest city revenue generators in Monterey Park.[40] Ocean Star, owned by Robert Y. Lee, had 800 seats and was one of the largest Chinese restaurants in the San Gabriel Valley.[41] Embedded in the rapid growth of the food and restaurant business was the vision of the post-1965 Chinese immigrants about their life in America. While willing to settle down and embrace American culture, many new immigrants were reluctant to abandon their own cultural traditions, especially food habits. With modest prices, authentic food, and familiar dishes, Chinese restaurants in Monterey Park made new immigrants feel at home and their adaptation in America a less painful process. Ethnic food helped immigrants settle down in their newly adopted country.

Food connected Chinese immigrants to their Asian cultural roots. In 1987, a *Los Angeles Times* restaurant review listed the top ten Chinese restaurants in Monterey Park and Alhambra. Wonder Seafood Restaurant was one of them. Dishes on its menu included abalone and duck hot pot, crystal shrimp with sweetened walnuts, and ground pigeon topped with plum sauce. But according to Ricky Wu, co-owner of the restaurant, his true culinary masterpiece was a three-snake soup, made from cobra, rattler, and a third snake for which Wu said there is no English name. "This legendary dish is considered a wintertime delicacy for its unique warming effect and mythical powers as an aphrodisiac." Wu confessed that it really should be five-snake soup, but it was difficult to get all the snakes in America.[42] Wu's masterpiece was not a new exotic delicacy. In Hong Kong and Guangzhou, many high-end restaurants served five-snake soup. Three-snake soup simply showed how Wu or other Chinese restaurants served Chinese customers authentic Chinese food.

Another famous dish at Wu's restaurant was Fo Tiao Qiang, which means "Buddha jumped over the wall" because "he smelled the soup, and it smelled so delicious." This is only one of three versions about the origin of this expensive entrée, the most famous dish in Fujian cuisine. In content, "this stew that serves 10 contains abalone, conch, soft-shell turtle, and a host of other ingredients."[43] With a number of seafood ingredients, this dish was a must at social dinners for many businessmen from Taiwan and Hong Kong. In Chinese culinary culture, most of the famous dishes originated from a family recipe or an unknown restaurant in a small town before they became nationally famous. Fo Tiao Qiang used to be such a dish in Fujian Province. When it spread to Guangzhou in the mid-1960s, the dish began to appear on the menu of government banquets for international VIPs, which boosted its reputation. Then it spread to Hong Kong in the 1980s. When eating out, business executives, movie celebrities, and upper-middle-class families all ordered it as a well-known delicacy.

Overseas Chinese restaurants across the world, especially in Southeast Asia, quickly learned the recipe and served the dish to local Chinese merchants. Many post-1965 immigrants in the Monterey Park area were immigrants from Taiwan who spoke the same dialect and shared similar cultural traditions with the people in Fujian Province. Due to their transnational business networks, merchant immigrants from Taiwan also frequently traveled to Guangzhou and Hong Kong. Many tasted this famous dish there with business friends. Now back home in Monterey Park, they could also enjoy it at Wonder Seafood Restaurant. Fo Tiao Qiang illustrates how Chinese restaurants in Southern California followed culinary trends in Asia.

Food is a tangible cultural symbol representing an ethnic group. According to the historian Huping Ling's cultural community theory, Chinese restaurants concentrated in Monterey Park were a phenomenon that reflected cultural congregation for ethnic identity.[44] The Chinese restaurant business in Monterey Park made that city a food destination during the weekend. "The presence of Chinese newcomers, who are spread throughout the city, is magnified each day by countless other Asians who live outside Monterey Park but crowd its streets to shop, bank, and entertain friends."[45] Chinese customers from all over Southern California drove long distances to shop, bank, and eat in Monterey Park. According to a *Los Angeles Times* story in 1991, the Zhou family drove from Valencia, in the San Diego area, about fifty miles round-trip every Saturday in order to have a good Chinese meal and shop at Ai Hoa Supermarket on North Atlantic Boulevard because there were no Asian supermarkets where they lived. Another family came from Thousand Oaks once a month for a dim sum meal and shopping in a Chinese grocery store where they could buy live fish and have the shopper assistants help them clean it inside out. Their shopping list included items like noodles, tofu, Chinese cabbage, fresh bamboo shoots, Chinese sausage, plum candy, canned litchis in syrup, oyster sauce, and Pop-pan, a popular breakfast cracker. It was a family activity, and the children loved it.[46]

Though there were also Chinese restaurants in the San Diego area or Thousand Oaks, Ventura County, the Zhou and Li families were still willing to drive all the way to Monterey Park. What they looked for was not only an authentic Chinese meal but also the Chinese cultural atmosphere there. Restaurants in Monterey Park functioned as connecting elements for dispersed Chinese immigrants. A 1995 *Los Angeles Times* article observed that "in Monterey Park, there are now so many Chinese restaurants that you could eat Chinese every weekend for more than a year and never hit the same place twice."[47] The significance of the Chinese restaurants in Monterey Park is not just the number. Different from their counterparts earlier and elsewhere that catered mainly to white clients, Chinese restaurants in Monterey Park served authentic Chinese food. They catered to mainly Chinese customers.

Food transmitted culture. Chinese restaurants, grocery stores, and other service businesses in Monterey Park reflected how the post-1965 Chinese community maintained their cultural traditions. When parents were too busy or exhausted from work to cook, they took their children to Chinese restaurants. A family meal gave Chinese parents a sense of "cultural authority" about the home country as they ordered and explained Chinese food to their children. For the American-born or -raised generation, eating Chinese food was a way to learn and maintain Chinese culture. When some American-born Chinese abandoned Chinese food, they would eventually abandon their cultural roots, even family traditions and community networks.

However, it did not mean Chinese immigrants totally detested Western cuisine. Post-1965 Chinese immigrants often expressed interest in American food. In fact, they were probably interested in hamburgers or pizza more than in Americanized Chinese dishes like chop suey, which they often considered as "fake" Chinese food. Many of them tried American food from time to time. A report from the *Los Angeles Times* on June 27, 1985, told a story of how thirty-five Chinese women in Monterey Park organized a luncheon outing at a Sizzler restaurant. Some of them had not been to an American restaurant due to the language and cultural barriers, though they had been in the United States for two years. The leader of the group helped translate the menu and advised how to order. They all seemed excited about this exploration of a mainstream American restaurant.[48] No doubt, language and cultural barriers could not be overcome just through a couple of visits to American restaurants. Nor was it too easy for anyone to abandon a food habit.

Monterey Park was not a Chinatown but a suburban American city with a large Chinese population. Post-1956 Chinese immigrants increasingly lived in integrated suburban neighborhoods. Chinatown was no longer the only cultural center for them. Serving new immigrants with genuine Chinese food, Chinese restaurants in Monterey Park set off a new trend and began a new chapter in Chinese culinary history. Similar to Taipei or big cities in mainland China, a cluster of restaurants featuring different regional cuisines constituted a translocal Chinese restaurant market. Recipes, ingredients, and cookery in the post-1965 Chinese restaurant businesses in America would follow closely their counterparts in Asia. The Chinese community remains transnational in its food culture.

SAN GABRIEL VALLEY AS A CHINESE FOOD CAPITAL

Monterey Park was only the beginning of much deeper and wider changes that would be brought about by Chinese immigrants in the San Gabriel Valley, a vast suburbia to the east of Los Angeles. When Fred Hsie predicted that Monterey Park would be comparable to Los Angeles's Chinatown and then surpass it, another Chinese merchant echoed his prediction by saying that in a decade, the entire San Gabriel Valley would be like Monterey Park as the Chinese purchased real estate properties heavily in Alhambra, Montebello, Rosemead, and El Monte.[49] Working as real estate agents, they foresaw this trend because the number of their Chinese clients kept growing. Less than a decade later, their prediction became true. Atlantic Boulevard does not end in Monterey Park but reaches northward to where Alhambra, San Marino, and South Pasadena intersect. Garvey Avenue goes eastward from Monterey Park through Rosemead and El Monte. Chinese restaurants and strip malls naturally expanded into these neighboring cities. Using Monterey Park as a model or an entry port, post-1965 Chinese immigrants quickly spread into many cities in the San Gabriel Valley.

After the 1965 immigration reform, the Chinese population in the area soared. According to a 1987 *Los Angeles Times* article, an estimated 100,000 Chinese and other Asians had moved into the western San Gabriel Valley area since 1980, more than doubling the number of Asians living in the twenty-seven cities and unincorporated areas of the San Gabriel Valley to an estimated 180,000 people. For every entering Asian, there would be a departing white American. Of the region's 327,000 residents, the white population dropped from 78 percent in 1970 to 56 percent in 1980 to an estimated 36 percent in 1987.[50] By 1990, the Chinese population in Southern California rose to 324,274, making it the largest Chinese community in the nation. By 2000, Southern California had become the home of 523,597 Chinese residents.[51]

About 50 percent of this population concentrated in the San Gabriel Valley area and spread from Alhambra, Rosemead, San Marino, South Pasadena, San Gabriel, and Arcadia, and all the way east to West Covina, Hacienda Heights, Rowland Heights, Diamond Bar, and Walnut. In some cities, the Chinese population reached over 30 to 40 percent. While Monterey Park's Chinese population constituted, for example, about 44.3 percent, San Marino had 43.4 percent; Arcadia, 36.3 percent; San Gabriel, 36.3 percent; Alhambra, 35.9 percent; Rosemead, 32.5 percent; and Rowland Heights, 31.5 percent (see Table 1).

All these cities had Asians as the largest population group.[52] The Chinese and Asian presence in the region significantly boosted the sagging real estate market in the early 1990s. Nearly one of five home buyers in Los Angeles County in 1992 had a Chinese last name.[53] The change has made not only Monterey Park but also the San Gabriel Valley home to the largest concentration of Chinese Americans

TABLE 1.   Chinese Restaurants and Ratio to the Chinese Population
in Nine San Gabriel Valley City/Areas

City/Areas	Restaurant Number			Total Population in 2000	Chinese Population in 2000	% Population	Ratio of Chinese Restaurants to Chinese Population*
	1988	1997	2007				
Alhambra	28	49	57	85,804	30,836	35.9%	1:540
Arcadia	5	11	35	53,054	19,274	36.3%	1:550
Chinatown	58	43	44	15,000	n.a.	n.a.	1:340
Hacienda Heights	7	15	28	53,122	13,090	24.6%	1:467
Monterey Park	48	57	72	60,051	26,582	44.3%	1:369
Rosemead	4	26	27	53,505	17,372	32.5%	1:643
Rowland Heights	1	37	65	48,553	15,273	31.5%	1:234
San Gabriel	13	55	96	39,804	14,460	36.3%	1:150
San Marino	1	1	2	12,945	5,616	43.4%	1:2,808
Total	165	294	426				1:677

SOURCES: The number of Chinese restaurants was based on *Chinese Yellow Pages* (华商年鉴) 1988, 1997, and 2007, and *Chinese Consumer Yellow Pages* (华人工商) 1997 and 2007. Chinese population information is from www.census.gov. Chinatown population information is from "Selling the Taste of Chinatown," *Los Angeles Times* June 14, 2004, and the number of Chinatown restaurants is identified based on their street locations.
* The ratio compares the number of Chinese restaurants in 2007 with the Chinese population in the city/area based on 2000 census data. The ratio in Chinatown compares the number of Chinese restaurants with the total population.

in the nation. Many non-Asian residents in this region had to learn how to live as a minority in America and tasted a life that they had probably not experienced before.

While the Chinese population was spreading into the San Gabriel Valley, Monterey Park, called the "first suburban Chinatown" by the sociologist Tim Fong, gradually lost its leading status as the Chinese dining center. Many other cities in the region began to look like Monterey Park. Chinese mini-malls, shopping plazas, financial and real estate services, and other retail businesses proliferated. Chinese restaurants took the lead in such business expansion and often clustered on the major streets in those cities. In many cases, wealthy merchants from Hong Kong, Taiwan, or Southeast Asia purchased commercial blocks, let go the old business tenants, remodeled the buildings, and then leased them out to Chinese restaurant proprietors and other retail or service business owners. "There's a Chinese restaurant in Rosemead where the Builder's Emporium used to be, a Chinese restaurant in Alhambra in what once was the Chowder House. The Edwards Drive-In in San Gabriel is now an enormous stucco mall. It has fifteen restaurants in it, all Chinese."[54] Following this pattern, post-1965 Chinese immigrants have transformed the social landscape in the San Gabriel Valley. At the same time, backlash by other residents against Chinese food and other businesses eventually slowed down the uncontrolled growth of Chinese restaurants in Monterey Park. City officials and many residents, including the Chinese, wanted to attract more high-end mainstream retail businesses to the city.

Though there were numerous Chinese restaurants in the San Gabriel Valley, each city with concentrated Chinese residents has a few famous Chinese restaurants as an anchor business attraction. Monterey Park has the Ocean Star and Harbor Village. Arcadia has the celebrated Din Tai Fung dumpling house. San Gabriel has the high-end restaurant Mission 261. Rowland Heights has the Sea Harbor Seafood Restaurant and Sam Woo Seafood Bistro. Famous Chinese restaurants follow wherever the immigrants have congregated. Sam Woo, for example, also has branch operations in Monterey Park, San Gabriel, and Irvine, which is not in the San Gabriel Valley but has a large Chinese population.

In order to attract business, Chinese restaurants cluster on certain streets rather than spreading out evenly in most of these San Gabriel Valley cities. "Rosemead has 50 restaurants jammed into five square miles. Rowland Heights has 30, give or take one or two."[55] Main Street in Alhambra, Valley Boulevard in San Gabriel, the cross streets of Baldwin and Duarte Road in Arcadia, and Colima Street in Rowland Heights have become what Atlantic Boulevard is in Monterey Park. Concentrated Chinese restaurants have formed a dining destination in each city. In a few decades, Chinese strip malls or shopping centers, often with a number of restaurants as anchor businesses, have been sprawling across the entire stretch of the San Gabriel Valley, from Monterey Park in the west to Diamond Bar in the east.

The most visible dining destination, however, is not a single city but Valley Boulevard, which goes through Alhambra, San Gabriel, and Rosemead. "The boulevard—a bustling swath of Asian supermarkets, about 100 Asian restaurants and scores of small shops selling products as varied as woodsilk towels and chrysanthemum tea—is not only a regional shopping district, but also has put San Gabriel on the international destination map."[56] Its only counterpart is probably

Main Street in Flushing, New York. Most of the 100-plus Chinese restaurants are crammed together on a two-mile "golden stretch" in the city of San Gabriel and a couple of blocks of Alhambra. In 1982, land on Valley Boulevard in Alhambra sold for $20 a square foot. Five years later, the price had doubled or tripled. "One local banker said a customer paid $8 million for property on Valley Boulevard in 1985 and sold it a year later for $12 million."[57]

Numerous Chinese restaurants border each other on both sides of the street, while many others are crowded inside a dozen of strip malls on the boulevard. Together, they draw huge crowds of customers during the lunch and dinner hours, especially on the weekends and holidays. In order to survive the competition, each restaurant claims its regional tradition or special flavor, maintains its own cuisine style, develops its own unique dishes, and offers its own special deals. Business relationships among the Chinese restaurants on Valley Boulevard are a subtle interaction. While competing with each other for clientele, the restaurants also bond together to create a visible Chinese cuisine hub. Valley Boulevard today is far more famous and attractive as a Chinese food epicenter than Monterey Park and Los Angeles's Chinatown.

SAM WOO RESTAURANT AND CHINESE GROCERY STORES

Sam Woo B.B.Q. and Seafood Bistro is a big name in the Chinese restaurant world. Many Chinese in Southern California like to have family meals at this restaurant during the weekend. Its founding partner Tam Chek Cheung was an immigrant from Hong Kong and arrived in Los Angeles in 1979. When he settled in Chinatown, Cheung opened a modest barbecue restaurant filled with lacquered ducks, marinated pork, and chickens brushed with a distinctive blend of star anise, ginger, garlic, and other traditional Chinese barbecue spices—the same kind of barbecued food he used to cook in Hong Kong. When his commercial in the local Chinese newspapers "offered a dollar dinner special built around a big bowl of soup, Sam Woo restaurant drew crowds of homesick immigrants and Chinese graduate students from nearby colleges and universities."[58]

Cheung's barbecued duck signaled a new trend in the Chinese American restaurant business at that time. Genuine Cantonese food was going to replace chop suey and egg foo yong, which were still served as typical Chinese dishes by restaurants like Golden Pagoda or General Lee's in Chinatown. Soon Cheung opened another Sam Woo in Monterey Park, and then one more in Alhambra. Instead of American customers, Sam Woo targeted new immigrants from Taiwan and Hong Kong who desired genuine Chinese food. Sixteen years later, there were eighteen Sam Woo restaurants stretching from San Diego, Irvine, Van Nuys, and Las Vegas to Canada.[59] Of the eighteen, some became upscale, full-service seafood restaurants. Some continued to be inexpensive, cash-only Sam Woo B.B.Q. restaurants. A full-service and a B.B.Q. restaurant were often located in the same shopping plaza as they represent different service. By 1997, Sam Woo developed its twenty-third chain.[60] It even opened a chain store in South Coast Plaza, Orange County, one of the largest and most famous upscale malls in the United States.

"Sam Woo" in Cantonese means "*san he*," or "Three Harmonies." In Chinese culture, people believe that success often depends on three elements—right opportunity or timing (*tian shi*), good location (*di li*), and smooth human relationships or solidarity (*ren he*). The "Three Harmonies" principle seemed to guide Sam Woo's expansion and choice of locations. Following the Chinese congregation in Monterey Park, Sam Woo quickly opened a store on 634 West Garvey Avenue. A couple of years later, it opened another store in the neighboring city of Alhambra, which also had a large Chinese population. In Sam Woo's operation, "*ren he*" sometimes meant forming partnerships with other Chinese businesses. When Roger Chen, an immigrant from Taiwan and owner of the 99 Ranch Supermarket, decided to diversify in real estate and build the shopping mall named San Gabriel Square on Valley Boulevard, Sam Woo established a strategic relationship with this largest Chinese supermarket chain. While the 99 Ranch Supermarket was the anchor grocery store, Sam Woo became its anchor restaurant.[61] Together, they drew dozens of other retail and service stores and restaurants and made it a destination for shopping and eating. The mall was so crowded during the weekend that it was often difficult to find a parking spot. With seating for 900, Sam Woo in the San Gabriel Square mall was probably the largest of its chain. Partnership between Sam Woo and the 99 Ranch continued to develop. Wherever the 99 Ranch Supermarket built a new store, Sam Woo would be there. Then less famous Chinese restaurants, cafeterias, or teahouses and other retail businesses would quickly join the two partners. The chain reaction generated one after another visible Chinese strip malls in Southern California. Cities with large Chinese populations like Monterey Park, Alhambra, Arcadia Cerritos, Van Nuys, Rowland Heights, and Irvine all had Sam Woo restaurants and the 99 Ranch Supermarkets opening chain stores in the same business locations.

The 99 Ranch Supermarket in the San Gabriel Square mall was actually the company's eighth store. A landmark Chinese mall, San Gabriel Square was a twelve-acre, 220,000-square-foot multilevel mega-shopping center and featured a variety of Chinese and Asian restaurants—from Shanghai cuisine, Taiwan local flavor, Chinese Muslim food, Korean tofu, Japanese sushi, and Thai food. Like most Chinese supermarkets, the 99 Ranch carried a huge selection of produce, especially Asian vegetables and fruits; a variety of live fish, crabs, and lobsters; and other daily necessities. Initially, many items were from Taiwan, as the owner was a Taiwanese immigrant. As the number of immigrants from mainland China grew, more and more things from China began to appear on its shelves.

Across the street from the San Gabriel Square mall was a $60 million Hilton Hotel adjunct with a new cluster of restaurants and retail businesses. The hotel was owned by Chinese merchant immigrant Sunny Chen, who had made a fortune through two large retail centers. Located in the city of San Gabriel, which used to be famous for its Spanish mission, the hotel rooms all bear the names of California missions—for example, the San Miguel Room and the San Diego Room.[62] Contemporary looking, this custard-colored Hilton received 5,500 monthly guests, half of whom were from mainland China, Taiwan, or Hong Kong. Over 70 percent of the staff were Asian. The head chef was from Shanghai, and the food had to be good as there were hundreds of Chinese restaurants nearby. According to the hotel's general manager, Chinese guests could tell if the fish was fresh by tasting it.[63] San Gabriel Square was well known among Chinese in Southern California and Asia.

Not too far away from the 99 Ranch Supermarket were located two other big Chinese supermarkets—Hawaii Supermarket and San Gabriel Superstore. Geographical proximity between the big three was amazingly close. The 99 Ranch Supermarket in the San Gabriel Square mall was located just west of Del Mar Avenue. Across the street on the east side of Del Mar was the Hawaii Supermarket. Just a little bit farther east, on the corner on San Gabriel Boulevard, was the San Gabriel Superstore. Opened in 1990 and 15,000-square-feet large, the Hawaii Supermarket was the largest in size and reportedly received 8,000 customers every weekend. Gerard Yang, the owner, was a Cambodian Chinese refugee who arrived in Southern California in the late 1980s. Targeting working-class or low-income Chinese and other Asian customers, his store boasted the largest produce section, and sold everything unwrapped for a low price.[64] "This is our corridor," Yang observed, "Chinese, Cambodian, Laotian, Vietnamese—everyone comes to Valley Boulevard."[65] His store carried food products for all of them—from Thailand fragrant rice, to Vietnamese fish sauce, to coconut milk and pineapples for sweet Malay curries, to golf-ball-size eggplants for dipping in pungent Cambodian anchovy dips.

Yang's refugee experience, his business, and his clients reflected important aspects of the Asian community in the San Gabriel Valley. Immigrants from Vietnam, Cambodia, and Laos were refugees fleeing from political instability and persecution in their home countries. Among them many were ethnic Chinese. Tang Kim Chuy, a refugee from Cambodia, arrived penniless in 1978 and spent four months on welfare. With the help of friends and relatives, he was able to establish several Chaozhou cuisine restaurants in Los Angeles's Chinatown and the San Gabriel Valley. As a successful businessman, he taught the management skills to other Cambodian refugee immigrants who wanted to open restaurants.[66] Though from Cambodia, his ethnic origin was Chaozhou in Guangdong Province, which had its own distinguished food tradition. In the late 1980s, Chaozhou flavor was a trendy cuisine in Hong Kong and mainland China, and then spread to North America. Like Tang, many Chinese and Asian immigrants to the United States were twice displaced and relocated.

Though the 99 Ranch Supermarket was smaller than the Hawaii Supermarket in size, it was the largest Chinese supermarket chain, with several dozen stores across the nation. Its expansion often reflected the growth of the Chinese population in a city or a region. Many Chinese restaurants and other retail Chinese businesses followed its lead in choosing their business location. Family-operated small businesses did not have research capability for marketing and development. By following the 99 Ranch, small, independent Chinese restaurant owners could determine how to find areas where Chinese congregated and where to locate their business. They knew that the 99 Ranch drew Chinese customers. They joked that wherever the 99 Ranch went, Chinese restaurants would follow. Actually, they provided more options for Chinese families from other suburban cities who would eat after shopping in the 99 Ranch Supermarket. It was often a routine part of Chinese families' weekend agenda.

FOOD AND IDENTITY

Post-1965 Chinese restaurants followed some of the operational traditions of chop suey houses. They provided tea as a free drink and fortune cookies as part of the meal. Both Chinese and non-Chinese customers took these two features for granted when eating at a Chinese restaurant. However, post-1965 Chinese immigrants were far more diverse in social backgrounds than early Cantonese immigrants. As a 1993 *Los Angeles Times* article reported, Chinese Americans in Southern California had diverse cultural roots. One in four was born in the United States, while a similar proportion was born in China and immigrated here—either directly or, more likely, by way of Taiwan or Hong Kong. The percentage distribution was actually 25 percent from mainland China, 24 percent from the United States, 22 percent from Taiwan, 11 percent from Vietnam, 8 percent from Hong Kong, 7 percent from other parts of Asia, and 3 percent from the rest of the world.[67]

This diversity reflects the history of Chinese migration in the late nineteenth century and the first half of the twentieth century. Foreign invasion and civil wars drove numerous Chinese overseas. After the Opium War of 1839–1842, a huge number of Chinese went to Southeast Asia, North America, South America, Europe, and Africa. Some became contract laborers; most were free immigrants. The Japanese invasion of China in the 1930s also pushed many Chinese from South China to Vietnam, Laos, and Cambodia. The civil war between the Nationalists and Communists caused a further outflow migration to Hong Kong and Taiwan. When the Communist government defeated the Nationalist government in 1949, one to two million officials, employees, their families, and other followers of the Nationalist government escaped to Taiwan.[68] As a result, Chinese Diaspora communities are now located almost all over the world.

Food is an expression of ethnic resilience. Different flavors in the Chinese restaurant business reflected the diverse subcultures of the new immigrants. In Chinese food culture, northerners prefer steamed bread or noodles as a staple food. Southerners like rice or rice noodles. Geographic ecology, farming tradition, and regional culture have shaped local tastes. Food habits are different from region to region. Furthermore, Chinese immigrants came from Hong Kong, Taiwan, and mainland China. Consequently, Chinese restaurants along Valley Boulevard feature all kinds of Chinese regional cuisines. "From the pot stickers and succulent dumplings of the northern provinces to the peppery Sichuan dishes of the west to the rich, sweetened Shanghai specialties of the east to the steamed and quickly stir-fried seafood of the south, virtually every form of Chinese regional cooking is represented in the restaurants of Monterey Park, Alhambra, and San Gabriel."[69] The diverse regional roots and Diaspora background of Chinese immigrants have made the Chinese restaurant business a colorful world.

Different from early Cantonese immigrants, post-1965 Chinese immigrants did not create isolated ethnic enclaves in America. Their arrival has changed and enriched the local communities with new cultures and new economic activities. For example, the famous restaurant Yu Zhen Lou in the city of San Gabriel simply used its street address, Mission 261, as its English restaurant name. The restaurant occupies a mission-style historic building, which is under a 150-year-old grapevine and on the 100-year site of the town's city hall. The historic architecture remains unchanged. The previous tenant of the building was a famous Mexican restaurant named Panchito's Mexican Kitchen. Its owner, Frank Ramirez, had run it for forty years. When the historic site failed to attract enough tourists and prosper after the city spent about $2.6 million in state and local funds to renovate it in the early 1990s, Panchito's eventually closed.[70]

Its closing took place when the Chinese population was rapidly growing in the area. Three Chinese immigrant brothers from Hong Kong—Harvey, Lewis, and York Ng—grasped the opportunity and switched from their real estate business to a restaurant career. Since its opening, Mission 261 has been ranked as one of the best dim sum and full-service sit-down Chinese restaurants in Southern California. The most famous dishes include "the ones shaped like small animals: 'ducklings' of fried taro, 'bees' of minced shrimp molded around bits of salted egg (with 'stripes' of finely sliced seaweed), seafood dumplings shaped like baby carp, custard-filled dumplings molded like inquisitive little rabbits."[71] In Mission 261, we see continuities and discontinuities in California history. Its Chinese name, Yu Zhen Lou (Royal Treasure House), reminds us of the name Man Jen Low, the oldest Chinese restaurant in Chinatown. Its English name embodies the legacy of the Mission San Gabriel Archangel built in 1771. The building bears the memory of the landmark Panchito's restaurant and its famous margaritas. But the food illustrates how the San Gabriel Valley has emerged as an Asian cultural hub since the 1980s.

A TRANSNATIONAL WORLD, A DIVERSE COMMUNITY

Food habits reflect how transnational culture is deeply rooted in Chinese family life. What people eat when they are young often determines their taste preferences and food habits. As the saying goes, we are what we eat. Many Chinese parents cook Chinese meals at home, and teach and advise their children what to order at a Chinese restaurant. When children learn the names and become familiar with the flavor of famous Chinese dishes, cultural values will be transmitted through the restaurant experience. When An Mei Lin moved to the United States from Taiwan in 1983, her friends had already advised her to settle in Monterey Park. But she decided to rent an apartment in South Pasadena, enrolled in English-language classes at Pasadena Community College, and passed civil service examinations for both Los Angeles County and the state of California. However, when she cooked pizza and hamburgers, her children complained that the food tasted Chinese. Despite her openness to American culture, Lin preferred and mostly cooked Chinese food at home. She wanted her children to "think American but feel Chinese."[72] Her remark represented the cultural sensibilities of many new immigrants. Lin wanted her children to survive and succeed as Americans but still remember their cultural traditions. In food culture, we see ethnic resilience rather than assimilation.

Many post-1965 Chinese immigrants have maintained their Asian lifestyle and ethnic identity while working and living in the United States. They do not see this preference as conflicting with their American life. At work, they speak English, crack jokes with their colleagues, and comfortably behave as typical Americans. At home, however, they speak Mandarin, Cantonese, Fujianese, or other Chinese dialects. About 49.6 percent of the Chinese speak their native language at home when their English is not fluent. But another 35.8 percent of them, with fluent English ability, still use Chinese at home. Only 14.5 percent Chinese Americans speak just English at home.[73] They also eat Chinese food, listen to Chinese-language radio stations, watch Chinese-language television channels, and read Chinese-language newspapers.[74] By the mid-1990s, the Southern California Chinese community supported at least twenty-three different daily and weekly Chinese-language newspapers, and there were seven daily Chinese-language newspapers and three TV stations in San Francisco.[75] However,

Chinese communities in the San Gabriel Valley are not isolated ethnic ghettos like traditional Chinatowns. They are integrated American neighborhoods with a high percentage of Asian residents.

Post-1965 Chinese immigrants are transnational in culture. Chinese media outlets typically keep the Chinese American community attuned to developments in all home areas—Hong Kong, Taiwan, and mainland China. The Chinese media also inform the community about events related to the Chinese community in Canada, Australia, Europe, South America, and Southeast Asia, as many contemporary Chinese have relatives and friends in those places. Many of the San Gabriel Valley cities have Chinese populations that make up between one-quarter and nearly half of their total residents, and more and more Chinese Americans have been elected as city council members, mayors, or members of the board of education for the local school districts. Compared with a homogeneous American neighborhood, those cities are probably more sensitive to cultural diversity issues, more informed about international events, and more dynamic in economic activities. As part of the global village, those cities reflect the dramatic changes that Asian immigrants have brought to American society in the last few decades.

The Chinese are not the only Asians in the area. There are Vietnamese, Koreans, Japanese, Filipinos, and immigrants from Thailand, Burma, or Indonesia. "The number of non-corporate U.S. businesses owned by Asians and Pacific Islanders grew by 30 percent from 1992 to 1997, four times faster than the nation's overall business growth rate, according to U.S. census data released today. Not surprisingly, California—especially Southern California—continued to dominate the Asian business landscape, with California claiming more than one-third of all such businesses in the nation."[76] Like the Chinese, most of these Asian groups maintain their ethnic resilience while becoming part of America. The coexistence and interaction between them makes Southern California a diverse and globalized society. While Chinese supermarkets also feature Vietnamese, Indonesian, Thai, Philippine, and Japanese foods, Chinese customers frequent Korean grocery stores and barbecue restaurants, go to Vietnamese noodle or sandwich shops, or enjoy Thai soft drinks. There were already about 30,000 Vietnamese Americans living in the forty-five-square-mile western San Gabriel Valley by the 1980s. In contrast, an estimated 65,000 Vietnamese Americans lived in Orange County.[77] In Los Angeles's Chinatown, refugee immigrants from Vietnam gradually replaced traditional Chinese Americans in owning and running restaurants and other retail businesses. West Covina had a "Filipino Hill" that featured a Filipino doctor's office, a real estate firm, a print shop, two Filipino restaurants, and three Filipino markets where residents shop for specialty items such as dried fish and a noodle called pancit.[78] In Rowland Heights, Korean grocery markets, restaurants, and other retail stores existed side by side with their

Chinese counterparts. Blended Asian neighborhoods and businesses spread into the entire San Gabriel Valley.

Asian Americans have multiple cultural backgrounds. Some Vietnamese immigrants were ethnic Chinese. Some Filipino families had Chinese ancestors. Among Koreans were some Chinese whose families originated from Shangdong Province in northern China. Many immigrants from Indonesia, Malaysia, or Thailand were ethnic Chinese who had lived in Southeast Asia for several generations. They spoke more than one language and knew a variety of food cultures. In Southern California, it was common to see an ethnic Chinese from Vietnam run a Lee's Sandwich store or a Phu restaurant; a Chinese refugee immigrant from Cambodia own a doughnut shop; a professional immigrant from Taiwan operate a sushi bar; or a Chinese-Korean immigrant manage a buffet restaurant that served Korean, Chinese, and Japanese food. In their nightlife, mixed American-born Asian teenagers shuttled from one Asian restaurant to another, helped each other communicate with the waiters and order food according to their own ethnic background, and advised each other where to eat. To cater to a pan-Asian group, some Chinese restaurants also offered Asian fusion food. Embedded in the restaurant culture is a colorful picture of how contemporary Asian groups have blended into each other's culture and become a new generation of Asian Americans.

8 · WHO OWNS CULTURE?

"WITH SIX YOU GET EGGROLL"

In 1968, the movie *With Six You Get Eggroll* featured a family comedy of a remarried middle-aged white couple with four children. The movie had nothing to do with the Chinese, but the title reflected a common expectation of American customers about Chinese restaurants. Eating out in Chinese was always a bargain. "Just pick up the kids from school, head over to the local Chinatown and order the Number 2 Special."[1] The special would include large portions of egg foo yong, chop suey, moo goo gai pan, and egg drop soup. Back then, a dinner for a family of six at a Chinese restaurant cost less than $15.

In the 1960s, Cecelia Chiang was probably the first restaurateur in San Francisco who wanted to introduce authentic Chinese cuisine with a variety of regional flavors.[2] She opened her first Mandarin Restaurant on Polk Street in San Francisco's Chinatown in 1962. Born in Beijing and raised in Shanghai, she had tasted many well-known Chinese dishes from various regional cuisines. Her menu listed over 300 items, including sizzling rice soup, smoked tea duck, beggar's chicken, and Mongolian lamb. But local and tourist customers had consumed chop suey, chow mein, and egg foo yong for decades. When Chiang asked for lamb from butchers in Chinatown, they found her request strange. At that time, even ingredients such as sesame oil or mushrooms had to be imported from Taiwan.[3] In the late 1960s, mushrooms from Taiwan were rationed and also in great demand by mainstream grocery stores. While the quota system allowed about 800,000 cases annually, Chinese wholesale trading companies in America were allocated 50,000 cases to supply to Chinese restaurants. As a result, each Chinese restaurant only received 200 to 300 cases of much-needed mushrooms a year. Some Chinese restaurants had to use mushrooms imported from Japan or France. The situation was not improved until the mid-1970s.[4]

During the first year and a half, the Mandarin Restaurant attracted few customers. It was losing money and close to bankruptcy. Johnny Kan, of the famous

Kan's Restaurant in Chinatown, kindly suggested to Chiang: "Change your cooking style. People are happy with chop suey and pressed duck. Besides, nobody has even heard of pot-stickers." Chiang's sister also advised her to close the restaurant.[5] But one day Herb Caen, a Pulitzer Prize–winning columnist for the *San Francisco Chronicle*, dropped by and tasted her food. Shortly after Caen declared his discovery of real Chinese food in his column, the Mandarin Restaurant received hundreds of phone calls for reservations. The business took off overnight. Eight years later, the Mandarin Restaurant moved out of Chinatown to Ghirardelli Square and expanded into a 300-seat high-end restaurant. On the evening of its grand opening, a $250-a-person banquet completely sold out.[6] No Chinese restaurant in America had ever charged that much.

The Mandarin's golden days began with the banquet. Businessmen, celebrity guests, tourists, and middle-class families all came to eat Chiang's authentic Chinese food. Her menu did not feature one particular regional flavor but a selection of famous dishes from several regional cuisines. American customers had no difficulty accepting most of them whether the dishes were southern, eastern, northern, or northwestern Chinese, or tasted spicy or sour-sweet. Chiang's cooking classes had students like Julia Child, James Beard, Alice Waters, Marion Cunningham, Jeremiah Tower, and Danny Kaye.[7] For decades, her restaurant was one of the few high-end Chinese restaurants that offered authentic Chinese food. Even after her retirement in 1991, she was still a sought-after restaurant consultant all over the United States. She helped establish many famous restaurants, such as Shanghai 1930.[8] But Chiang's success was a bittersweet story. Her Chinese food could only reach mainstream American customers after Caen's endorsement. Previous slow business was obviously not a flavor, palate, or culinary issue. Middle- and upper-class American patrons needed to be assured by their own food and cultural critics that it was all right to eat real Chinese food.

In 1975, Chiang opened another Mandarin Restaurant in Beverly Hills, California. Her son, Philip Chiang, joined her and eventually took over the management in 1989. In addition to this restaurant, Philip also owned the Mandarette in West Hollywood and the Lucky Duck on La Brea Avenue in Los Angeles.[9] Philip Chiang faced the similar attitude of American customers when he tried to offer authentic Chinese food. Linda Loi described a typical battle Philip had with his customers over sweet-and-sour pork. It was one of his most popular dishes, and Philip was proud of its ungreasy and unfatty version. But he wanted to change the sauce. When he stopped using ketchup and decreased the use of starch in order to bring out a more authentic flavor, the customers began to panic and phone him, complaining: "What is going on here? We liked it the way it was!" Even when he replaced Western-style broccoli with Chinese broccoli or string beans with Chinese long beans, his customers would catch him and resist. His customers often reminded him: "Well, you're a Chinese restaurant right? You're supposed to have chow mein."[10] To make things worse, customers were all used to low prices at a Chinese restaurant. "It drives us crazy," said co-owner Serry Osmena. "Some of our customers happily pay $11.95 for pasta with basil and olive oil down the street, but they balk at paying $12.50 for a chicken dish at our restaurant." Customers took for granted lower prices at Chinese restaurants even though Chinese restaurant owners paid the same price buying the same ingredients as other restaurants. "We pay $18.00 a pound for crab just like every other Westside restaurant," complained Robert Rogness, maître d' and wine director of the Mandarin.[11]

Philip Chiang was fighting many losing battles when offering authentic Chinese dishes. Low-cost Americanized Chinese food had already shaped American customers' tastes and expectations at a Chinese restaurant. Ironically, he was able to make a radical change and start all over again only after a fire destroyed the restaurant in 1988. "It was like having a clean slate, like getting a new restaurant," said Philip.[12] Of the new restaurant, he remarked: "The colors are brighter, and a new open kitchen dominates the main dining room. Here you can watch as Peking duck—the best I've had in the city—is pulled from the oven, its skin brown and crisp and delectable."[13]

P. F. CHANG'S AS A NEW CONCEPT

Though talented and having a passion for authentic Chinese food, Philip Chiang could not single-handedly change the image of Chinese restaurants until he became a partner in P. F. Chang's China Bistro founded by Paul Fleming, a white American restaurateur who had owned four Ruth's Chris Steak House franchises. From steakhouse to Chinese restaurant was a visionary transfer of business interest. On a trip to Los Angeles, Fleming ate at the Mandarin Restaurant in Beverly Hills owned by Philip Chiang and was deeply impressed by its food. In 1993, he opened his first P. F. Chang's in the Fashion Square shopping center in Scottsdale, Arizona, and invited Philip to be his partner.[14] Like Cecilia and Philip Chiang, Paul Fleming wanted to establish a high-end restaurant that provided authentic Chinese food. When the restaurant was named P. F. Chang's China Bistro, "P. F." stood for Paul Fleming and "Chang" for Chiang. Philip purposely changed "Chiang" into "Chang." With a more contemporary romanization of his last name, Philip expressed his determination to offer authentic Chinese food rather than the old-fashioned chop suey type of meals. Cecilia, along with Chinese cookbook author Barbara Tropp, created the menu for P. F. Chang's. Tropp was a China historian and restaurateur, and author of *The Modern Art of Chinese Cooking: Techniques and Recipes*, which won the prestigious Julia Child Award for Best International Cookbook.[15]

P. F. Chang's was a new concept in the Chinese restaurant business. Like most high-end American sit-down restaurants, it was not only a place to eat but also a destination for social gatherings, business events, and romance dates. It provided a comfortable eating atmosphere that made mainstream American customers want to come back. Though each chain store's exterior and interior design was different, none of them looked like a traditional Chinese restaurant in Chinatown. There was no mock Chinese pagoda architecture design or a Buddha figure at the entrance of the restaurant. Instead, the stylish interior featured hand-painted murals depicting ancient Chinese landscapes and sculptures representing life and society of the Tang and Ming Dynasties. Hardwood furniture and the stone floor gave a contemporary feel. Describing Fleming's store in Irvine, California, a *Los Angeles Times* article in 1996 pointed out that "this place is simply stunning. The main dining area, as big as a Vegas showroom, includes a parquet floor, replicas of Xi'an terra-cotta statuary standing guard on pedestals, stylish Diva lights and—one of the chain's design trademarks—giant off-white canvas disks hanging suspended from the ceiling, otherworldly shapes with an odd iridescence. The inspired concept of this place is to fuse authentic Chinese cooking with the amenities of a fine Western restaurant."[16] Though its decor and furniture were not as luxurious as Fleming's Ruth's Chris Steak Houses, it looked elegant and attractive to middle- and upper-middle-class customers.

P. F. Chang's offered authentic Chinese food. It did not drastically change the ingredients, flavor, or dispensation of Chinese dishes to suit the American palate. P. F. Chang's menu features five major Chinese regional cuisines— Guangdong, Hunan, Mongolian, Shanghai, and Sichuan. As early Chinese immigrants came from Guangdong, Cantonese cuisine had more influence in America than any other Chinese regional cuisine. Brought over by immigrants from Taiwan, Hunan cuisine was also popular in the 1970s. Though Mongolian cuisine was not a major Chinese food tradition, Mongolian lamb was a long-time house special on the Mandarin's menu. P. F. Chang's offered some of the best-known dishes from those regional cuisines, as the owners recognized that Chinese food culture consisted of different regional cuisines. "We're constantly confirming that we're keeping it as close to what they're doing in China as possible," P. F. Chang's executive chef, Paul Muller, said. Initially, Muller tried to modify traditional Chinese dishes to fit non-Chinese patrons. But then he decided to prepare the food as close as to what he saw and learned in China. When P. F. Chang's opened a new restaurant, he observed that his patrons frequently commented: "This is way too salty. This is way too oily."[17] But the customers still kept coming back. American customers readily accepted genuine Chinese food in a mainstream corporate-owned and -operated Chinese restaurant. Food did not have to be less Chinese there.

A WHITE EXECUTIVE CHEF

While Paul Fleming was the mastermind of offering authentic Chinese food by a national chain, Paul Muller was the executive chef to deliver the idea in the chain stores. Muller grew up in Long Island, New York, and had no background in cooking Chinese food before he worked for P. F. Chang's. But his grandfather was a chef at Hellman's Deli in New York. "The cooking he was weaned on, however, was clambakes and grilled fish, not dumplings and stir-fry." In his early days at P. F. Chang's, Muller had a hard time learning to use a wok. When he was hired to open the company's third store in La Jolla, California, he recalled: "The wok handles are three times the diameter of a saute pan, so I always would grab everything so tightly. Sometimes at the end of my training day, in the middle of the night, my hands would just curl up into a claw shape and cramp up."[18]

Though not from a Chinese cooking background, Muller had gained valuable experience working in high-volume, high-end restaurants. After graduating with a culinary degree from the New York Institute of Technology, he won a fellowship to teach at the school. He also had internships, including working at Manhattan's Waldorf-Astoria hotel. He worked there as one of the best chefs and rotated through the hotel's various kitchens. Such fine-dining experience was a valuable asset when he became an executive chef for P. F. Chang's. He was also willing to take risks. Fleming promised to establish the corporate executive chef position only after Muller successfully learned Chinese cooking and managed the chain's kitchen well.

To help Muller learn Chinese cooking, Philip Chiang let him spend time with the chefs at the Mandarin, took him to tour Chinatowns across the United States, and arranged for him to visit Hong Kong and mainland China for months. There Muller met Chiang's relatives "and really got to understand that what we were doing at P. F. Chang's was authentic and traditional but still innovative."[19] Philip introduced Muller to Chinese culinary traditions. This was the first step to become a good Chinese chef. As the chain's director of culinary operations and corporate executive chef, Muller traveled to China every fourteen to sixteen months to follow culinary developments there. The company still imports its water chestnuts and bamboo shoots from China, as well as many of its sauce bases, such as black-mushroom soy, plum, and hoisin.[20] Chinese food at P. F. Chang's may still not taste exactly like its counterpart in China, but it has made real Chinese food a visible option in the contemporary American sit-down restaurant market and available to a wide range of middle-class American customers. This is an accomplishment that many Chinese restaurants pursued but failed to achieve.

P. F. Chang's entered the Chinese restaurant market at the right time. By the 1980s, ethnic restaurants constituted 10 percent of all restaurants in the United States. They were mostly located in the Northeast and on the West Coast. The

Chinese restaurant business made up 30 percent of the total number of eth-nic restaurants in the United States. Chinese, Italian, and Mexican represented 70 percent of all ethnic restaurants.[21] In New York City, for example, the num-ber of Chinese restaurants was 304 in 1958, but there were nearly 800 in 1988.[22] However, there were no standardized chain sit-down Chinese restaurants for mainstream middle-class Americans at that time. Fleming's vision was to carve out a niche for such clientele. Restaurant culture was often class sensi-tive. Patrons of different classes usually did not want to mix when eating out. Chinese restaurants congregated in Chinatowns and Chinese-concentrated neighborhoods such as the San Gabriel Valley in Southern California or Flush-ing in Queens and Sunset Park in Brooklyn in New York. Some of the Chi-nese restaurants in those areas were stylish, elegant, and offered authentic Cantonese, Hunan, Sichuan, or Shanghai cuisine. Many middle-class Chinese American families or wealthy Chinese merchants visited them "to feel the cul-tural atmosphere associated with their home country." However, 90 percent of the customers of these restaurants were Chinese.[23] Middle-class mainstream American customers did not feel comfortable eating there, especially when they dined out for a social life.

For most Chinese patrons and operators, a restaurant was mainly an eating place. The strategy of many Chinese restaurants was to attract as many customers as possible. Food items on the menu could be a dim sum dish for $1.50 or bird's nest soup for $75 to $100. With prices ranging from 50 cents to $50 per dish for a dinner, a proprietor targeted customers of all social classes. In many Chinese-owned Chinese restaurants, the furniture looked mediocre and the restrooms were filthy. Cutthroat competition often affected food quality. Such business concepts and practices prevented many Chinese restaurants from attracting a critical mass of mainstream American upper- or middle-class patrons. Flem-ing foresaw a niche in the Chinese restaurant market for high-end clientele that small, independent, family-owned Chinese restaurants failed to occupy. He was fully aware of the thriving restaurant business in the San Gabriel Valley and in Flushing and Queens in New York. Nevertheless, he insisted that Phoenix, though not a recognized center of Chinese cooking, would be a good barometer for mainstream American customers for Chinese food.[24] Richard Federico, hired as the company's president in 1996, shared the same vision and remarked: "We looked at the restaurant universe and Chinese wasn't represented. . . . There were only independent operators. The whole country was available for the concept."[25]

P. F. Chang's tried to avoid some of the common problems associated with Chinese restaurants. Their dishes were usually not greasy and heavy. MSG was absolutely forbidden. The restaurant emphasized the use of fresh ingredients. "That includes all meats, seafood, and poultry. Vegetables are all hand cut every day. Every dumpling, every spring roll is made by hand every day. We probably use 40-some sauces plus and we make every one of those every day."[26] As a chain restaurant business, the size of P. F. Chang's stores ranged from 4,500 square feet to 8,000 square feet and accommodated inside seating for 210 to 225 customers; some locations offered patio dining. The kitchen was always open and standardized. One executive said: "We're not having to go in and figure out how to operate. All functions are identical."[27] In terms of flavor, cookery, and palatability issues, P. F. Chang's philosophy was to be as close as possible to the Chinese food tradition. In business operation, its franchise stores are similar to other American corporate restaurant chains. Their service style aims mainly at middle- and upper-middle-class mainstream American customers.

WHO OWNS CULTURE?

In 1996, P. F. Chang's made a strategic decision. The restaurant purchased back all its original stores managed and partially owned by other people, hired a management team led by Richard Federico as president and Robert Vivian as chief financial officer, and opened new stores in Denver, Las Vegas, and Houston. In 1998, when P. F. Chang's had ten stores, it filed an IPO at $12 a share, which jumped to $32.75 in March 2000. By then, the chain had developed thirty-nine stores and had thirteen in development.[28] Its speed of growth was set at thirteen to fifteen new restaurants each year. As of December 2014, P. F. Chang's owned and operated 210 full-service Bistro restaurants and 200 quick casual Pei Wei restaurants across the country. It is also pursuing opportunities to open restaurants in more than twenty-two countries and claims to import ingredients, herbs, and spices directly from China and features traditional Chinese dishes.[29] In American food history, P. F. Chang's China Bistro is the first and so far the only sit-down Chinese restaurant that has become a publicly traded stock on Nasdaq. This is an important landmark in Chinese restaurant history in America.

P. F. Chang's success is a mixed blessing for Chinese Americans. Through P. F. Chang's expansion, more and more American customers got to know genuine Chinese food. While mainstream American customers tended to stay away from independent, small, and family-owned Chinese restaurants for social dinners, they have accepted genuine Chinese food at P. F. Chang's. This is an accomplishment that Chinese American restaurateurs failed to achieve in their long history in America. Perhaps this goal can be only accomplished by a giant, mainstream American corporation. As a big player in the food business, P. F. Chang's has the financial resources to provide a trendy, comfortable dining environment in order to attract young and middle-aged professionals and middle-class families as its clients. As a sit-down restaurant, P. F. Chang's is in the same price range as Olive Garden, California Pizza Kitchen, or the Cheese Cake Factory. It represents a new image of the Chinese restaurant business. As a public company with standardized chain stores, it has enabled real Chinese food to be part of the high-end American restaurant market.

The P. F. Chang's phenomenon poses a serious question to Chinese Americans—who owns culture?[30] Food was related to their ethnic identity in America. For a long time, they worked hard to make their food part of the American restaurant market. The result turned out to be chop suey, egg foo yong, or other American-ized dishes. Real Chinese food had no market in America. Some individual Chinese restaurants, like Cecilia Chiang's Mandarin Restaurant, were struggling with real Chinese dishes, and they became successful only after mainstream American food critics endorsed them. Chinese American restaurateurs were not in control of their own culture in the American food market. P. F. Chang's success lies not only in its ability to occupy part of the sit-down, high-end restaurant market but also in its power to deliver authentic Chinese food and represent Chinese culinary culture as corporate America.

Culture is often considered as a soft power of a community or an ethnic group. Culture seems hereditary or primordial. But in reality, culture, especially culinary culture, is a "public domain" in which every participating agent or insti-tution could have access to or even own it. A piece of culture does not necessar-ily belong to those who originated it. To make authentic Chinese food part of the mainstream American restaurant market requires no ethnic association or intrinsic linkage to the Chinese American community. Food is both a culture and commodity. But when food becomes a commodity, it is no longer an inher-ited culture. Corporate America could easily appropriate it from the Chinese community.

PANDA EXPRESS AS A BREAKTHROUGH

Compared with P. F. Chang's, the success of Panda Express has a different sig-nificance. If P. F. Chang's is a case of how the mainstream America food business embraced authentic Chinese culinary culture, Panda Express shows how the Chinese restaurant business has integrated the American fast-food concept. As one food critic put it, "*Panda Express* is a real innovation. Where most attempts at Chinese fast-food have settled for egg rolls, rice, and chow mein, *Panda Express* offers orange-flavored chicken, tofu with black mushrooms, beef with broccoli, and many other dishes conceived by Chinese chefs and prepared on site by trained cooks."[31]

Officially called Panda Restaurant Group, it was established in 1983 by Andrew and Peggy Cherng, an immigrant couple from Taiwan and Hong Kong. It is the largest fast-food Chinese restaurant chain and the fastest-growing Asian restaurant business in the United State. As of December 2014, it had over 1,500 chain stores in forty-two states, Puerto Rico, and Mexico.[32] Through Panda

Express, Chinese food reached many more American customers at a much faster speed compared to P. F. Chang's.

Andrew Cherng came to attend Baker University, a small Methodist college in Baldwin City, Missouri, southwest of Kansas City, in 1966. He earned degrees in applied mathematics from Baker and from the University of Missouri. It was at Baker that he met Peggy, who was studying electrical engineering and computer science as a Ph.D. student from Hong Kong and later found a job as a software developer for McDonnell Douglas.

In 1972, Andrew Cherng bought a shuttered coffee shop on Foothill Boulevard in Pasadena, California, and turned it into the sit-down restaurant Panda Inn as his parents were about to migrate to the United States in 1973. His father, Ming-Tsai Cherng, was a native of Jiangsu Province and worked as a chef in Shanghai, Taipei, and Yokohama, Japan, before coming to the United States.[33] Andrew was actually born in Jiangsu, China. Instead of chop suey, their restaurant in Pasadena served genuine Chinese food and attracted mostly white American customers. With good service and quality food, Panda Inn was one of the most popular restaurants in the city. In 1983, a returning customer and a real estate developer in Glendale, California, asked Andrew if he would be interested in opening a store in the Galleria shopping mall. Andrew agreed but realized that he had to adapt his Panda Inn restaurant operation to a fast-food setting in the mall. He did so, using recipes originated by his late father, who died in 1981. Panda Express became an instant success.[34]

Panda Express started in Southern California, the birthplace of American fast-food restaurants. McDonald's, Carl's Jr., and In-N-Out are some of the big names in this area. Rising in the 1950s in Southern California, fast-food restaurants with drive-thru service "helped turn the once lowly hamburger into America's national dish. Ray Kroc's decision to promote McDonald's as a restaurant chain for families had a profound impact on the nation's eating habits. Hamburgers seemed an ideal food for busy professionals, budget-tight students, skilled laborers, technicians, or even small children as they were convenient, inexpensive, hand-held, and easy to chew."[35] In the automobile culture of Southern California, grabbing a burger in one hand and controlling the steering wheel with the other while driving was often the lifestyle of time-pressured youngsters and professionals. Holding a rice bowl in one hand or eating chow mein while driving was hardly possible. As the journalist food critic Matt Krantz put it, Chinese food did not "quite fit the on-the-go lifestyle that fast food caters to."[36]

Competing in the fast-food restaurant business was a formidable task for a Chinese restaurant business. Cooking a Chinese dish required many more ingredients and seasonings than cooking a hot dog or hamburger. Many Chinese dishes needed long preparation and cooking processing times. Running a Chinese fast-food restaurant could be far more challenging than running a

McDonald's or a Burger King. Moreover, hamburger was a familiar food to many Americans. When working at a hamburger restaurant, many American teenagers already knew how to flip a burger on a grill in the backyard of their parents' home. But they had no idea on how to chop vegetables or stir-fry rice or beef with broccoli. Different from cooking hotdogs or hamburgers, cooking Chinese food was less familiar to American youngsters and required more complicated preparation and handling. As Dennis Lombardi, executive vice president of Technomic, put it, "A wok is not something a lot of American cooks are used to. There needs to be a premium on keeping the turnover in that category low so that your training costs don't get out of line."[37] When Panda Express joined McDonald's, Pizza Hut, and Burger King in the American fast-food market, it met with more challenges than its American fast-food competitors.

Standardized operation is the key in the fast-food business. At Panda Express restaurants, each dish had a fixed formula for preparation, cooking, and serving. The formula clearly described the amount of each ingredient and seasonings, and the expected flavor as well as the cooking procedure and the time required in each step of the cooking. Vegetables must be chopped in the same shape and style. Seasonings must be precisely proportioned and carefully mixed for the right flavor.[38] A full-size replica of a restaurant was established at the company's headquarters, where restaurant managers are brought in to learn the names and ingredients of various Chinese dishes and the way to cook them. In actual operation, Panda Express's cooks constantly fill and refill a number of bins with a dozen of different food items. Customers look at the dishes and order whichever appeal to them even if they are not familiar with the names. The employees then scoop the correct portions on plates for them. The training of the employees is a challenging task because they are learning a piece of Asian culture.

Panda Express has adapted itself well in the American fast-food business competition. In 1997, Panda Express opened its first drive-thru restaurant in Hesperia, California, which paved the way for more than 300 drive-thru stores by 2009.[39] In 2001, it surpassed In-N-Out, the most popular hamburger chain store in Southern California, in growth.[40] In 2004, when expanding in Texas, it developed freestanding street stores with drive-thru service rather than just outlets in shopping malls.[41] In fact, it has become one of the fastest-growing restaurant chains in the United States. In 2006, for example, Panda Express established three new stores every week, tripling the number of restaurants that Burger King built weekly.[42]

Locating in shopping malls, airports, theme parks, sport stadiums, street plazas, university campuses, hospital cafeterias, and even military camps, Panda Express has targeted mainly mainstream American customers. As American customers are often worried about food safety, the company has banned the use of MSG and categorically assured the customers that none of its entrées or side dishes contain MSG.[43] It has emphasized the use of fresh ingredients in its products, clean equipment in operation and cooking, and strict hygiene standards. Panda Express seldom establishes stores in Chinese-concentrated neighborhoods, though Chinese American customers in general should have no problems eating its food.

As a visible option in the American fast-food market, Panda Express has become increasingly popular among mainstream American customers. In 2008, QSR (Quick-service and Fast Casual Restaurant News and Information) magazine ranked the top fifty quick-service and fast-casual concepts in the American restaurant industry. Panda Express ranked twenty-third, the only Asian restaurant on the list.[44] After Peggy Cherng served as CEO from 1998 to 2004, Panda Express hired former Taco Bell executive Tom Davin as Panda Express's president and CEO. Its long-term goal was to have 10,000 restaurants across the nation. Outside of Andrew Cherng's office was a map of the United States showing which states had Panda Express stores and which did not. His ambition was to fill in all the gaps, including places like Alaska and Montana. The company also owned five Panda Inn traditional restaurants and nine Hibachi-San Japanese fast-food outlets. In 2005, the company sold $735 million worth of Chinese food, tripling the combined sales of Pei Wei Asian Diner and Pick Up Stix, the second and third most powerful players, respectively, in the Chinese fast-food business.[45] In a study of consumers' familiarity with the fast-food business in the Los Angeles area in 2008, more than 90 percent of those surveyed were aware of Panda Express, and 70 percent of them had eaten there.[46]

It is difficult to say if Panda Express serves authentic or somewhat Americanized Chinese food. The chain restaurant claims that it has offered Sichuan, Mandarin, or other regional food and dishes based on Andrew Cherng's father's recipes, who once worked as a chef in mainland China and Taiwan. However, some of its dishes look familiar to American customers as they were previously available in chop suey houses. For example, one of the popular dishes on its menu is Kung Pao chicken. Prepared with marinated diced chicken, crunchy peanuts, diced red bell peppers, and sliced zucchini, and seasoned with ginger, garlic, and chilies, it has been one of the most popular Chinese dishes in America. Most independent Chinese restaurants also offer it. In fact, it is so well known that California Pizza Kitchen, a mainstream sit-down restaurant chain, has offered a hybridized dish called Kungpao Pasta together with Peking duck pizza. On the Panda Express menu there are also dishes such as baked dumplings, fried spring rolls, and cheese rangoons.[47] Customers also get a free fortune cookie, which they used to get in chop suey houses in the past.

The Cherngs knew that it was still difficult for mainstream American customers, especially outside of the metropolitan areas, to accept a Chinese dish in its original form and flavor. Thus most of the Panda Express dishes were modified to fit Americans' taste. Orange chicken, the restaurant's most famous and popular dish, is a case in point. Prepared with lightly battered boneless chicken bites and seasoned with ginger and chilies, the dish came allegedly from Hunan cuisine in South China. Its original flavor was supposed to be salty and spicy. However, Andrew Cherng invented a new sweet and spicy orange sauce for the chicken. As the seasoning gave the dish a bit of a sweet flavor, the invention became a great success. For many years since its initial offering, orange chicken remained the best seller in the restaurant. In 2006 alone, the chain restaurant sold thirty-nine million pounds of orange chicken.[48] Today, orange chicken is not only a Panda Express's dish but also a frozen Chinese food in grocery stores like Trader Joe's. Many independent Chinese restaurants in American also offered this dish in modified version. Cream cheese rangoon was another invention by Panda Express. Made of crisp wonton skin, the rangoon used to be a fried dim sum with a salty flavor. But at Panda Express, it was made with cream and cheese, which was based on a Jewish dish.[49]

Though the food at Panda Express may not match the precise flavor of its counterpart in China, its Chinese culinary identity is clear and visible. China is the cultural home of Chinese restaurants in America. Customers in California, Nevada, and Arizona accounted for 70 percent of the chain's sales. Its highest-volume store was actually in Hawaii. Sales in North Carolina and Georgia did not do as well. As one executive of the company put it, "The closer we get to China the better we do."[50] Andrew and Peggy Cherng did not want to lose the company's Chinese identity. Like other American corporate executives, they engaged in philanthropic activities. But many of their donations were aimed at promoting Asian or Chinese culture. In 2001, they donated $1 million to the United Way of Greater Los Angeles during Asian American Heritage Month.[51] In 2006, Panda Express funded Chinese New Year parties at more than seventy-five California elementary and middle schools. At the parties, while enjoying Chinese food with chopsticks, the children also learned Chinese history and Chinese Lunar New Year traditions.[52]

CHINESE FOOD IN THE FAST-FOOD BUSINESS

Panda Express entered the American fast-food market at a crucial time. As the food historian Donna Gabaccia pointed out: "Perhaps no sector better represents the popularity of ethnic foods in contemporary American eating than the fast-foods industry. By the 1980s, a typical American ate fast food nine times a month, and left most of his money in the hands of a few corporate purveyors of a few standard fast-food items."[53] As one of the fastest-growing food businesses, Asian fast-food restaurants were increasing at a 20 percent annual rate. "Customer traffic grew a third from 1987 to 1990 in Asian-cuisine restaurants, while it declined slightly during the same period in hamburger, chicken, and fast-food stands, according to the restaurant association."[54] In New York City, for example, Chinese fast-food takeout restaurants were "rapidly expanding into non-Chinese neighborhoods to compete with customers with mainstream fast-food business such as McDonald's and Burger King."[55]

However, most of the Chinese restaurants in America were small, independent, family-owned businesses. During the 1980s and 1990s, there were no big Chinese fast-food chain restaurants in the country. Many large American food corporations were tempted to enter the Chinese fast-food market. As an executive of a big restaurant corporation eagerly put it in 1992: "It's not a niche. It's a gaping hole."[56] By 2006, P. F. Chang's, for example, had about 150 fast-food Pei Wei Asian Diner stores in fifteen states.[57] By 2009, Pick Up Stix, started in 1989 by Charlie Zhang, a Chinese immigrant, had 125 stores in California, Nevada, and Arizona.[58] But some corporations quickly ended their initial efforts, as running Chinese fast-food restaurants was not as easy as they assumed. Paul Fleming, of the P. F. Chang's China Bistro, started his lower-priced Paul Lee's Chinese Kitchen joint venture with Outback Steakhouse, but closed it down after opening just four locations. Giant restaurant chains Yum Brands, which owns Pizza Hut and Taco Bell; Chili's owner Brinker; and Darden, the company behind Olive Garden, all tried to get involved in the Chinese fast-food business but gave up trying after their initial efforts.[59]

Smaller in size but growing at a steady speed, many other Chinese fast-food restaurant chains followed Panda Express and also entered the mainstream American fast-food market. Manchu Wok, for instance, was a Chinese fast-food chain established by a Hong Kong immigrant in Canada in 1980 and is now owned by Hong Kong–based Cafe de Coral Holdings Ltd. By 2009, it had about 200 franchises in the United States, Canada, San Rita, Guam, and Okinawa, Japan. Most of Manchu Wok stores are located in shopping malls.[60] The list of the competitors with Panda Express is much longer than in the 1990s, and many of them are also either based in the Pacific Coast states or established stores there. According to a 1992 *Los Angeles Times* article, Ho-Lee-Chow, a Chinese food company based in Canada, for example, sold more than 270 franchises nationally, including 14 in the greater Los Angeles area.[61]

Rice Garden, established by two former Panda Express employees in 1994, had established over eighty chain stores by 2009.[62] Though a much smaller Chinese fast-food chain business, Rice Garden was able to spread into a dozen different states and often established stores in shopping malls, on college campuses, or next door to movie theaters. The company had about 500 employees, and the average staff per store was six people. It also provided health benefits, dental insurance, and a 40K retirement fund to its employees. Like Panda Express, all its stores were ranked A in hygiene standard and had signs of "No MSG

ADDED."[63] Mark Pi's Express was based in Columbus, Ohio, and by 2009 had twenty fast-food outlets, eight China Gate Gourmet Restaurants, and one Feast of the Dragon Buffet operating mostly in the Midwest.[64] Among the competitors in Southern California, there were also Wok Spirit, operated by Urban Foods Inc., which opened its first takeout and delivery location in Costa Mesa, Orange County, and Wok Fast, which is based in the west Los Angeles area.[65] However, none of them has reached the same level of Panda Express in the fast-food restaurant business.

Rapid expansion of Panda Express and the existence of many Chinese fast-food restaurants indicated a change in the American diet or eating habits, which have become increasingly multicultural. In this transformation, Panda Express has actively promoted itself among young and educated Americans. Opening its chain units on university campuses seemed to be its priority. When Panda Express makes its products a natural pick for a quick lunch for American college students, a top choice for American travelers at airports, or an easy preference by American shoppers at malls, Chinese food longer looks too ethnic and alien. If twenty-first-century Americans can order Chinese food as comfortably as the baby-boomer generation ordered a drive-thru hamburger, it will become a truly American food. Panda Express's success is highly significant in Chinese American history. As Shun Lu and Gary Alan Fine pointed out: "While cooperate food industry kept dominating American restaurant market and profession as a standardized and regulated field, ethnic restaurant operators never stopped competing for their shares of food market."[66] Like P. F. Chang's, Panda Express serves mainly non-Chinese customers. The significance of its popularity is not how close its food tastes to food in China but the fact that it has made Chinese cuisine a visible option for American fast-food consumers across the United States.

A DOUBLE STANDARD IN THE CHINESE RESTAURANT BUSINESS

In 2005, Councilman Joaquin Lim of Walnut City in Los Angeles County established a Chinese Restaurant Health Standards Task Force hoping to improve the situation in which most Chinese restaurants were rated at B or lower in the county's hygiene grading system established seven year earlier. He loved Chinese food and knew where to get the tastiest dim sum and the freshest fried noodles in the San Gabriel Valley but was frustrated that C often stood for a Chinese restaurant in the grading system.[67] Chinese restaurants were numerous in cities with high concentrations of Chinese, such as Monterey Park, Alhambra, Arcadia, Rosemead, San Gabriel, and Rowland Heights in the San Gabriel Valley in Southern California. While Chinese residents could taste all kinds of Chinese flavors here, congestion and sanitary conditions are two major issues confronting the Chinese restaurant world today.

The number of Chinese restaurants was growing at a rapid speed from the 1980s to the 2000s. In 1988, Monterey Park had forty-eight Chinese restaurants. The number grew to seventy-two in 2007. With a Chinese population of 26,582, it meant that there was one Chinese restaurant for every 369 Chinese residents. The ratio was even more skewed in the city of San Gabriel, which had ninety-six Chinese restaurants for a Chinese population of 14,460. That was one Chinese restaurant for every 150 Chinese residents. In the city of Hacienda Heights, the ratio was one Chinese restaurant for every 467 Chinese residents, and in Rowland Heights one Chinese restaurant for every 234 Chinese residents (see Table 1). For restaurant owners, the large Chinese population in the San Gabriel Valley meant potential patrons and an unlimited supply of cheap labor. With modest capital and free family labor, some new immigrants hoped to realize their American dream through the restaurant business. Many others relied on restaurant jobs for a living due to language barriers or a lack of marketable professional skills.

Offering a bonus dish over a certain amount of spending or a free dessert during the weekend is a common strategy employed by Chinese restaurants. Some Chinese restaurants spy on each other's menus and recipes or undercut each other's prices. Fierce competition has made change of ownership or bankruptcy a frequent phenomenon in the Chinese restaurant business. It is a dilemma for Chinese restaurant operators. When they bond together to create a visible Chinese cuisine hub, they draw more business. But on the other hand, competition among individually owned restaurants often went uncontrolled.

However, in San Marino, one of the wealthiest neighborhoods in Southern California, with a 43.4 percent Chinese population, there were only two Chinese restaurants, one of which, Lollicup, was a kind of drink/snack-type establishment. Two other restaurants seemed to have Chinese owners, though neither was a Chinese restaurant. According to the city directory, there were fourteen restaurants in San Marino in total.[68] The wealthy Chinese residents were obviously not interested in seeing many restaurants in their multi-million-dollar-house neighborhood. San Marino's geographic proximity to other West San Gabriel Valley cities allows its residents to meet their culinary needs in neighboring cities. Pasadena was another West San Gabriel Valley city with about fourteen Chinese restaurants out of ninety-five total restaurants.

Many Chinese restaurants in the San Gabriel Valley had unsatisfactory sanitary conditions due to congested business and intense competition. When eating in a Chinese restaurant, customers could easily notice a tainted carpet, cheap dinnerware, mediocre furniture, and filthy restrooms. Since most Chinese restaurants have closed kitchens, customers had no idea of the sanitary conditions inside. The Los Angeles County Department of Health Services regularly sent health inspectors to score restaurants on a 100-point scale. Inspectors would check everything from inadequate cooling or heating of food to the chef's personal hygiene, the use of leftovers, or unclean equipment. An A grade was granted when a restaurant scored between 90 and 100 points, a B for 80 to 89 points, and a C for 70 to 79 points. Below 70, a restaurant would be ordered to close. According to the county's restaurant ratings in 2007, 80.9 percent of the non-Chinese restaurants in eight cities/areas of Los Angeles County received an A, while Chinese restaurants fell far behind, with only 33.6 percent of them rated as A and 60.5 percent rated as B. In comparison, only 18 percent of non-Chinese restaurants received a B (see Table 2).[69] Proper hygiene was a gripping issue for the Chinese restaurant businesses.

Neither the Chinese proprietors nor the Chinese customers seemed to take the hygiene issue seriously. On September 28, 2005, Los Angeles County health officer Siu-Man Chiu conducted a three-hour inspection of a popular Chinese dim sum eatery in the heart of the San Gabriel Valley. "She noted the uncovered glass left in the food preparation area. No paper towels by the hand sink. A moldy refrigerator. Dead bugs in a plastic container used to hold pig's blood." Furthermore, the cooks left seven pounds of cooked red beans cooling overnight on a food preparation table to make desserts for the next day.[70] Chiu was upset because bacteria growth could reach an unacceptable level if food was placed for three hours at room temperature. The restaurant's current grade was already a B. When Chiu was tabulating violations, she was predicting about a C. But neither the manager nor the customers seemed to care. As the lunch hour came, customers swarmed in, and the manager told to her to finish up the inspection. Chiu said, "Some of the violations you see again and again, and they're still making good business. Even with a C, Chinese people don't care."[71] Another popular Chinese café in Monterey Park had been repeatedly cited for health violations and had recently received a C from Chiu. But customers were still coming. "I've been coming here forever," said Melvin Jin, twenty-five, as he headed for lunch. "I'm getting the fried rice. It's quick, it's easy. Besides, my friend used to work here and he says it's OK." Michael Ke, a thirty-year-old University of Southern California student who also frequented this restaurant, replied: "I don't even know where they post the letters. B and C is so much gray area."[72]

Chinese restaurant operators often argued that food preparation was complicated in Chinese cookery, that they had to deal with many more ingredients and equipment than their non-Chinese counterparts, and that they merely followed the thousand years' tradition of Chinese cooking. "We've been cooking like this for 5,000 years," said Harvey Ng, owner of the famous Mission 261 in San Gabriel. "Why do we have a problem now?"[73] They were probably right.

TABLE 2.   Los Angeles County Restaurant Ratings in Selected San Gabriel Valley City/Areas (2006–2007)

Restaurant	Number	A	B	C	D	Total
Chinese Restaurants in Eight Cities/Areas						
Alhambra	54	37%	57%	6%	0	100%
Arcadia	44	36%	62%	2%	0	100%
Hacienda Heights	24	42%	58%	0	0	100%
Monterey Park	74	23%	69%	8%	0	100%
Rosemead	43	26%	60%	12%	2%	100%
Rowland Heights	87	31%	60%	8%	1%	100%
San Gabriel	113	42%	57%	1%	0	100%
San Marino	2	0	50%	50%	0	100%
Total Chinese Restaurants in the Eight Cities/Areas	441	33.6%	60.5%	5.4%	0.5%	100%
Total Non-Chinese Restaurants in the Eight Cities/Areas	857	80.9%	18%	1.1%	0	100%
All Restaurants in the Eight Cities/Areas	1,298	64.8%	32.4%	2.6%	0.2%	100%
Chinese Restaurants in LA Chinatown*	69	48%	51%	1%	0	100%
Panda Express	106	100%	0	0	0	100%
Chinese Fast Food in Los Angeles County						
P. F. Chang's China Bistro	7	100%	0	0	0	100%
In Los Angeles County						
Pasadena	14	78.6%	21.4%	0	0	100%

SOURCES: Rating information are restaurants inspected and rated by the Los Angeles County Public Health Department during 2006 and 2007, with a few inspected in 2005, from website: www.lapublichealth.org. Chinese restaurants are identified based on compiled information from the *Chinese Consumer Yellow Pages* (华人工商) *2007*; *Chinese Yellow Pages* (华商年鉴) *2007*; *California Yellow Pages* (加州彩页) *2007–2008*; and *Chinese E-Search Yellow Pages* (华商大全) *2006–2007*. Citywide dining list from City of Alhambra website www.cityofalhambra.org, and dining in Arcadia from City of Arcadia website www.ci.arcadia.ca.u. Pasadena rating data is from City of Pasadena website, www.cityofpasadena.net.
Rating Criteria: A=90–100; B:=80–89; C=70–79
* Chinatown data is identified by zip code CA 90012 and the location of the restaurants.

Different from other cuisines, many Chinese dishes could not be previously prepared and semicooked before the service. For example, when a customer ordered a steamed fish, the chef had to show the fish alive to the customer first, then scrubbed it inside and out, and then marinated it with shredded ham or bacon, mushrooms, sliced ginger, green onion, and other seasoning for ten or more minutes before he or she steamed it. But high hygiene standards are not an impossible mission for the Chinese restaurant businesses. Almost as a pattern, sanitary conditions and hygiene standards remained consistently higher at those Chinese restaurants that served mostly non-Chinese clients. Panda Express had 106 stores in Los Angeles County. All of them were ranked A. P. F. Chang's China Bistro had seven restaurants in the West Los Angeles area, and all of them were ranked A. The hygiene issue was mainly a problem for Chinese restaurants in communities with large concentrations of Chinese. No doubt food at some of family-owned, independent Chinese restaurants is more authentic than food at Panda Express or P. F. Chang's. That is how they attract new and returning Chinese customers. But sanitary conditions at those restaurants make mainstream customers nervous about their food and push them to go to Panda Express or P. F. Chang's.

CONCLUSION

Chinese cuisine has become one of the most popular ethnic foods in the United States. In the 2000s, there were more than 40,000 Chinese restaurants across the nation—a number much larger than the total number of McDonald's (13,774), Wendy's (6,300), and Burger King (7,482) in the United States combined.[74] The rapid growth in the number of Chinese restaurants reflected Americans' constantly changing and often multiethnically blended eating habits. Unlike in the San Gabriel Valley in Southern California, the majority of the clientele for the Chinese restaurant business outside of Chinatowns or suburban neighborhoods with concentrated Chinese residents are non-Chinese customers. The multicultural food market in America today is very different from that in the nineteenth century and the first half of the twentieth. Interest in Chinese food is increasing daily. But authentic flavor is not the only thing customers look for. A good eating environment, decent sanitary conditions, healthy ingredients, professional cookery, and good service are all relevant. The success of P. F. Chang's and Panda Express and the competition in the restaurant business in areas with a high concentration of Chinese reveal the complexity of cultural and economic negotiations between mainstream Americans and Asian Americans, between struggling, family-owned small businesses and giant, publicly traded American corporations.

9 · DIN TAI FUNG AS A GLOBAL DUMPLING HOUSE

THE RISE OF SHANGHAI CUISINE IN TAIWAN

On December 4, 2007, the Taiwan government sponsored Din Tai Fung, a steamed dumpling house in Taipei, to hold a gastronomic demonstration in Paris as a diplomatic event to promote its "soft power."[1] Though the cooking show was held by a pro-independence regime, the restaurant actually featured Shanghai cuisine rather than local Taiwanese food, which originated in the southern Fujian Province. With franchises in Japan, Singapore, Indonesia, South Korea, Malaysia, Australia, Hong Kong, mainland China, and the United States, Din Tai Fung was probably the most famous Shanghai steamed dumpling house in the world. Its international reputation has exceeded that of many its of counterparts, such as Nanxiang Bun Shop in Shanghai.[2] Media reports in Taiwan claimed that the *New York Times* rated it as one of the top ten restaurants in the world in 1993.[3] Din Tai Fung's success is an illuminating example of how the Chinese restaurant business became a global phenomenon following the growth of overseas Chinese communities, especially in the United States.

Shanghai cuisine is distinguished from other Chinese regional flavors by a number of famous dishes such as steamed meatballs, sweet-and-sour spare ribs, Shanghai stir-fried noodles, crispy chicken, or "da zha xie," a special crab found in the Changjiang (Yangtze) River. However, the most famous Shanghai delicacy is "xiao long bao"—little steamed dumplings. Steamed in bamboo baskets, the dumplings are small buns filled with several kinds of stuffing, including ground pork, ground chicken, ground pork mixed with crabmeat, ground pork mixed with shrimp, and chopped vegetables. The stuffing is carefully blended with green onions, salt, and chicken broth, which plays a key role in the stuffing's flavor. The dumplings are served with vinegar and shredded ginger soaking in the vinegar. When eating, a customer is supposed to take a bite, sip the soup when it cools down a little bit, and then dip the dumpling in the vinegar. Well-made steamed dumplings should be able to hold up in the soup until the dumpling is bitten.

Elegant steamed dumplings have been a delicacy in Shanghai since the late nineteenth century. As dumpling houses compete in quality and prices, many stores claim to be descendant stores of the first dumpling house in Shanghai and represent the original flavor, as authenticity is a selling point. The most famous dumpling house in Shanghai is Nanxiang Bun Shop, which has a history of over 100 years in Yu Yuan Park and is a well-known name across the country. During lunch or dinnertime, local customers and tourists often line up for a seat or a table. In fact, it has become a point of comparison for other dumpling houses in Shanghai and other areas. Historically, Shanghai cuisine, like any other big city's food, has been influenced by food traditions in its surrounding areas, such as Jiangsu and Zhejiang Provinces. Both provinces are known for their fine cuisines and culinary traditions. Steamed dumplings, for example, have long existed in Yangzhou City in Jiangsu Province and Hangzhou City in Zhejing Province. They are still popular in these cities today.

In the 1960s, Taipei was known as a capital of Chinese cuisine. Numerous restaurants with regionally flavored cuisines and food stores selling all kinds of dried fruits, cookies, snacks, or other food items quickly spread in the city. Shanghai cuisine was also popular in Taiwan. Among the Nationalist Party followers were some wealthy merchants, officials, and their families from Shanghai. Hengyang Road in Taipei became a "Little Shanghai" in the 1950s when mainlanders from Shanghai, Zhejiang, and Jiangsu Provinces settled and started restaurants, food stores, and other retail businesses there. Many changes have taken place since then, but tourists today can still find a pharmacy/general store called Wu Zhong Hang that was established there in 1950. It carried Shanghai-flavored snacks and other commodities for more than sixty years. There were also a couple of long-time Shanghai-flavored restaurants on the same street.[4] By the 1970s, there were numerous Shanghai-flavored restaurants in Taipei.

However, the best-known Shanghai cuisine restaurants were located to the east of Zhonghua Road in the Xi-Men-Ting (Ximen ding) area, one of the most famous shopping plazas in Taipei since the 1950s. Some Shanghai cuisine restaurants like Three-Six-Nine originated in Shanghai and were particularly attractive to those wealthy merchants, government officials, and their wives from the Shanghai area, as it reminded them of their old days in this most prosperous and Westernized city in China. As the anthropologist E. N. Anderson pointed out, Three-Six-Nine in Shanghai or other famous restaurants such as the Winter Garden in the 1930s catered to warlords and international bankers, serving banquets that could cost five to six figures in modern times.[5] "The Forever Yi Xueyan," a short story by the California-based Taiwanese novelist Bai Xianyong, vividly described how Shanghai refugees from mainland China spent their nightlife playing mahjong games, window-shopping in the Xi-Men-Ting area, watching Shaoxing (in Zhejiang) regional operas, and eating sweet rice ball soup at Three-Six-Nine. This was how they were recollecting their old life in Shanghai.[6]

THE MAKING OF DIN TAI FUNG DUMPLINGS

Din Tai Fung's founding owners, Yang Pin Ying and his wife, Li Pam Mae, were not Shanghai natives. Yang was born in 1927 in Shanxi Province in North China. Li was a Hakka Chinese born in Taiwan. In the 1940s, Yang first enlisted in a local warlord army, where his uncle on his mother's side served as a company commander. Soon he was tired of military life and wanted to go to Taiwan, where he had another uncle on his mother's side. So he left Shanxi and traveled to a number of cities until a relative (another uncle) in the city of Qingdao helped him get a ship ticket from Shanghai to Taiwan. In the summer of 1948, Yang left Shanghai for Taiwan. The following year, the Nationalists retreated from the mainland. Their confrontation with the Communist government made his stay in Taiwan permanent.

With the help of his aunt-in-law in Taiwan, Yang became a delivery boy for a Wang family's food oil business in Taipei. This family came from Shanghai, as did Yang's aunt-in-law.[7] His diligence and hardworking spirit soon earned him the position of the store manager and let him into the oil business network. It seemed that many merchants in the oil business came from Shanghai. Through working for the Wang family, Yang became familiar with Shanghai culture. Yang got to know his wife, Li Pam Mae, when she also worked for the Wang family. When the store went bankrupt in a few years, Yang started his own oil business in 1958 and named its store Din Tai Fung. His oil business was not very successful, so in 1972 Yang tried the restaurant business using the same store name.

Competition in the restaurant business was intense in Taiwan. Yang and Li had a Shanghai chef as a partner for a short while. When the chef left, they hired a local Taiwanese chef who also knew how to make steamed dumplings and other Shanghai snacks.[8] When their store's dumpling business became stable, Yang permanently closed his oil business and focused on his restaurant operation. Most restaurants in Taipei were small business operations in which family members pooled their time and energy. Though Li Pam Mae was a Hakka, she played an important role in running the family's Shanghai restaurant. Hardworking and talented, she was multilingual, speaking Hakka, Taiwanese (or Southern Fujianese) dialect, Shanghai dialect, and the Japanese language.[9] Her friendly and warm personality helped the restaurant retain a stable team of chefs and employees. A recently Taiwan-produced fictional TV series about Din Tai Fung featured Li as the prominent character in the family business.[10] Din Tai Fung's success showed how different Chinese regional food traditions became rooted in Taiwan.

Neither Yang nor Li was a Shanghai native. They learned the trade themselves through a lot of consultation and experimenting. To get the right texture for the dough, for example, kneading flour was a long and tedious job. They gradually developed the use of semi-risen flour, which was different from non-risen flour steamed dumplings in Shanghai. For stuffing, they chose ground pork meat that came from freshly slaughtered pigs, a special brand of chicken broth, and other local ingredients. They continuously improved and modified the stuffing, and tested the customers' responses to its flavor in the market. The recipe was a family secret when the dumplings became more and more popular. The key ingredients were precisely controlled by Luo Lunbing, one of the oldest and pioneer assistants of the Yang family. Only Luo and Yang Chi-hua, the elder son of Yang, knew the recipe.[11] Like that of Nanxiang Bun Shop in Shanghai, the nicely flavored soup remained inside until the dumpling was bitten.

In Taipei, the restaurant market was a translocal business in which Shanghai cuisine was an important part. Din Tai Fung was competing vigorously with other local Shanghai cuisine restaurants. After years of competition, it eventually became the most well known Shanghai steamed dumpling restaurant in Taipei. Sales soared and customers came in crowds. The restaurant expanded from a four-table capacity to a 300-seat restaurant in a narrow, four-story building on Hsin Yi Road. During the weekend, there could be 50 to 100 groups of guests waiting in line, and the waiting time could be as long as one and a half hours.[12] Din Tai Fung was often regarded as a point of comparison for other dumpling houses, like Nanxiang Bun Shop in Shanghai.

Many Nationalist leaders became its loyal customers. The list of its elite fans included the late general Chiang Wei-guo, son of the late president Chiang Kai-shek; Jiang Xiaowu and Jiang Xiaoyong, grandsons of Chiang; former Nationalist president Lian Zhan; former defense minister and prime minister Hao Bocun and his son; Taipei mayor Hao Longbin; and many other officials of Shanghai or Zhejiang natives and their children or grandchildren. Interestingly, pro-independence Taiwan government leaders like Li Denghui and Chen Shuibian never ate in the restaurant.[13] When Ang Lee, one of the most famous Chinese American directors, made his movie *Eat Drink Man Woman*, Din Tai Fung's steamed dumpling was a visible food item on the main character Chef Chu's dining table. Yang Chi-hua's cooking skills actually earned him an appearance as a double for Chef Chu.[14] When filming how to roll the wrapper, put in the filling, fold the wrap, and pleat the edge of the wrapper in a stylish fashion, Lee asked Yang to shave the hair on his hands so that they looked like those of Chef Chu in the movie.[15]

In 2000, Din Tai Fung became an incorporated company with 50 percent of its stock shares for outside investors. It hired a professional management team that master-planned a central kitchen located in Zhonghe City, streamlined supply sources, and manufactured most of the food items, except for the hand-made dumplings.[16] The restaurant rolled out fifteen million steamed dumplings annually and in 2007 reported revenue of 700 million New Taiwan dollars, which was about U.S.$21.63 million.[17] In addition to the flagship store, the restaurant soon established two branch stores at Zhongxiao East Road, and another branch at Xinyi Road in Taipei. More important, the business went global. Din Tai Fung established franchise stores in Japan, mainland China, Singapore, Indonesia, South Korea, Malaysia, and Australia. The store would soon expand to New York, London, and Paris, as all those metropolitan cities have a number of internationally recognized authentic Chinese restaurants.

Din Tai Fung's authenticity was sometimes challenged. After all, it was a Shanghai dumpling house that was established in Taiwan. During a gastronomic demonstration in Japan in 1986, a local chef from China was hired to help Yang Chi-hua. The chef came from Yangzhou City, Jiangsu Province, where steamed dumpling was a native delicacy for a long time. In his preparation, the chef made the dumplings a little bit bigger than required. Yang immediately noticed the difference and asked him to do the work again. The chef insisted that his own way was right, but Yang threw all the dumplings away. The chef finally followed what he was told.[18] The authenticity of Din Tai Fung's dumping as Shanghai cuisine was obviously established in Taipei.

Few people in Taiwan had actually tasted the original flavor of steamed dumplings in Nanxiang Bun Shop or other famous dumpling restaurants in Shanghai. In fact, most customers in Taiwan had no idea whether Yang Pin Yin and Li Pam Mae were Shanghai natives. They probably did not care as long as their dumplings tasted delicious. Taiwanese consumers' collective memory about Shanghai steamed dumplings allowed Din Tai Fung to maintain certain core elements in its cookery. But the dumplings' flavor as a Shanghai cuisine was shaped in Taipei. It was the taste and judgment of the customers there rather than those in Shanghai that determined Din Tai Fung's dumplings' authenticity. That is also probably true of other famous Chinese regional cuisine restaurants in Taiwan.

DIN TAI FUNG IN SOUTHERN CALIFORNIA

Din Tai Fung opened a franchise in Arcadia, in Southern California, in 2000. Different from its franchise stores in other metropolitan regions in the world, which are usually run by hired managers, the Southern California store is owned and managed by Frank (Guohua) Yang, the second son of Yang and Li. Frank opened his store in Arcadia with a careful consideration. He had promised his father not to enter into a restaurant career when he migrated to the United States. His father had advised him that the restaurant hours were too long and the work too hard. In fact, Frank had worked for thirteen years as a garment inspector before opening his store. But he noticed that at least two restaurants had used Din Tai Fung's name for their businesses since his arrival in America.[19] Din Tai Fung, as an authentic Shanghai restaurant in Taipei, tempted some immigrant restaurant operators to take advantage of its reputation.

Frank Yang's store in Southern California became an immediate success. Located in Arcadia, a city where many middle-class and wealthy Taiwanese immigrant families lived, the restaurant quickly attracted loyal customers. Though it served 2,000 dumplings a day, the waiting line was always long. During the weekend, it took at least thirty to forty-five minutes to get a table. Arcadia was a right location. Frank Yang's store obviously had Taiwanese customers in mind when it opened there. Seventy years earlier, Arcadia was the city where the first McDonald's restaurant was opened by Richard and Maurice McDonald. They then moved it to San Bernardino three years later. In the 2000s, Arcadia was a city with over 37 percent Chinese population; many of them came from Taiwan and had been to Din Tai Fung in Taipei. A customer recollected how years ago she saw a waiter carried a customer with a disability to the third-floor dining room because there was no elevator in the old Taipei store. She also insisted that the dumplings in the Taipei flagship store tasted better than the dumplings in the Arcadia store.[20]

Authentic flavor was also an important issue to Frank Yang. He did not want to ruin the reputation of his family business and disappoint his fellow Taiwanese immigrant customers. In fact, his elder brother was concerned about the quality issue when Frank Yang decided to open a chain store in the Los Angeles area.[21] Competition in the Chinese restaurant business in Southern California was intense. Many restaurants were operated by struggling immigrants who could not find a decent job and became self-made cooks. Food quality and hygiene conditions were often an issue in such restaurants. Failure in competition could affect Din Tai Fung's reputation in Taiwan, as the contemporary Chinese American community was transnational in nature. Cultural and social contact between Taiwanese immigrants in Southern California and their friends and relatives in Taiwan was frequent.

Frank worked very hard to maintain the original flavor and quality of the dumplings. Din Tai Fung milled a special combination of medium- and low-gluten flour to get the right texture for the dough. The secret of its dumplings was actually the appropriate mix of flours so that the wrapper would be transparently thin yet resilient. Frank continued that cooking tradition. He also ordered custom-made stainless steel steamers built in Taiwan to match exactly the shape and size of the bamboo steamers they used in Taipei. To his regret, the Los Angeles County Department of Health Services forbade using bamboo steamers. In spite of many hard efforts, Frank Yang still believed that the flavor of his products was only 80 percent like that of Taipei.[22]

Frank's diligent efforts to maintain Taipei standards was more than the spirit of entrepreneurship. Authenticity was an emotional issue for his Taiwanese customers. Food was not only an expression of ethnic resilience but also a cultural comfort for immigrants when they settled down in their adopted country. Din Tai Fung and other brand-name Taiwanese restaurants made immigrants from Taiwan in Southern California feel at home and gave them a sense of community. The original flavor that Frank tried to retain, and the authenticity that the Taiwanese customers expected, was not based on dumplings in Shanghai but on the products of its flagship store in Taipei. In 2000, there were several dozens of Shanghai restaurants in the San Gabriel Valley in Southern California. Some were operated by Taiwanese and others by immigrants from mainland China. But none of them could offer the same kind of steamed dumplings that Din Tai Fung served, and none had the same international reputation it had.

Din Tai Fung attracted non-Chinese clients as well. Shortly after Frank Yang opened his store, it became one of the most famous Chinese restaurants in Southern California. Mainstream newspapers, magazines, and television programs featured the restaurant in their food coverage. The number of non-Chinese customers was growing steadily for Din Tai Fung's variety of juicy, hand-made steamed dumplings. During the weekend lunch or dinner hours, the restaurant has typically seven to eight tables of non-Chinese guests out of thirty to forty tables. Among the customers are often Chinese American college students or young professionals eating there with their non-Chinese friends. To serve the increasing number of customers, the restaurant recently opened a new store in the neighboring plaza just behind the old store. The restaurant functions as a bridge for anyone who is interested in Chinese culinary culture and in getting to know more regional flavors of Chinese food.

Like some of the trendy restaurants in America, Din Tai Fung (the old store) has an open kitchen. Through the glass of its open kitchen, customers can watch chefs or kitchen helpers standing around a big chopping block working as a team. Some are swiftly tugging off dough into numerous small, rounded pieces of similar size. Others are skillfully rolling dough out into thin, round wrappings with finger-thick wooden rollers. Still others are filling the wrappings with the same amount of thoroughly ground pork or crab ingredients. Finally, someone else will mold them into elegant dumplings ready to be steamed. Among the kitchen staff, waiters and waitresses are immigrants from Taiwan, mainland China, Mexico, or other South American countries. Many immigrants joined the local menial service job market when they first arrived in America. Using an open kitchen and relying on immigrant workers reflect how

Din Tai Fung or many other restaurants—Chinese or non-Chinese—operate in the United States.

Din Tai Fung is not the only restaurant transplanted from Taiwan. Hundreds of Chinese restaurants in the San Gabriel Valley are either chain stores from their flagship restaurants in Taiwan, Hong Kong, or mainland China, or are affiliated to the original stores by using the same restaurant names and cooking the same kind of food. A & J Restaurant (Banmu Yuan in its Chinese name) in Alhambra, Good Time Café (Hao Nian Dong Taiwan Xiaochi in its Chinese name) in Arcadia, Dragon Mark Restaurant (Yitiaolong Beiping Miandian in its Chinese name), and Yung Ho Restaurant (Yonghe Doujian Canting in its Chinese name) in San Gabriel were all from Taiwan. While operating the American stores independently, immigrant entrepreneurs wanted to use a brand name because the original store had already established its reputation back in the home areas. The original name represents the authenticity of their food. They may initially appeal only to homesick Taiwanese customers. But if they are good, they will attract mainland Chinese or any customers who like Chinese food. As immigrant customers eat and debate if the food is authentic enough, they feel less isolated in America and realize that they are part of a social network connected through food, grocery stores, Chinese banks, real estate or other financial services, newspapers, radio, and television. Their American experience is not straight-line assimilation. While adapting themselves to mainstream American culture at work, they can live their own cultural life at home or off work. The multicultural American society they are living in is not a totally strange world because it also includes their culture as a component.

OPENING IN SHANGHAI

The year 2000 was a turning point in Din Tai Fung's history, as it was no longer a family-owned business but an incorporated company with 50 percent outside stock shares. It was during this year that Din Tai Fung established stores in mainland China. Surprisingly, it chose to open its first chain store in Shanghai, the birthplace of steamed dumplings.[23] The choice of Shanghai for its first store in mainland China was both challenging and logical. The city had many dumpling restaurants as well as a booming Taiwanese community. When the relationship improved between Taiwan and mainland China in late the 1980s, thousands of tourists, businesspeople, professionals, and students from Taiwan, or Taiwan immigrants from North America and other parts of the world, rushed there to build factories, open business offices, establish joint venture companies, invest in the local economy, or attend schools. "Two-way trade between Taiwan and China in the year 2000 came to US$32 billion, accounting for 11 percent of Taiwan's total export. Estimates of Taiwan investment in the mainland range from

$40–$100 billion as of mid-2001, making Taiwan the fourth largest investor in China. Taiwan's investment is especially heavy now in the Shanghai area. . . . Every day, some 10,000 Taiwanese business people enter the PRC."[24]

For these returning or remigrating Taiwanese immigrants, the United States was not necessarily their final destination in migration, or the only location of their cultural, social, and economic activities. Din Tai Fung's opening in Shanghai could be seen as part of this "reverse migration" by Taiwanese immigrants. By 2000, over 300,000 Taiwanese were working and living in Shanghai and formed their own networks, community organizations, and even school systems. Many of them were probably Nationalist expatriates or descendants of such expatriates driven away from mainland China in 1949. In a reverse and circular migration pattern, they were back to their cultural roots and began a new chapter of their career or business. When Din Tai Fung opened its store in Shanghai, it not only "returned" to its symbolic home but also became part of the booming Taiwanese community in Shanghai. As a brand-name Taiwan restaurant, it joined the Taiwanese return-migration movement to mainland China.

Opening a store in Shanghai could be an uphill challenge for Din Tai Fung, as the city was the very birthplace of steamed dumplings. The famous Nanxiang Bun Shop has a history of over 100 years in the local restaurant market. Many other local dumpling houses are competitive in price and quality. To prepare its operation, Din Tai Fung's master chef, Shao Guanglong, allegedly tasted dumplings of all the famous Shanghai restaurants but was still confident in establishing a store in Shanghai. According to a report in 2003, 30 percent of Din Tai Fung's customers were local people. On the other hand, Nanxiang Bun Shop still received an average of 3,000 customers per day.[25]

Located in a high-end mall and charging a much higher price than most of the local steamed dumpling restaurants, Din Tai Fung's store in Shanghai is trendy and upscale in decoration. Different from chop suey, which also returned to China in the 1940s but failed miserably as it only fit the taste of American patrons, Din Tai Fung's dumplings were not foreign food to the Chinese, and Din Tai Fung had an international fame that other local Shanghai dumpling restaurants did not have. Its authenticity was clear and simple: the restaurant offered brand-name Taiwan-made Shanghai dumplings. It would survive and succeed as an upper-scale restaurant in Shanghai.

While expanding to China, Din Tai Fung has also successfully opened stores in Singapore, Indonesia, Malaysia, and Australia, where Chinese food is popular and the Chinese population is large. As early as in 1996, with a franchise agreement with Takashimaya, a Japanese department store, Din Tai Fung opened five chain stores in Japan. Shortly after its opening, Shanghai steamed dumplings became trendy food in Japan. Din Tai Fung attracted many enthusiastic Japanese patrons. As a global enterprise, it has developed a modern operation standard in a Chinese restaurant. In addition to its flavor, tastefulness, and good service, Din Tai Fung has established standardized hygiene, food preparation, and cookery procedures that many other Chinese restaurants fail to develop. Chefs at each new location in Japan need to complete a vigorous three-month training in the Taipei kitchen in order to create the original recipes.[26] Din Tai Fung's store in Shanghai sometimes has Japanese tourists due to its reputation in Japan. Din Tai Fung also opened stores in Beijing, Shenzhen, Guangzhou, and Tianjin. By 2009, it had opened three stores in Shanghai, two in Beijing, three in Shenzhen, one in Tianjin, and one in Hong Kong.[27]

All of its chain stores in mainland China are high-end, sit-down restaurants well known among local, tourist, or Western customers, especially among Chinese American professionals and students working and studying in China. Many Chinese young, white-collar, middle-class patrons come to the restaurant through the recommendation of their overseas Chinese or international friends. With its competitive edge and international reputation, Din Tai Fung began to impact the Chinese steamed dumpling business. Many steamed dumpling restaurants in China, for example, imitated Din Tai Fung in having open kitchens. Din Tai Fung's success in China further boosted its reputation as serving authentic Shanghai cuisine.

Din Tai Fung is not the only Chinese restaurant transplanted from Taiwan to America, and then to mainland China. Banmu Yuan (Half-acre Farm), Yonghe Doujiang (Forever Harmony Bean-curd Milk), San-Liu-Jiu (Three Six Nine), Lu Yuan (Green Garden), Jiazhou Niu Rou Mian (California Beef Noodle), and a number of other Chinese American food enterprises established chain stores in China. Banmu Yuan was established in 1971 in Taipei during the restaurant business boom in Taiwan and soon established chain stores in several counties and cities there. In 1984, it opened branch stores in Los Angeles and San Jose. In Taiwan, Banmu Yuan was known for its authentic northern Chinese food such as steamed buns, noodles, or baked pan cakes. A few years after it expanded in California, Zhang Taike, the owner, met Zhao Bingsheng, another immigrant from Taiwan, on a business trip, and asked Zhao if he would be interested in joining the business and opening a chain store in mainland China. Zhao was interested because his father was a northerner from Shangdong Province. Though he had never been to China, he was always interested in going and wanted to explore his opportunities there. In 1994, the first branch store of Banmu Yuang opened in Shuangyu Shu, Haidian District, in western Beijing. It was a university area where many middle-class and professional Chinese lived. As one of the earliest Taiwan restaurants established in Beijing, Baimu Yuan attracted the attention of many local media, and its guests included Chinese movie celebrities like Zhang Yimou and Gong Li. By 2007, Baimu Yuan had opened twenty-seven stores in

Beijing and Shanghai.[28] Meanwhile, it has also opened a store in Maryland and another one in Virginia.[29]

Similarly, Yonghe Doujiang and Jiazhou Niu Rou Mian both have hundreds of chain stores in China. Those immigrants from Taiwan never expected that their modest American restaurant business could develop into such huge restaurant chains in mainland China. Through his stay in China, Zhao Bingsheng met his wife in Beijing, who also came from Taiwan and worked for a Taiwan company there. She originally planned to work there for three months. The marriage made her settle down in Beijing. Zhao also invited his aging father to join him in Beijing from Taiwan. It seemed that he established a home away from home in Beijing. The global economy and rapid economic growth in China made many Chinese Americans transnational citizens. Their life and work often involved more than one location and culture—from America to Taiwan, Hong Kong, or mainland China. The immigrant boom has marked the beginning of the globalization of Chinese communities and food culture.

After Din Tai Fung, Baimu Yuan, and Yonghe Doujiang opened stores in Shanghai, Guangzhou, Shenzhen, Beijing, and other metropolitan cities in mainland China, authenticity in Chinese food culture has become an increasingly complex issue. Returning to the birthplace of steamed dumplings, can Din Tai Fung claim its dumplings as authentic Shanghai cuisine? Who represents the best Shanghai dumplings: an internationally famous brand name or a native store 100 years old? As transnational businesses in China, the culinary identities of Din Tai Fung, Banmu Yuan, and Yonghe Doujiang are different from their business identities and status in the United States. In China, they are not struggling ethnic food businesses depending or surviving on cheap prices, ethnic customers, and the use of immigrant or underpaid family labor. Instead, they are high-end chain restaurants with an international reputation and higher hygiene standards. Many middle-class or professional customers in mainland China prefer them to other local restaurants because of their California and Taiwan backgrounds. Their transnational Chineseness does not make their culinary identity marginal in mainland China.

CONCLUSION

The restaurant business is an old profession in China. Chinese food is one of the best in the world. Chinese immigrants are among the earliest arrivals in California. Canton Restaurant was a landmark food institution during the gold rush. Food history illustrated who Chinese pioneer immigrants were. Chinese "forty-niners" were founders of San Francisco. Following the merchants came hundreds of thousands of Chinese immigrants of lesser means who joined the gold rush, pioneered the fishing industry, operated many small businesses, worked as agricultural laborers, and built the Central Pacific Continental Railroad. Chinese Americans were also laundrymen and restaurant operators.

While the Chinese changed the social landscape of the United States, racial America also changed them. Work competition, racial hostility, and the exclusion laws made the Chinese forever foreigners. Food was used as a tool in racial rhetoric. American newspapers, journals, and literary writings disseminated stereotypes on Chinese food culture. In the last three decades of the nineteenth century, the Chinese restaurant business experienced stagnant growth in California when racism against the Chinese reached its peak. Meanwhile, Chinese laundries were everywhere in American cities. As the Chinese were denied many job opportunities, menial service occupations became their only option. This was the historic context into which Chinese Americans invented chop suey and made it popular in American society. Chop suey was an innovative way for the Chinese to survive in racial America.

The Chinese restaurant business changed again when new immigrants came after the Immigration and Nationality Act of 1965. Authentic Chinese food replaced chop suey meals. Numerous Hunan, Sichuan, Mandarin, and Shanghai restaurants appeared on the East Coast. But General Tso's chicken, the most famous dish in Hunan restaurants, was actually invented in Taiwan. Many regional-flavored Chinese restaurants were brought over by immigrants from Taiwan rather than mainland China. Embedded in this history is a complicated, bittersweet story of Chinese migration. Authenticity in Chinese food history is more than a culinary issue.

Contemporary Chinese immigrants and their families are a new generation of Asian Americans. Congregated Chinese restaurants, grocery stores, and other retail and service businesses in the San Gabriel Valley, in Southern California, or in Flushing and Queens, in New York, are visible examples of their transnational lifestyle, which does not prevent them from making America their home. Across the country, thriving Chinese restaurant businesses have considerably enriched American food culture. The rapid growth of P. F. Chang's as a full-service Chinese restaurant and Panda Express as a fast-food Chinese restaurant reflects Americans' constantly changing and often multiethnically blended eating habits. Chinese food is an indispensable part of the American restaurant market today.

NOTES

INTRODUCTION

1. I refer to both Chinese immigrants and their descendants as Chinese Americans in this book.
2. Chinese immigrants in the nineteenth century came mainly from seven counties in Guangdong Province, South China.
3. Kevin Starr, *Golden Dreams: California in an Age of Abundance, 1950–1963* (New York: Oxford University Press, 2009), 453.
4. Gaye Tuchman and Harry G. Levine, "Safe Treyf," *Brandeis Review* 24 (1993): 382.
5. James Flanigan, "Cooking Up a Powerhouse of Chinese Fast Food," *Los Angeles Times*, October 8, 2001.
6. Tu Wei-ming, "Cultural China: The Periphery as the Center," in *The Living Tree: The Changing Meaning of Being Chinese Today*, ed. Tu Wei-ming (Stanford, Calif.: Stanford University Press, 1994), 13–18.

CHAPTER 1   CANTON RESTAURANT AND CHINESE FORTY-NINERS

1. This gathering was mentioned by many early and contemporary writings about Chinese migration. See *Daily Alta California*, December 10, 1849; Ellen Rawson Wood, "*California and the Chinese: The First Decade. A Thesis for University of California*" (1961; reprint, San Francisco: R & E Research Associates, 1974), 21; Gunther Barth, *A History of the Chinese in the United States, 1850–1870* (Cambridge, Mass.: Harvard University Press, 1964), 64; Boji Liu, *Meiguo huaqiao shi* (A History of Overseas Chinese in America) (Taipei: Taiwan Books, 1958), 41.
2. *Daily Alta California*, May 12, 1851, cited in Wood, *California and the Chinese*, 20.
3. I borrow the term from Ronald Takaki's book *Strangers from a Different Shore: A History of Asian Americans* (Boston: Little, Brown, 1989), 12.
4. Elizabeth Sinn, *Pacific Crossing: California Gold, Chinese Migration, and the Making of Hong Kong* (Hong Kong: Hong Kong University Press, 2013), 55.
5. Geoffrey C. Ward, *The West: An Illustrated History* (New York: Little, Brown, 1996), 121.
6. Ibid., 134, 164.
7. James O'Meara, "The Chinese in Early Days," *Overland Monthly*, May 1884, 477.
8. Ibid.
9. According to Mary Roberts Coolidge, there were 54 Chinese in California in 1848; 325 arrived at the San Francisco Custom House in 1849; 450 arrived in 1850. See Mary Roberts Coolidge, *Chinese Immigration* (New York: Henry Holt, 1909), 498. See also Thomas Chinn, Him Mark Lai, and Philip Choy, eds., *A History of the Chinese in California: A Syllabus* (San Francisco: Chinese Historical Society of America, 1969), 9; Liu, *Meiguo huaqiao shi* (A History of Overseas Chinese in America), 99.
10. Barth, *History of the Chinese*, 64.
11. Coolidge, *Chinese Immigration*, 498–499. Coolidge estimated that by 1851, the Chinese population on the West Coast was 7,370, and that it increased to 25,116 in 1852, to 46,897 in 1860, to 71,083 in 1870, to 104,991 in 1880, and to 132,300 in 1882.

12. This pattern did not apply to Chinese labor migration to South America or to the Caribbean islands in the nineteenth century.

13. Sinn, *Pacific Crossing*, 51.

14. James P. Delgado, *To California by Sea: A Maritime History of the California Gold Rush* (Columbia: University of South Carolina Press, 1996).

15. Sandy Lydon, *Chinese Gold: The Chinese in the Monterey Bay Region* (Capitola, Calif.: Capitola Book Company, 1985), 14.

16. The Canton System was a system where the Chinese emperor designated ten to thirteen merchant families as the only licensed companies for international trade in 1757. The families were among the wealthiest people in the country.

17. For the Hong merchants, see Liang Jiabin, *Guangdong shisan hang kao* (The Thirteen Hongs of Canton) (Guangzhou, China: Guangdong People's Press, 1999); Weng Eang Cheong, *Hong Merchants of Canton: Chinese Merchants in Sino-Western Trade, 1684–1798* (Curzon Press, printed in Britain, in 1997).

18. William Hoffman, *The Monitor; or, Jottings of a New York Merchant during a Trip Round the Globe* (New York: Carleton, 1863), 41.

19. J. G. Kerr, *The Guide to the City and Suburbs of Canton* (Hong Kong: Kelly and Walsh, 1904), 10. This is an updated reprint of the early version about Canton. John Kerr stayed in China for twenty-three years as a missionary doctor and established the famous Po-chi Hospital in Canton in 1859. He delivered a speech to the Young Men's Christian Association (YMCA) on November 13, 1877, on Chinese culture and history. He refuted point by point racist objections against Chinese migration, denial of entrance of Chinese children into San Francisco public schools, and high import duties on rice from China. J. G. Kerr, *The Chinese Question Analyzed: A Lecture Delivered in the Hall of the Young Men's Christian Association, November 13, 1877* (San Francisco, 1877).

20. John Henry Gray, *China, A History of the Laws, Manners, and Customs of the People* (London: Macmillan, 1878), 64, cited in Andrew Coe, *Chop Suey: A Cultural History of Chinese Food* (New York: Oxford University Press, 2009), 97.

21. The city was named Yerba Buena (meaning "good herb," a local plant with mint flavor).

22. *Daily Alta California*, May 11, 1850, cited by Tonia Chao, "Communicating through Architecture: San Francisco Chinese Restaurants and Cultural Intersections, 1849–1984" (Ph.D. diss., University of California, Berkeley, 1985), 46.

23. Sinn, *Pacific Crossing*, 55.

24. Loren W. Fessler, ed. and China Institute in America, Inc., comp., *Chinese in America: Stereotyped Past, Changing Present* (New York: Vantage Press, 1983), 24, 25, 59.

25. *Daily Alta California*, November 14, 1857.

26. Corinner K. Hoexter, *From Canton to California: The Epic of Chinese Immigration* (New York: Four Winds Press, 1976), 9.

27. Xiao-huang Yin, *Chinese American Literature since the 1850s* (Urbana and Chicago: University of Illinois Press, 2000), 24.

28. O'Meara, "Chinese in Early Days," 478.

29. Hoexter, *From Canton to California*, 9.

30. Ibid., 44.

31. Sucheng Chan, *Asian Americans: An Interpretive History* (Boston: Twayne, 1991), 47.

32. *Daily Alta California*, July 20, 1852; Wood, *California and the Chinese*, 21.

33. Liu, *Meiguo huaqiao shi* (A History of Overseas Chinese in America), 110.

34. A. W. Loomis, "The Old East in the New West," *Overland Monthly*, October 1868, 36.

35. Liu, *Meiguo huaqiao shi* (A History of Overseas Chinese in America), 110–112.

36. Yin, *Chinese American Literature*, 24.

37. Ibid., 19.

38. Chinese merchants may have gotten some help from missionaries like Selim E. Woodworth, but the ideas in the letter were obviously theirs.

39. Liu, *Meiguo huaqiao shi* (A History of Overseas Chinese in America), 112–113.

CHAPTER 2   FLAGS OF YELLOW SILK

1. Waverly Root and Richard de Rochemont, *Eating America: A History* (New York: Ecco Press, 1981), 177.

2. Elizabeth Sinn, *Pacific Crossing: California Gold, Chinese Migration, and the Making of Hong Kong* (Hong Kong: Hong Kong University Press, 2013), 154.

3. Tonia Chao, "Communication through Architecture: San Francisco Chinese Restaurants as Cultural Intersections, 1894–1984" (Ph.D. diss., University of California, Berkeley, 1985), 43; Bayard Taylor, *Eldorado; or, Adventures in the Path of Empire: Comprising a Voyage to California, Via Panama; Life in San Francisco and Monterey; Pictures of the Gold Region, and Experiences of Mexican Travel* (New York: George P. Putnam, 1850), 116–117, cited in Loren W. Fessler, ed., and China Institute in America, Inc., comp., *Chinese in America: Stereotyped Past, Changing Present* (New York: Vantage Press, 1983), 26–27.

4. Taylor, *Eldorado*, 117.

5. Fessler, *Chinese in America*, 26–27.

6. Yong Chen, *Chinese San Francisco: 1850–1943: A Trans-Pacific Community* (Stanford, Calif.: Stanford University Press, 2000), 55.

7. *The Oriental* 2, nos. 1 and 12 (February 1865), cited in Chao, "Communication through Architecture," 48. See also "Chinese Directory" listed in the *Oriental*, February 8, 1856, English section; Thomas W. Chinn, H. M. Lai, and Philip Choy eds., *A History of the Chinese in California: A Syllabus* (San Francisco: Chinese Historical Society of America, 1969), 10.

8. Joseph R. Conlin, *Bacon, Beans and Galantines: Food and Foodways on the Western Mining Frontier* (Reno: University of Nevada Press, 1987), 190–192, quoted in J. A. G. Roberts, *China to Chinatown: Chinese Food in the West* (London: Reaktion Books, 2000), 136.

9. William Shaw, *Golden Dreams and Waking Realities; Being the Adventures of a Gold-Seeker in California and the Pacific Islands* (London: Smoth, Elder, 1851), 39–40; David G. Gutierrez, "Seeing the Elephant: Myth and Myopia: Hispanic People and Western History," in *The West: An Illustrated History*, ed. Geoffrey C. Ward (New York: Little Brown, 1996), 147.

10. James Ayers, *Gold and Sunshine: Reminiscences of Early California* (Boston: R. G. Badger, 1922), 30.

11. Root and Rochemont, *Eating America*, 177.

12. Daniel J. Boorstin, *The Americans: The National Experience* (New York: Vintage Books, 1965), 146.

13. William Redmond Ryan, *Personal Adventures in Upper and Lower California in 1848–9, with the Author's Experiences in the Mines* (London: W. Shoberl, 1850), cited in Fessler, *Chinese in America*, 24.

14. Ryan cited in Fessler, *Chinese in America*, 25.

15. Donna R. Gabaccia, *We Are What We Eat: Ethnic Food and the Making of Americans* (Cambridge, Mass.: Harvard University Press, 1998), 103.

16. Peter J. Blodgett, *Land of Golden Dreams: California in the Gold Rush Decades, 1848–1858* (San Marino, Calif.: Huntington Library, 1999), 73.

17. Ryan cited in Fessler, *Chinese in America*, 24.

18. Fessler, *Chinese in America*, 26–27.

19. Gabaccia, *We Are What We Eat*, 102.

20. Alexander McLeod, *Pigtails and Gold Dust* (Caldwell, Idaho: Caxton Printers, 1948), 20.

21. James O'Meara, "The Chinese in Early Days," *Overland Monthly*, May 1884, 477–478.

22. J. H. Bates, *Notes of a Tour in Mexico and California* (New York: Burr Printing House, 1887), 119.

23. Andrew Coe, *Chop Suey: A Cultural History of Chinese Food in the United States* (New York: Oxford University Press, 2009), 123, 125.

24. O'Meara, "Chinese in Early Days," 477–478.

25. Ibid.

26. McLeod, *Pigtails and Gold Dust*, 32.

27. Jacques Gernet, *Daily Life in China: On the Eve of the Mongol Invasion 1250–1276* (Stanford, Calif.: Stanford University Press, 1970), 51.

28. Thomas Robertson Stoddart, *Annals of Tuolumne County* (Sonora, Calif.: Mother Lode Press, 1963), 67.

29. Sylvia Sun Minnick, *Samforw: The San Joaquin Chinese Legacy* (Fresno, Calif.: Panorama West Publishing, 1988), 36.

30. Mary Coolidge, *Chinese Immigration* (New York: Henry Holt, 1909), 21.

31. J. A. G. Roberts, *China to Chinatown: Chinese Food in the West* (London: Reaktion Books, 2000), 136.

32. Sinn, *Pacific Crossing*, 309–311.

33. Ibid., 145.

34. Ibid., 149.

35. Robert F. G. Spier, "Food Habits of 19th Century California Chinese," *California Historical Society Quarterly* (March 1958): 9–84, 126–136.

36. Sinn, *Pacific Crossing*, 151.

37. Sucheng Chan, *This Bittersweet Soil: The Chinese in California Agriculture, 1860–1910* (Berkeley: University of California Press, 1986), 84.

38. Ibid., 86, 93.

39. Gabaccia, *We Are What We Eat*, 111.

40. Chan, *This Bittersweet Soil*, 88.

41. Charles Morley, trans. with foreword, "The Chinese in California as Reported by Henryk Sienkiewicz," *California Historical Society Quarterly* 34 (1955): 308, 301–316.

42. Gabaccial, *We Are What We Eat*, 11.

43. Kevin Starr, *Golden Dreams: California in an Age of Abundance, 1950–1963* (New York: Oxford University Press, 2009), 453.

44. Coe, *Chop Suey*, 123.

CHAPTER 3   "CHINAMEN LIVE ON RICE"

1. For the description of the banquet, see Samuel Bowles, *Our New West* (Hartford, Conn.: Hartford, 1869), 410–411, cited in Corinne K. Hoexter, *From Canton to California: The Epic of Chinese Immigration* (New York: Four Winds Press, 1976), 69–70. See also Andrew Coe, *Chop Suey: A Cultural History of Chinese Food* (New York: Oxford University Press, 2009), 104–106.

2. For a general description and different perspective of British food history, see Colin Spencer, *British Food: An Extraordinary Thousand Years of History* (New York: Columbia University Press, 2003). For Chinese food history, see Eugene N. Anderson, *The Food of China* (New Haven, Conn.: Yale University Press, 1988); Thomas O. Höllmann, *The Land of the Five*

Flavors: A Cultural History of Chinese Cuisine (New York: Columbia University Press, 2013). For a description of a royal banquet in China, see Renqiu Yu, "Imperial Banquets and the Emperor's Meals in Qing China," *Flavor & Fortune* (Summer 2000): 7.

3. Cited in Jonathan D. Spence, "Food," in *Chinese Roundabout: Essays in History and Culture* (New York: W. W. Norton, 1992), 171.

4. Joanna Waley-Cohen, "The Quest for Perfect Balance," in *Food: The History of Taste*, ed. Paul Freedman (London: Thames & Hudson, 2007), 107.

5. Charles Benn, *Chinese Golden Age: Everyday Life in the Tang Dynasty* (Oxford: Oxford University Press, 2002), 132, see especially chapter 6, "Food and Feast," 119–147.

6. Jacques Gernet, *Daily Life in China: On the Eve of the Mongol Invasion 1250–1276* (Stanford, Calif.: Stanford University Press, 1970), 134.

7. For a description of Chinese cuisine in the Ming Dynasty, see Su, Heng'an (蘇恆安), *Culinary Arts in Late Ming China: Refinement, Secularization and Nourishment: A Study on Gao Lian's Discourse on Food and Drink* (Taipei: SMC Publishing, 2004).

8. Anderson, *Food of China*, 1.

9. Mei Yuan, *Sui Yuan Shi San* (随园食单) (Beijing: Zhong Hua Shu Ju (中华书局) 2010).

10. Noah Brooks, "Restaurant Life in San Francisco," *Overland Monthly*, November 1868, 472.

11. Daniel J. Boorstin, *The Americans: The Democratic Experience* (New York: Vintage Books, 1965), 322.

12. Harvey Levenstein, *Revolution at the Table: The Transformation of the American Diet* (Berkeley: University of California Press, 2003), 3.

13. Lawrence Waters Jenkins, *Bryant Parrott Tilden of Salem, at a Chinese Dinner Party* (Princeton, N.J.: Princeton University Press, 1944), 18–27, cited in Coe, *Chop Suey*, 14, 35–36.

14. Coe, *Chop Suey*, 2, 35–36.

15. Ibid., 106.

16. Levenstein, *Revolution at the Table*, 21.

17. Ibid., 15.

18. Walter Prescott Webb, *The Great Plains* (Lincoln: University of Nebraska Press, 1959), 216–226. For Joseph G McCoy, see Ralph P. Bieber, ed., *Joseph G. McCoy: Historic Sketches of the Cattle Trade of the West and Southwest* (Glendale, Calif.: A. H. Clark, 1940).

19. Boorstin, *Americans*, 318.

20. Ibid., 5.

21. David M. Potter, *People of Plenty: Economic Abundance and the American Character* (Chicago: University of Chicago Press, 1954), 91–110.

22. Bryan R. Johnson, "Let's Eat Chinese Tonight," *American Heritage* 38, no. 8 (December 1987).

23. Alexander Young, "Chinese Food and Cookery," *Appleton's Journal* (September 14, 1872), 292.

24. Jennifer 8. Lee, *The Fortune Cookie Chronicles: Adventures in the World of Chinese Food* (New York: Hachette Book Group, 2008), 54. The pamphlet was published again in 1908, entitled *Meat vs. Rice: American Manhood against Asiatic Cooliehood*. See also Anita Mannur, "Asian American Food-Scapes," *Amerasia Journal* 32, no. 2 (2006): 1–5.

25. U.S. Senate, 57th Cong., 1st sess., Doc. No. 137 (Washington, D.C.: Government Printing Office, 1902), 24, cited in Levenstein, *Revolution at the Table*, 24.

26. *New York Times*, March 1, 1917.

27. "Tell of Food Needs in 5th Av. Ballroom," *New York Times*, March 6, 1917.

28. For Gold Rice, see Richard Schulze, *Carolina Gold Rice: The Ebb and Flow History of a Lowcountry Cash Crop* (Charleston, S.C.: History Press, 2005).

29. *Daily Alta California*, June 18, 1853.

30. Walter Rose, "A Chinese Dinner," *Appleton's Journal* 7, no. 148 (January 27, 1872): 95–96.

31. Alexander Young, "Chinese Food and Cookery," Appleton's Journal 8, no. 181 (September 14, 1872): 291–293.

32. Mark Twain, *Roughing It* (Berkeley: University of California Press, 1972), 353–355.

33. Louis Beck, *New York's Chinatown: A Historical Presentation of People and Places* (New York: Bohemia, 1898), 296.

34. Limin Chu, *The Images of China and the Chinese in the Overland Monthly, 1868–1875, 1883– 1935* (San Francisco: R & E Research Associates, 1974), 75.

35. James O'Meara, "The Chinese in Early Days," *Overland Monthly*, May 1884, 478.

36. "Wong Chin Foo," *Harper's Weekly*, May 26, 1877.

37. By the late nineteenth century, the Krupp family in Germany became a leading manufacturer of cannons and other military products in Europe.

38. See the card at the Daniel K. E. Ching Collection at the Chinese Historical Society of America Museum and Learning Center in San Francisco. See also http://www.chsa.org/.

39. J. A. G. Roberts, *China to Chinatown: Chinese Food in the West* (London: Reaktion Books), 147. This book is the most comprehensive research on the Western perception of Chinese food and eating habits.

40. Estelle T. Lau has a brief comment on the rhyme. See Estelle T. Lau, *Paper Families: Identity, Immigration Administration, and Chinese Exclusion* (Durham, N.C.: Duke University Press, 2006), 45.

41. The information is based on "New York Chinese Protest 'Mouse' in Takeout Report," *Sing Tao Daily*, February 5, 2007, http://news.newamericamedia.org/news/view_article.html ?article_id=6cce2d1ec2be3029d6ea54a4776d9a38; on "Mei huaren canyin yezhe nuchi laoshu rou baodao" (New York Chinese Restaurant Operators Denounced "The Rat Meal" News), February 1, 2007, http://www.chinaqw.com//hqhr/hrdt/200702/01/60155.shtml; and on "Laoshu rou shijian renu meiguo huaren" (The Rat New Angered Chinese Americans), http://www .chinaqw.com//hqhr/hrdt/200702/09/61250.shtml. Detailed coverage of this event was also carried by *Shijie Ribao* (World Journal News) on February 3, 4, and 5, 2007.

42. "'Rats Gone Wild' in NYC Restaurant," Associated Press, February 23, 2007.

43. Noah Brooks, "Restaurant Life in San Francisco," *Overland Monthly*, November 1868, 465–473.

44. Waverly Root and Richard de Rochemont, *Eating America: A History* (Hopewell, N.J.: Ecco Press, 1981), 349.

45. Donna R. Gabbacia, *We Are What We Eat: Ethnic Food and the Making of Americans* (Cambridge, Mass.: Harvard University Press, 1998), 96.

46. Brooks, "Restaurant Life in San Francisco," 473.

47. Ibid., 465–473.

48. Root and de Rochemont, *Eating America*, 349.

49. Ibid., 350.

50. Tonia Chao, "Communicating through Architecture: San Francisco Chinese Restaurants as Cultural Intersections, 1849–1984" (Ph.D. diss., University of California, Berkeley, 1985), 226, Table 4.

51. Brooks, "Restaurant Life in San Francisco," 470.

52. Ibid.

53. Levenstein, *Revolution at the Table*, 7.

54. Yong Chen, *Chinese San Francisco, 1850–1943: A Trans-Pacific Community* (Stanford, Calif.: Stanford University Press, 2000), 55, 58, 59.

55. Ibid., 59–63.

56. Chao, "Communicating through Architecture," 37.

57. Roger Daniels, *Asian America: Chinese and Japanese in the United States since 1850* (Seattle: University of Washington Press, 1988), 36.

58. Ibid.

59. Alexander Saxton, *The Indispensable Enemy: Labor and the Anti-Chinese Movement in California* (Berkeley: University of California Press, 1971), 105.

60. June Mei, "Socioeconomic Developments among the Chinese in San Francisco, 1848–1906," in *Labor Immigration Under Capitalism: Asian Workers in the United States before World War II*, ed. Lucie Cheng and Edna Bonacich (Berkeley: University of California Press, 1984), 377.

61. Ronald Takaki, *Strangers from a Different Shore: A History of Asian Americans* (Boston: Little, Brown, 1989), 92, 240.

62. Paul Ong, "Chinese Laundries as an Urban Occupation in 19th Century California," in *The Annals, of the Chinese Historical Society of the Pacific Northwest*, ed. Douglas W. Lee (Seattle: Chinese Historical Society of the Pacific Northwest, 1983), 71.

63. Ibid. See also Chao, "Communicating through Architecture," 38.

64. Chao, "Communicating through Architecture," 40.

65. Clarence Edwards, *Bohemian San Francisco: Its Restaurants and Their Most Famous Recipes* (San Francisco: Paul Elder, 1914).

66. Gabbacia, *We Are What We Eat*, 103.

67. Ibid., 104.

68. Mei, "Socioeconomic Developments among the Chinese in San Francisco," 377.

69. Sucheng Chan, *This Bittersweet Soil: The Chinese in California Agriculture, 1860–1910* (Berkeley: University of California Press, 1986), 362.

70. Gabaccia, *We Are What We Eat*, 113.

71. Chan, *This Bittersweet Soil*, 365.

CHAPTER 4   CHOP SUEY AND RACIAL AMERICA

1. "Couldn't Tell about the Chicken," *Los Angeles Times*, April 16, 1917.

2. Wong Chin Foo, "The Chinese in New York," *Cosmopolitan* 5 (March–October 1888): 297–311.

3. Allan Forman, "New York's China-town," *Washington Post*, July 25, 1886, quoted in Andrew Coe, *Chop Suey: A Cultural History of Chinese Food* (New York: Oxford University Press, 2009), 158.

4. For example, in the student cafeteria at the University of Hong Kong, a two-song meal means a meal that consists of cooked rice with two dishes.

5. Li Shu-fan (1887–1966) was a famous doctor in Hong Kong.

6. Irish Chang, *A History of Chinese in America: A Narrative History* (New York: Viking Penguin, 2003), 14.

7. Calvin Lee, *Chinatown USA* (New York: Doubleday, 1965), 71.

8. Waverly Root and Richard de Rochemont, *Eating America: A History* (Hopewell, N.J.: Ecco Press, 1981), 277.

9. Renqiu Yu, "Chop Suey: From Chinese Food to Chinese American Food," in *Chinese America: History and Perspectives* (San Francisco: Chinese Historical Society of America, 1987), 87–100.

10. "Viceroy Li While at Sea," *New York Times*, August 29, 1896.

11. "Dinner in Honor of Li," *New York Times*, September 5, 1896.

12. "The Viceroy Their Guest," *New York Times*, August 30, 1896.

13. Wong Chin Foo, "Chinese Cooking," *Brooklyn Eagle*, July 1884.

14. Yu, "Chop Suey," 93.

15. Louis Beck, *New York's Chinatown: A Historical Presentation of People and Places* (New York: Bohemia, 1898), 47–54.

16. *Webster's Ninth New Collegiate Dictionary* (Springfield, Mass.: Merriam-Webster, 1988), 237.

17. Beck, *New York's Chinatown*, 50.

18. "Chop Suey Resorts," *New York Times*, November 15, 1903.

19. Ibid.

20. Beck, *New York's Chinatown*, 54.

21. Hanna Miller, "Identity Takeout: How American Jews Made Chinese Food Their Ethnic Cuisine," *Journal of Popular Culture*, no. 3 (2006): 446.

22. Beck, *New York's Chinatown*, 12, 58.

23. "Chop Suey Resorts."

24. He was also known as "Diamond Charley Boston" as he often wore big diamond rings on his fingers. See Bruce Edward Hall, *Tea That Burns: A Family Memoir of Chinatown* (New York: Free Press, 1998), 158–159; Mary Ting Yi Lui, *The Chinatown Trunk Mystery: Murder, Miscegenation, and Other Dangerous Encounters in Turn-of-the-Century New York City* (Princeton, N.J.: Princeton University Press, 2005), 65; "Hold Chinaman as Head of Opium Ring: Charley Boston, Reputed Brains of Smuggling Syndicate, Seized in Chinatown," *New York Times*, January 31, 1911.

25. "Chop Suey Resorts."

26. Liang Qichao, *Xindalu Youji* (Diary of Traveling in the New World) (Japan: Xinmingchong-hao, 1904; reprint, Changsha, China: Hunan Renming Chubanshe, 1981), 52.

27. "Heard About Town," *New York Times*, January 29, 1900.

28. "How to Make Chop Suey," *New York Times*, November 3, 1901.

29. Ibid.

30. Lewis A. Erenberg, *Steppin' Out: New York Nightlife and the Transformation of American Culture* (Chicago: University of Chicago Press, 1984), 50.

31. "Chop Suey Resorts."

32. Ibid.

33. See a photo in Mary Ting Yi Lui's book *The Chinatown Trunk*, (Princeton, N.J.: Princeton University Press, 2005), 66.

34. "Chop Suey Resorts."

35. Ibid.

36. Ibid.

37. Ibid.

38. "Chop Suey Injunction: Lem Sen of 'Frisco Here to Allege Copy-right Infringement," *New York Times*, June 15, 1904.

39. "Chop Suey Resorts."

40. Sinclair Lewis, *Main Street: The Story of Carol Kennicott* (New York: Harcourt, Brace and Howe, 1920), chapter 8.

41. Imogene I. Lim and John Eng-Wong, "The Chow Mein Sandwich: Chinese American Entrepreneurship in Rhode Island," in *Origin and Destinations: 41 Essays on Chinese America* (Los Angeles: Chinese Historical Society of Southern California, 1994), 417. See also Imogene I. Lim, "The Chow Mein Sandwich American as Apple Pie," *Radcliffe Culinary Times* 3, no. 2 (Autumn 1993): 4–5.

42. To view Hopper's painting, see http://www.artchive.com/viewer/z.html.

43. Harvey Levenstein, *Paradox of Plenty: A Social History of Eating in Modern America* (New York: New York University Press, 1993), 185.

44. Bertram Reinitz, "Chop Suey's New Role," *New York Times*, December 27, 1925.

45. Ibid.

46. Huping Ling, *Chinese Chicago Race, Transnational Migration, and Community since 1870* (Stanford, Calif.: Stanford University Press, 2012), 24–57.

47. William Mason, "The Chinese in Los Angeles," *Museum Alliance Quarterly* 6, no. 2 (Fall 1967): 16 (Los Angeles County Museum of Natural History).

48. Ching Chao Wu, "Chinatowns: A Study of Symbiosis and Assimilations" (Ph.D. diss., University of Chicago, 1928), 87.

49. *Pasadena City Directory* (1920), 268.

50. Tonia Chao, "Communicating through Architecture: San Francisco Chinese Restaurants as Cultural Intersections, 1849–1984" (Ph.D. diss., University of California, Berkeley, 1985), 223.

51. Ibid., 98.

52. Ibid., 115.

53. Bureau of the Census, 1920 report, Population Table 18, 75.

54. Chao, "Communicating through Architecture," 95. See also "Chinatown, My China-town," *Business Week*, March 12, 1938.

55. Chao, "Communicating through Architecture," 95.

56. Ruth Hall Whitfield, "Public Opinion and the Chinese Question in San Francisco, 1900–1947" (Master's thesis, University of California, Berkeley, 1947), 39–40.

57. Lorraine Dong, "The Forbidden City Legacy," in *Chinese America: History and Perspectives* (San Francisco: Chinese Historical Society of America and Asian American Studies, San Francisco State University, 1992), 139.

58. *San Francisco Chronicle*, August 16, 1924.

59. Laura A. Kirkman, "Chinese Chop Suey in the Guest Luncheon Menu," in Efficient Housekeeping column, *Los Angeles Times*, April 15, 1922.

60. About thirty to forty food review articles published chop suey recipes during this period. See, for example, Marion Harland, "Common Sense in the Home: Chop Suey and Some Rice Dishes," *Los Angeles Times*, October 12, 1913.

61. Levenstein, *Paradox of Plenty*, 122.

62. "Eisenhowers Keep Yen for Chop Suey: Send Out for Dish to Capital Restaurant That Has Been Their Favorite since 1930," *New York Times*, August 2, 1953.

63. Ibid.

64. James J. Nagle, "The Twain Meet in Middle West: Chun King of Duluth Turns Out Chinese Delicacies," *New York Times*, March 17, 1957.

65. Donna R. Gabaccia, *We Are What We Eat: Ethnic Food and the Making of Americans* (Cambridge, Mass.: Harvard University Press, 1998), 166.

66. James J. Nagle, "Nation's Tastes: Italian, Chinese and Jewish Specialties Now Favored by All Classes Here," *New York Times*, February 15, 1955.

67. Gabaccia, *We Are What We Eat*, 166.

68. "Paulucci Named Entrepreneur of the Year," *NIAF News* 19, no. 1 (January 31, 2003): 4.

69. This information is based on a phone interview with Gilbert Hom, a longtime member of Chinese Historical Society of Southern California, on May 20, 2007.

70. Nagle, "Twain Meet in Middle West."

71. "Chow Mein Package Patented," *New York Times*, September 5, 1957.

72. "Long Ago and Far Away," published by *Frozen Food Digest*, October 1, 2007, http://www.entrepreneur.com/tradejournals/article/print/170414529.html.

73. Lilian Ng, "Yeo Takes a Bite of American Market," *Asia Business* 25, no. 12 (December 1989): 18.

74. "Long Ago and Far Away."

75. Lim, "Chow Mein Sandwich," 106.

76. Malcolm Gay, "St. Louie Chop Suey: You Are What You Eat: The Story of a Culture, Told through Its Cuisine," November 15, 2006, St. Louis Riverfronttimes.com. See http://rftstl.com/2006–11–15/news/st-louie-chop-suey/.

77. "China Has Most Things Chinese, But Chop Suey Isn't to Be Found There," *Los Angeles Times*, March 25, 1924.

78. "Chop Suey, Popular Here, Is Hardly Known in China," *New York Times*, November 11, 1928.

79. Frank G. Carpenter, "Old China as Seen in Canton," *Los Angeles Times*, November 9, 1924.

80. Ibid.

81. "China Disowns Chop Suey," *Los Angeles Times*, April 21, 1937.

82. Root and de Rochemont, *Eating America*, 277.

83. "China Has Most Things Chinese."

84. Yu, "Chop Suey," 96.

85. Grace Zia Chu, *The Pleasure of Chinese Cooking* (New York: Simon and Schuster, 1962), 52.

86. Root and de Rochemont, *Eating America*, 277.

87. "Chop Suey Café in Peking Fails—Untraveled Chinese Don't Know About Dish; It's American," *Los Angeles Times*, October 28, 1928.

88. "Chop Suey, Popular Here, Is Hardly Known in China."

89. "Li on American Hatred," *New York Times*, September 3, 1896.

90. Garding Lui, *Inside Los Angeles Chinatown* (Los Angeles: n.p., 1948), 174.

CHAPTER 5   KUNG PAO KOSHER

Though revised extensively, this chapter is based on "Kung Pao Kosher: Jewish Americans and Chinese Restaurants in New York," *Journal of Chinese Overseas* 6, no. 1 (2010): 80–101.

1. Ronald L. Eisenberg, *The 613 Mitzvot: A Contemporary Guide to Commandments to Judaism* (Rockville, Md.: Schreiber Publishing, 2008).

2. Gaye Tuchman and Harry G. Levine, "'Safe Treyf': New York Jews and Chinese Food," in *The Taste of American Place: A Reader on Regional and Ethnic Foods*, ed. Barbara G. Shortridge and James R. Shortridge (New York: Roman and Littlefield, 1997), 163–184.

3. For Jewish Americans' tradition of eating Chinese food on Christmas, see Joshua Eli Plaut, *A Kosher Christmas: 'Tis the Season to Be Jewish* (New Brunswick, N.J.: Rutgers University Press, 2012), especially chapter 3, "We Eat Chinese on Christmas," 65–86.

4. Bill Ong Hing, *Making and Remaking Asian America through Immigration Policy, 1850–1990* (Stanford, Calif.: Stanford University Press, 1993), 47.

5. Roger Daniels, *Coming to America: A History of Immigration and Ethnicity in American Life* (New York: Harper Perennial, 1990), 223–226.

6. "Chinese Play 'King David': Oriental Actors Perform for the Benefit of Jews in Russia," *New York Times*, December 4, 1904.

7. Anna Miller, "Identity Takeout: How American Jews Made Chinese Food Their Ethnic Cuisine," *Journal of Popular Culture* 39, no. 3 (June 2006): 437.

8. Daniels, *Coming to America*, 226.

9. "Child Disappears with His Chinese Friend; Police Find Them Happy in a Movie Theatre," *New York Times*, August 13, 1925.

10. Ibid.

11. Donna R. Gabaccia, *We Are What We Eat: Ethnic Food and the Making of Americans* (Cambridge, Mass.: Harvard University Press, 1998), 69–70.

12. Louis Beck, *New York's Chinatown: A Historical Presentation of People and Places* (New York: Bohemia, 1898), 70.

13. Wong Chin Foo, "The Chinese in New York," *Cosmopolitan* 5 (March–October 1888): 297–311.

14. Gabaccia, *We Are What We Eat*, 104.

15. Beck, *New York's Chinatown*, 49–50.

16. Elizabeth H. Pleck, *Celebrating the Family: Ethnicity, Consumer Culture, and Family Rituals* (Cambridge, Mass.: Harvard University Press, 2000), 97–98.

17. "Yule Stirs Chinese to Aid Jewish Home: Eng Shee Chuck Gives Chow Mein Dinners and Tells Fairy Stories to Children," *New York Times*, December 26, 1935.

18. Roger Nash, *In the Kosher Chow Mein Restaurant* (Sudbury, Ont.: Your Scrivener Press, 1996).

19. Molly Katz, *Jewish as a Second Language* (New York: Workman, 1991), 67.

20. Donald Siegael, *From Lokshen to Lo Mein: The Jewish Love Affairs with Chinese Food, the Kosher Chinese Cookbook* (New York: Gefen Publishing House, 2005).

21. David Margolick, "Jewish Comics Make It a Not So Silent Night," *New York Times*, December 24, 1994.

22. Alex Witchel, "For Some, It Was a Very Moo Shu Christmas," *New York Times*, December 17, 2003.

23. Jennifer 8 Lee, *The Fortune Cookie Chronicles: Adventures in the World of Chinese Food* (New York: Hachette Book Group, 2008), 96.

24. Margolick, "Jewish Comics."

25. Plaut, *Kosher Christmas*, 78.

26. Ibid., 84.

27. Jenna Weissman Joselit, *The Wonders of America: Reinventing Jewish Culture, 1880–1950* (New York: Hill and Wang, 1994), 214.

28. Michael Luo, "As All American as Egg Foo Yong," *New York Times*, September 24, 2004.

29. Mimi Sheraton, "Moo Goo Gai Pan and Strictly Kosher," *New York Times*, December 27, 1980.

30. Mimi Sheraton, "A Jewish Yen for Chinese," *New York Times*, September 23, 1990.

31. Ibid.

32. Mimi Sheraton, "Restaurants: Japanese-French and Chinese-Jewish," *New York Times*, March 11, 1977.

33. Miller, "Identity Takeout," 453.

34. Paul Lukas, "The Right Chinese Food for Christmas," *New York Sun*, December 20, 2006.

35. Ted Roberts, "There's Nothing New under the Sun (Especially Chicken Feet)," www.jewishworkreview.com/0298/chicken.html.

36. Pete Cherches, "Chinese Food, the Early Years," http://petercherches.blogsort.com/2007/07chinese-food-early-years.html.

37. This information is based on an e-mail exchange from Laurie Shrage on May 21, 2007.

38. Beth Kressel, "Adaptation Helps Diners Enjoy Jewish Holiday," *Hillsborough Beacon*, October 23, 2003.

39. Ching-Ching Ni, "The Challenge of Keeping China Kosher," *Los Angeles Times*, February 5, 2008.

40. Lee, *Fortune Cookie Chronicles*, 97.

41. Gabaccia, *We Are What We Eat*, 64.

42. Ibid., 81.

43. Ibid.
44. *Chop Suey* is one of most famous pieces of art by Edward Hopper, who painted it 1929.
45. Tuchman and Levine, "Safe Treyf," 73.
46. Miller, "Identity Takeout," 456.
47. Richard J. Hooker, *Food and Drink in America: A History* (New York: Bobbs-Merrill, 1978), 323.
48. Bruce Edward Hall, *Tea That Burns: A Family Memoir of Chinatown* (New York: Free Press, 1998).
49. A-Cheng, *The Jews in Harbin: He Shangdi yiqi liulang; youtai ren ha-er-bin binan ji* (Traveling with God: Jews' Exile Life in Harbin) (Chongqing: Chongqing Publishing Group, 2008), 307. Harbin is a city in northeast China.
50. Luo Suwen, *Jindai Shanghai: Dushi shehui yu shenghuo* (Modern Shanghai: Metropolitan Life and Society) (Beijing: Zhonghua Press, 2006), 218.
51. Miller, "Identity Takeout," 458.

CHAPTER 6   GENERAL TSO'S CHICKEN MADE IN TAIWAN

1. Jennifer 8 Lee, *The Fortune Cookie Chronicles: Adventures in the World of Chinese Food* (New York: Hachette Book Group, 2008), 81–82.
2. Franklin Ng, *The Taiwanese Americans* (Westport, Conn.: Greenwood Press, 1998), 124.
3. For a description of Chinese regional cuisines from a culinary perspective, see Francine Halvorsen, The Food and Cooking of China: An Exploration of Chinese Cuisine in the Provinces and Cities of China, Hong Kong, and Taiwan (New York: J. Wiley, 1996).
4. Jacques Gernet, *Daily Life in China: On the Eve of the Mongol Invasion 1250–1276* (Stanford, Calif.: Stanford University Press, 1970), 134.
5. Jonathan D. Spence, "Food," in *Chinese Roundabout: Essays in History and Culture* (New York: W. W. Norton, 1992), 203.
6. Mark Swislocki, *Culinary Nostalgia: Regional Food Culture and the Urban Experience in Shanghai* (Stanford, Calif.: Stanford University Press, 2009), 147.
7. Most of those restaurants are still open in Beijing.
8. Craig Claiborne, "For Food Lovers Enamored of Chinese Cooking, Taipei Is the Place to Visit," *New York Times*, December 23, 1968.
9. Murray A. Rubinstein, "Taiwan's Socioeconomic Modernization, 1971–1996," in *Taiwan: A New History*, ed. Murray A. Rubinstein (New York: M. E. Sharpe, 2007), 377–378.
10. Peter Chen-main Wang, "A Bastion Created, Regime Reformed, Economy Reestablished, an Economy Reengineered, 1949–1970," in Rubinstein, *Taiwan*, 329.
11. Iris Chang, *A History of Chinese in America: A Narrative History* (New York: Penguin Group, 2003), 286.
12. Huping Ling, *Surviving on the Gold Mountain: A History of Chinese American Women and Their Lives* (Albany: State University of New York Press, 1998), 150.
13. Zhuang Guotu, *Huaqiao huaren yu zhongguo de guanxi* (Relationship between Overseas Chinese and China) (Guangzhou, China: Guangdong High Education Press, 2001), 480. According to another source, from 1950 to 1974 a total of 30,765 students from Taiwan came to American colleges and universities. See Ling, *Surviving on the Gold Mountain*, 150.
14. David M. Reimers, *Still the Golden Door: The Third World Comes to America* (New York: Columbia University Press, 1985), 103.
15. Ronald Takaki, *Strangers from a Different Shore: A History of Asian Americans* (Boston: Little, Brown, 1989), 422.

16. Charles C. Wong, *Monterey Park: A Community Transition* (Pullman: Washington State University Press, 1998).

17. Ng, *Taiwanese Americans*, 2.

18. For a dramatic description of the Nationalists' escape, see the best seller Lung Ying-tai *Da Jiang Da Hai 1949* (Big River, Big Sea—Untold Stories of 1949) (Taibei: Tian xia za zhi gu fen you xian gong si, 2009).

19. Chang, *Chinese in America*, 283; Ng, *Taiwanese Americans*, 10. See also Zhiqing Cui, "Taiwan: lishi, xianzhuan he qianzhan (Taiwan: History, Status quo and Future)" April 17, 2007, http://www.njass.org.cn.

20. See Bai Xianyong *Taibei Ren* (Taipei Residents) (Guangzhou, China: Huacheng Press, 2004); Jiang Xun, *Tiandi you da mei* (Great Beauty on Earth) (Nanning, Guangxi: Guangxi Normal University Press, 2006); Zhu Tianxin, *Xiang wo juancun de xiongdi men* (I Miss My Buddies in the Military Quarter) (Taipei: Maitian Press, 1992); and Su Weizhen, *Youyuan qianli* (Sheer Luck) (Taipei: Hongfan Press, 1993).

21. Dihua is a city in Xinjiang Province.

22. John Bodnar, *Remaking America: Public Memory* (Princeton, N.J.: Princeton University, 1992), 15. Bodnar offers an insightful theoretical discussion on public memory. However, the concept of "public memory" is different from that of "collective memory" used in this chapter. While "public memory" is mainly associated with the government's political agenda, "collective memory" is about cultural traditions that followed the mainlander emigrants to Taiwan.

23. Wang, "Bastion Created," 325.

24. John Liu and Lucie Cheng, "Pacific Rim Development and the Duality of Post-1965 Asian Immigration to the United States," in *The New Asian Immigration in Los Angeles and Global Restructuring*, ed. Pual Ong, Edna Bonacich, and Lucie Cheng (Philadelphia: Temple University Press, 1994), 76.

25. Chang, *Chinese in America*, 292.

26. Wang, "Bastion Created," 333.

27. Jack F. Williams, "Who Are the Taiwanese? Taiwan in the Chinese Diaspora," in *The Chinese Diaspora: Space, Place, Mobility, and Identity*, ed. Laurence J. C. Ma and Carolyn Cartier (New York: Rowman & Littlefield, 2003), 178.

28. Chen Benchang, *Meiguo Huaqiao Canguan Gongye* (Chinese Restaurant Business in America) (Taipei: Taiwan Far-East Publisher, 1971), 162, 216.

29. The best description of various restaurants in Taipei are in Shu Guozhi, Qiongzhong tan chi: Taiwan wushi nian chifan zhi jianwen (How to Eat When Being Poor: Fifty Years of Anecdotes from Frequenting Taiwan Restaurants) (Taipei: Lianhe Wenxue Press, 2008); Shu Guozhi, Taiwan xiaochi zhaji (Taiwan Food Market) (Taipei: Huangguan Press, 2007).

30. David Y. H. Wu, "McDonald's in Taipei: Hamburgers, Betel Nuts, and National Identity," in *Golden Arches East: McDonald's in East Asia*, ed. James L. Watson (Stanford, Calif.: Stanford University Press, 1997), 111.

31. Bai Xianyong (Hsien-yung Pai) is the son of a famous Nationalist general, Bai Chongxi, a Guangxi native. Changchun is a city in Jilin Province in northeast China.

32. Bai Xianyong, "Huaqiao Rong Ji" (Huaqiao Rong Family Restaurant), in *Bai Xianyoung zi xuan ji* (Self-Selected Anthology of Bai Xianyoung) (Guangzhou, China: Huacheng Publisher, 2009), 171–180.

33. Fox Butterfield, "Echoes of China Just Off the Mainland China: In Taiwan, Culinary Pleasures and Artistic Treasures," *New York Times*, September 16, 1984.

34. David Y. H. Wu and Sidney C. H. Cheung, "Introduction: The Globalization of Chinese Food and Cuisine: Markers and Breakers of Cultural Barriers" in *The Globalization of Chinese*

Food, ed. David Y. H. Wu and Sidney C. H. Cheung (Honolulu: University of Hawaii Press, 2002), 8.

35. Myron L. Cohen, "Being Chinese: The Peripheralization of Traditional Identity," in *The Living Tree: The Changing Meaning of Being Chinese Today*, ed. Tu Wei-ming (Stanford, Calif.: Stanford University Press, 1994), 96.

36. However, many food scenes were cut in the final version of the movie.

37. "Grandma's Kitchen: Eat Drink Man Woman—Starring . . . Food," http://www .jadedragon.com/archives/cooking/eatdrink.html.

38. Lin Huei-Yi, *Yinshi Nannu Shipu* (*Recipes of Eat Drink Man Woman*) (Taipei: Taolue, 1994).

39. http://ent.sina.com.cn/m/c/2006–06–19/14121128372.html. Cantonese cuisine characterizes the style of his movie *Pushing Hands*, Sichuan cuisine his *Wedding Banquet*, and Zhejiang cuisine his *Eat Drink Man Woman*.

40. David Y. H. Wu, "Cantonese Cuisine (Yue-cai) in Taiwan and Taiwanese Cuisine (Taicai) in Hong Kong," in Wu and Cheung, *Globalization of Chinese Food*, 87.

41. Fuchsia Dunlop, "Hunan Resources," *New York Times Magazine*, February 4, 2007, Section 6, 75; Michael Browning, "Who Was General Tso and Why Are We Eating His Chicken?," *Washington Post*, April 17, 2002.

42. See "Cooking General Tso's Chicken Again at the Age of 96 by the 'Royal' Chef of the Chiang Family" (Jiangjia "yuchu" 96 sui zaizuo "zuozongtang ji"), http://www.wenxuecity .com/news/2014/05/30.

43. Wang Gungwu, "Among Non-Chinese," in Wei-ming, *Living Tree*, 128.

44. Williams, "Who Are the Taiwanese?," 163.

45. The only exception was the famous Tan family cuisine developed by Cao Si (Cao Jinchen), a famous family chef of Governor Tan Yankai, the last Hunan governor in the late Qing Dynasty and the first prime minister of the Nationalist government. The famous Tan family cuisine was refined, was mild in flavor, and included seafood such as sharks' fins.

46. Shi Yinxiang, *Xiang cai jin ji* (A Collection of Hunan Recipes) (Changsha, Hunan: Hunan Kexu Jishu, 1983).

47. Barbara Tropp, *The Modern Art of Chinese Cooking Techniques and Recipes* (New York: Hearst Books, 1982), 140.

48. Zhou Sanjin, ed., *Zhong guo ming cai jing hua* (Taipei: Diteng Chuban Tushu Youxian, 1999), 209–211.

49. General Tso's chicken figured prominently in another Lee film, *Pushing Hands*.

50. Kenneth Lo, *Chinese Food: An Introduction to One of the World's Great Cuisines* (London: Penguin Group, 1972), 65.

51. Lee, *Fortune Cookie Chronicles*, 79.

52. Craig Claiborne, "A Chef Recalls the Long Road from Shanghai," *New York Times*, January 25, 1975.

53. *New York Times*, July 27, 1973.

54. Lynn Pan, *Sons of the Yellow Emperor: A History of Chinese Diaspora* (New York: Little, Brown, 1990), 334.

55. Mimi Sheraton, "Restaurants," *New York Times*, December 16, 1977.

56. Michael Luo, "As All American as Egg Foo Yong," *New York Times*, September 24, 2004.

57. Ralph Blumerthal, "Chinese Restaurants Flower Following Diplomatic Thaw," *New York Times*, July 27, 1972.

58. Andrew Coe, *Chop Suey: A Cultural History of Chinese Food* (New York: Oxford University Press, 2009), 240.

59. Blumerthal, "Chinese Restaurants Flower."

60. Williams, "Who Are the Taiwanese?," 163.

61. Alex Yannis, "Secretary Vance Get Wishes: Chinese Ties Cosmos," *New York Times*, October 9, 1977.

62. Patricia Brooks, "Skillfully Spiced Hunan Fare," *New York Times*, October 9, 1977.

63. M. H. Reed, "Sichuan Cuisine: Another Source," *New York Times*, November 9, 1980.

64. Brooks, "Skillfully Spiced Hunan Fare."

65. M. H. Reed, "A Convenient Hunan Restaurant," *New York Times*, November 9, 1986.

66. Lee, *Fortune Cookie Chronicles*, 82–83.

67. "Bei ma yingjiu shangshi: xiangmei Taiwan chuangye ji" (Hunan Girl's Business in Taiwan When Blessed by Ma Yingjiu), *Chengshi jinrong bao* (城市金融报 City Financial News), May 23, 2009, www.csjaw.cn.

68. Zhou Min, *Contemporary Chinese America: Immigration, Ethnicity, and Community Transportation* (Philadelphia: Temple University Press, 2009), 105.

69. http://www.restaurant.org/pressroom/.

70. Harvey Levenstein, *Revolution at the Table: The Transformation of the American Diet* (Berkeley: University of California Press, 2003), 206–207.

CHAPTER 7   SAN GABRIEL VALLEY AS A CAPITAL OF CHINESE FOOD

This chapter is based on an article published in 2009, although it has been considerably revised. Discussion on Sam Woo Restaurant, Chinese grocery stores such as 99 Ranch Supermarket, or other Asians in San Gabriel Valley is newly added information. See Haiming Liu and Lianlian Lin, "Food, Culinary Identity, and Transnational Culture: Chinese Restaurant Business in Southern California," *Journal of Asian American Studies* 12, no. 2 (June 2009): 135–162.

1. For the closing and history of General Lee's, see David Holley, "General Lee's Bows to Change after Century of Service," *Los Angeles Times*, October 11, 1985. However, according to another article, "From Chop Suey to Chiu Chow," by Charles Perry of the *Los Angeles Times*, February 21, 2007, the menu of this restaurant in the 1950s gave its founding date as 1890. By 1900, there were but two or three Chinese restaurants, frequented mostly by Chinese, in Los Angeles's Chinatown. Man Jen Low was one of them. The restaurant became known as General Lee's in the 1950s as the owner was a World War II veteran (but not a general) and was the grandson of the founder. The original Man Jen Low was first located outside Chinatown, then moved to a three-story building in the old Chinatown; it moved to New (that is, present-day) Chinatown after old Chinatown was torn down in 1933 to make way for the Union Station. New Chinatown was built in 1938.

2. William Mason, "The Chinese in Los Angeles," *Museum Alliance Quarterly* 6, no. 2 (Fall 1967): 16.

3. Ivan Light, "From Vice District to Tourist Attraction: The Moral Career of American Chinatown, 1880–1940," *Pacific Historical Review* 43 (1974): 367–394, quoted in J. A. G. Roberts, *China to Chinatown: Chinese Food in the West* (London: Reaktion Books, 2000), 148.

4. Henry Shih-shan Tsai, *The Chinese Experience in America* (Bloomington: Indiana University Press, 1986), 105. In Ronald Takaki's estimate, 12,559 out of 45,614 were laundrymen, and therefore there were probably more Chinese working in restaurants than in laundries. See Ronald Takaki, *Strangers from a Different Shore: A History of Asian Americans* (Boston: Little, Brown, 1989), 240. The 1920 census indicates that of the 45,614 Chinese employed, 11,438 were cooks, waiters, and/or restaurants operators.

5. Mai Liqian (Lai, Him Mark), *Cong huaqiao dao huaren: Ershi shiji meiguo huaren shehui fazhan shi* (From Overseas Chinese to Chinese Americans: A History of 20th Century

Chinese American Social and Economic Development) (Hong Kong: San Lian Press, Joint Publishing H. K. Co., 1992), 85.

6. Takaki, *Strangers from a Different Shore*, 267.

7. Mai, *Cong huaqiao dao huaren*, 393.

8. For the recipe and menu of these two and other Americanized Chinese dishes, see Alice Miller Mitchell, *Oriental Cookbook* (Chicago: Rand McNally, 1950), 11–12.

9. Chen Benchang, *Meiguo huaqiao canguan gongye* (Chinese Restaurant Business in America) (Taipei: Taiwan Far-East Publisher, 1971), 216.

10. Takaki, *Strangers from a Different Shore*, 421.

11. Zhuang Guotu, *Huaqiao huaren yu Zhongguo de guanxi* (Relationship between Overseas Chinese and China) (Guangzhou, China: Guangdong Gaodeng Jiaoyu Press, 2001), 480.

12. Karl Schoenberger, "Breathing Life into Southland from Mainland Millionaires to Grad Students, a 'New Wave' of Chinese Immigrants Is Invigorating the Economy," Los Angeles Times, October 4, 1993.

13. Min Zhou, *Chinatown: The Socioeconomic Potential of an Urban Enclave* (Philadelphia: Temple University Press, 1992), 14.

14. Tsai, *Chinese Experience in America*, 149.

15. Mai, *Cong huaqiao dao huaren*, 394.

16. According to Tsai, the percentage of Chinese in professional and technical occupations increased from 2.8 to 26.5 percent between 1940 and 1960. Tsai, *Chinese Experience*, 195. According to S. T. Yuan, the number of Chinese living in the Bay Area suburbs quadrupled. S. T. Yuan, *Chinese American Population* (Hong Kong: UEA Press, 1988), 61–62.

17. Daryl E. Lembke, "And More Immigrants Pour In," Los Angeles Times, December 18, 1966.

18. Jerry Hulse, "Chinatown Changing as Suburbs Call Residents," Los Angeles Times, October 26, 1959.

19. Jean Murphy, "Chinese Immigrants Learning English," Los Angeles Times, December 19, 1969.

20. Penelope McMillan, "L.A.'s Chinatown Turns from Tourists to the Chinese," Los Angeles Times, September 18, 1977.

21. Ibid.

22. I have learned this information from Gilbert Hom, a member of Chinese Historical Society of Southern California.

23. "Training Under Way to Ease Shortage of Chinese Cooks," Los Angeles Times, August 24, 1973.

24. Chen, *Meiguo huaqiao canguan gongye*, 207.

25. Lois Dwan, "Restaurants," Los Angeles Times, May 11, 1980.

26. Barbara Hansen, "All Lucky Asian Lure," Los Angeles Times, June 11, 1981.

27. This number is based on information collected from *Chinese Consumer Yellow Pages 1997* and *Chinese Yellow Pages 1997*. The actual number should be larger, as there were restaurants that did not advertise in these two telephone books.

28. Wei Li, "Building Ethnoburbia: The Emergence and Manifestation of the Chinese Ethnoburb in Los Angeles' San Gabriel Valley," *Journal of Asian American Studies* 2, no. 1 (February 1999): 7–8.

29. Ibid., 5.

30. Tim Fong, *The First Suburban Chinatown: The Making of Monterey Park, California* (Philadelphia: Temple University Press, 1994), 26. For the population, see Li, "Building Ethnoburbia," 5.

31. Penelope McMillan, "Influx in Monterey Park," Los Angeles Times, April 13, 1980.

32. Steve Harvey, "Sings the Blues without Locust's Song," *Los Angeles Times*, April 5, 1983.

33. Fong, *First Suburban Chinatown*, 43–44.

34. Mark Arax, "Monterey Park Nation's 1st Suburban Chinatown," Los Angeles Times, April 6, 1987.

35. Ibid.

36. Ibid.

37. Mike Ward, "Cities Report Growth—and Some Losses—From Asian Business," Los Angeles Times, April 19, 1987.

38. Fong, *First Suburban Chinatown*, 62.

39. Arax, "Monterey Park Nation's 1st Suburban Chinatown."

40. Li, "Building Ethnoburbia," 9.

41. Shawn Hubler, "A Feeding Frenzy in the 'New Chinatown,'" *Los Angeles Times*, December 5, 1995.

42. Mark Arax, "Family Elders Cling to Old Ways as Young Look to New," *Los Angeles Times*, April 16, 1987.

43. Max Jacobson, "Top 10: A Guide to the Middle Kingdom," Los Angeles Times, October 26, 1986.

44. Huping Ling, "Reconceptualizing Chinese American Community in St. Louis: From Chinatown to Cultural Community," *Journal of American Ethnic History* 24, no. 2 (Winter 2005): 65–101.

45. Arax, "Monterey Park Nation's 1st Suburban Chinatown."

46. Randye Hoder, "A Passion for Asian Foods Markets: City Officials Suspect That Many Non-Residents Flock to Monterey Park for Its Specialty Food Stores," Los Angeles Times, June 6, 1991.

47. Hubler, "Feeding Frenzy."

48. Mike Ward, "Monterey Park Is Truly All American City," Los Angeles Times, June 27, 1985.

49. McMillan, "Influx in Monterey Park."

50. Mark Arax, "Selling Out, Moving On, Some Old-Timers Flee the Congestion, Density, and Unfamiliarity of 'Little China,'" *Los Angeles Times*, April 12, 1987.

51. Asian Pacific American Legal Center of Southern California, *The Diverse Face of Asians and Pacific Islanders in Los Angeles County* (Los Angeles: Asian Pacific American Legal Center of Southern California, 2004), 49.

52. Ibid., 7. See also the 2000 census from www.census.gov.

53. Schoenberger, "Breathing Life into Southland."

54. Hubler, "Feeding Frenzy."

55. Ibid.

56. Stephanie Chavez, "New Look Reflects an Old Pattern," *Los Angeles Times*, July 25, 2004.

57. Ward, "Cities Report Growth."

58. Hubler, "Feeding Frenzy."

59. Ibid.

60. Max Jacobson, "Eats; O.C. ON THE MENU; Sam Woo Sees the Lite; 23rd Restaurant in Chain Breaks Rank in a Health-Conscious Way," *Los Angeles Times*, April 3, 1997.

61. Hubler, "Feeding Frenzy."

62. Chavez, "New Look."

63. David Pierson, "Dragon Roars in San Gabriel," *Los Angeles Times*, March 31, 2006.

64. Charles Perry, "Where the Action Is: From Dim Sum to Pastry, the New Hot Spot for Chinese Food Is San Gabriel's Valley Boulevard," *Los Angeles Times*, January 15, 2003.

65. Chavez, "New Look."

66. Mark Arax, "Family Finds Affinity for American Life," Los Angeles Times, April 19, 1987.

67. Schoenberger, "Breathing Life into Southland."

68. Iris Chang, The Chinese in American: A Narrative History (New York: Penguin Group, 2003), 283.

69. Arax, "Family Elders Cling to Old Ways."

70. Chavez, "New Look."

71. Charles Perry and Linda Burum, "Real Fireworks: A Burst of Innovation Has Electrified the Local Dim Sum Scene," Los Angeles Times, January 26, 2005.

72. Mark Arax, "Taiwanese Native Pursues American Ways: A Woman of Independent Mind," Los Angeles Times, April 6, 1987.

73. Terrance J. Reeves and Claudette E Bennett, We the People: Asians in the United States— Special Report (U.S Census Bureau, December 2004), 11.

74. The Los Angeles Times 1997 survey indicated that 79 percent of the Chinese in Southern California spoke Chinese at home. K. Connie Kang, "Chinese in the Southland: A Changing Picture," Los Angeles Times, June 27, 1997.

75. Joe Chung Fong, "Transnational Newspapers: The Making of the Post-1965 Globalized/ Localized San Gabriel Valley Chinese Community," Amerasia Journal 22, no. 3 (1996): 65–77; Mary Curtius, "A Coming of Age for S.F. Chinese," Los Angeles Times, October 11, 1999.

76. Karen Robinson-Jacobs, "Asian, Pacific Islander Firms Surging in U.S.," Los Angeles Times, May 22, 2001.

77. Mark Arax, "San Gabriel Valley Asian Influx Alters Life in Suburbia," Los Angeles Times, April 5, 1987.

78. Arax, "Family Finds Affinity for American Life."

CHAPTER 8   WHO OWNS CULTURE?

1. Linda Loi, "So We Don't End Up Like Chop Suey: Searching for Authentic Chinese Food in L.A.," http://www.sscnet.ucla.edu/aasc/classweb/fa1197/M163/loi5.html.

2. Johnny Kan himself tried to change the image of Chinese restaurants as cheap, convenient eateries. His Kan's Restaurant (Guan yuan) was a high-end dining destination for celebrities such as Herb Caen and tourists across the country. As an American-born Chinese, Kan featured mainly Cantonese cuisine, and many dishes were Americanized in flavor. According to Madeline Hsu, however, Kan's Restaurant in San Francisco's Chinatown should be considered the first Chinese restaurant to push for authentic Chinese food. See Madeline Y. Hsu, "From Chop Suey to Mandarin Cuisine: Fine Dining and the Refashioning of Chinese Ethnicity during the Cold War Era," in Chinese Americans and the Politics of Race and Culture, ed. Sucheng Chan and Madeline Yuan-yin Hsu (Philadelphia: Temple University Press, 2008), 173–193.

3. Much of the following information about Cecelia Chiang was based on the presentations by Emerald Yeh and others at the Eighth Annual Asian Pacific Fund Gala by board member and journalist Emerald Yeh. See http://www.asianpacificfund.org/awards/bio_chiang .shtml; Hsu, "From Chop Suey to Mandarin Cuisine"; and Cecilia Chiang with Lisa Weiss, The Seventh Daughter: My Culinary Journey from Beijing to San Francisco (Berkeley, Calif.: Ten Speed Press, 2007).

4. Chen Beichang, Meiguo huaqiao canguan gongye (Chinese Restaurant Business in America) (Taipei: Taiwan Far East Book, 1971), 298–314.

5. See http://www.asianpacificfund.org/awards/bio_chiang.shtml.

6. Ibid.

7. Ibid.

8. Ibid.

9. Ruth Reichl, "Mandarin: The Next Generation New Menu Spices Up Beverly Hills' Premier Chinese Restaurant," *Los Angeles Times*, February 26, 1989.

10. Loi, "So We Don't End Up Like Chop Suey."

11. Ibid.

12. Ibid.

13. Reichl, "Mandarin."

14. Joel Kotkin, "Will Chinese Food Go the Way of Pizza?," *New York Times*, March 26, 2000.

15. Barbara Tropp, *The Modern Art of Chinese Cooking: Techniques and Recipes* (New York: William Morrow, 1982).

16. Max Jacobson, "P. F. Chang's Explores New Dimensions but Stays Flat in Places," *Los Angeles Times*, March 21, 1996.

17. Bret Thorn, "Paul Muller: Creating a Stir and Frying Up a Storm at P. F. Chang's China Bistro," *Nation's Restaurant News*, January 27, 2003, http://www.findarticles.com/p/articles/mi_m3190/is_4_37/ai_97314555/pg_1.

18. Ibid.

19. Ibid.

20. Ibid.

21. Donna Gabaccia, *We Are What We Eat: Ethnic Food and the Making of Americans* (Cambridge, Mass.: Harvard University Press, 1998), 218.

22. Min Zhou, *Contemporary Chinese America: Immigration, Ethnicity, and Community Transformation* (Philadelphia: Temple University Press, 2009), 105.

23. Min Zhou, *Chinatown: The Socioeconomic Potential of an Urban Enclave* (Philadelphia: Temple University Press, 1992), 99.

24. Kotkin, "Will Chinese Food Go the Way of Pizza?"

25. Cynthia Mines. "Chinese Chain: Steaming with Success," May 1, 2000. http://retailtrafficmag.com/mag/retail_chinese_chain_steaming.

26. Ibid.

27. Ibid.

28. Kotkin, "Will Chinese Food Go the Way of Pizza?"

29. Company information: P. F. Chang's China Bistro, Inc., in *New York Times*, September 12, 2009, and www.pfcb.com.

30. For a theoretical discussion of cultural ownership, see Susan Scafidi, *Who Owns Culture? Appropriation and Authenticity in American Law* (New Brunswick, N.J.: Rutgers University Press, 2005).

31. James Flanigan, "Cooking Up a Powerhouse of Chinese Fast Food," *Los Angeles Times*, October 8, 2001.

32. www.pandar.com.

33. Flanigan, "Cooking Up a Powerhouse."

34. Ibid.

35. Eric Schlosser, *Fast Food Nation: The Dark Side of the All-American Meal* (New York: Houghton Mifflin, 2001), 198.

36. Matt Krantz, "Panda Express Spreads Chinese Food across USA," *USA Today*, September 11, 2006. See http://www.peiwei.com/#/home.

37. Julie Tamaki, "Far East Restaurant Battle Heating Up on West Coast; Asian Chains Are Competing to Dominate the Southland Market and Growing in Spite of Obstacles," *Los Angeles Times*, September 6, 2004.

38. Krantz, "Panda Express."

39. http://www.pandarg.com/default.asp?nav=about.

40. Leslie Earnest, "O.C. BUSINESS PLUS; HEARD ON THE BEAT / RETAIL; Chain Is Not Only In-N-Out, It Lands on Top in a Survey," *Los Angeles Times*, March 6, 2001.

41. Ron Ruggless, "Panda Express Takes to Street with Push for Freestanding Units," *Nation's Restaurant News*, August 9, 2004, http://findarticles.com/p/articles.

42. Krantz, "Panda Express."

43. Panda Express: Gourmet Chinese Food, "About Panda: Frequently Asked Questions," Panda Restaurant Group Inc., http://www.pandaexpress.com/contact/.

44. "The QSR 50," QSR Report, QSR magazine.com, http://www.qsrmagazine.com/reports/qsr50/2008/asian.phtml.

45. Krantz, "Panda Express."

46. Jerry Hirsch, "Want Rice with That? Serving up 45 Million Pounds of Orange Chicken a Year, Panda Express Has Become a Fast-Food Powerhouse," *Los Angeles Times*, August 13, 2008.

47. Panda Express: Gourmet Chinese Food, "Menu Items," Panda Restaurant Group, Inc., http://www.pandaexpress.com/menu/menu-items_flash.aspx.

48. Betty Shimabukuro, "Orange Chicken on the House: Panda Express Marks 20 Years in Hawaii with Major Plans for Expansion," *Star Bulletin*, January 17, 2007, Features section.

49. Panda Express: Gourmet Chinese Food, "Menu Items."

50. Hirsch, "Want Rice with That?"

51. "Cherng Gift," *City News Service*, May 25, 2001; Cecilia Kang, "Asian-American Philanthropist Determined to Share Money, Vision," *San Jose Mercury News*, August 16, 2002.

52. "Panda Express Hosts Chinese New Year Events for 8,000 Students at More Than 75 California Schools," *Business Wire*, January 20, 2006; "Andrew and Peggy Cherng of Panda Restaurant Group Receive City of Angels Award Honoring Contributions to the Los Angeles Area," *Business Wire*, February 8, 2008.

53. Gabaccia, *We Are What We Eat*, 170.

54. Chris Woodyard, "American Appetite for Asian Food Stirs a Rush to Set Up Fast-Food Chains," Los Angeles Times, December 13, 1992.

55. Zhou, *Contemporary Chinese America*, 98.

56. Woodyard, "American Appetite."

57. Krantz, "Panda Express."

58. http://www.pickupstix.com/about.php.

59. Flanigan, "Cooking Up a Powerhouse."

60. http://www.manchuwok.com.

61. Woodyard, "American Appetite."

62. http://www.ricegarden.biz/aboutus.php.

63. "12 nian qush youdao, 81 dian xinxian dangjia" (Twelve Years' Good Management and Eighty-one Store Ownership), *Zhongcan Tongxun* (Chinese Restaurant News) 12, no. 6 (June 2006): 12–16.

64. http://www.markpi.com/history.htm.

65. Woodyard, "American Appetite."

66. Shun Lu and Gary Alan Fine, "The Presentation of Ethnic Authenticity: Chinese Food as a Social Accomplishment," *Sociological Quarterly* 36, no. 3 (1995): 535–553.

67. David Pierson, "Pushing to Make the A-List: Chinese American Community Leaders Are Working to Alter the Attitudes of Restaurant Owners and Patrons Regarding Food Safety," *Los Angeles Times*, October 5, 2005.

68. See http://www.sanmarinochamber.org/directory.

69. See Los Angeles County's website: www.lapublichealth.org. Though the county's rating information did not differentiate types of restaurants according to their ethnic background, it was still possible to identify Chinese restaurants based on their names when I verified them in the *Chinese Yellow Pages.*

70. David Pierson, "Where 'A' Is Not on the Menu: Chinese Eateries in an L.A. County Enclave Struggle with Hygiene Ratings," *Los Angeles Times,* September 28, 2005.

71. Ibid.

72. Ibid.

73. Ibid.

74. "A Cultural Tour to Chinese Restaurants," *Zhongcan Tongxun* (June 2006): 164. *Zhongcan Tongxun* (Chinese Restaurant News) is a journal published by Smart Business Services, Inc. at 47428 Fremont Blvd., Fremont, CA 94538. According to another source, the total number of Chinese restaurants in the United States is 36,000. See "Chinese Immigrants Keep US Well Fed," in NY TIMES NEWS SERVICE, NEW YORK, October 9, 2005, 4, http://www .taipeitimes.com/News/world/archives/2005/10/09/2003275064. Most media reports about Chinese restaurants in the United States agreed to 40,000 as a total number of Chinese restaurants in the 2000s. In the same decades, the total number of McDonald's restaurants in the world was 30,000; Burger King, 11,100; and Wendy's, 6,600. Combined, the total number of the restaurants of these three companies was 47,700. However, the total number of McDonald's restaurants in the United States was only 13,774. The total number of Burger Kings in the United States and Canada was 7,482. The total number of Wendy's was 6,300. Combined, the total number of these restaurants is 27,556, which was obviously smaller than the total number of Chinese restaurants. See http://www.mcdonalds.com/corp/invest/pub/2006; Burger King Holdings, Inc. Second Quarter Fiscal 2008 Earnings, January 31, 2008, www.burgerking.com/bkglobal; and http://www.wendys-invest.com. Most of the McDonald's were outside the United States, and Burger King was trying to catch up, as it only had 3,800 restaurants overseas.

CHAPTER 9   DIN TAI FUNG AS A GLOBAL DUMPLING HOUSE

Though considerably revised, this chapter is based on my article "Flexible Authenticity: Din Tai Fung as a Global Shanghai Dumpling House Made in Taiwan," *Chinese America: History and Perspectives* (2011): 57–65.

1. http://www.nsc.gov.tw/int/ct.asp?xItem=12554&ctNode=2865; http://wwwga.epochtimes .com/b5/7/12/13/n1940660.htm.

2. Nanxiang is a suburb northwest of Shanghai City. In the late nineteenth century, a small restaurant owner, Huang Mingxian, in Nanxiang became famous for his delicious steamed breads and dumplings. Other restaurants in Nanxiang imitated his products, which gradually made the whole town famous for making steamed dumplings. Huang was later invited to open restaurants in Shanghai, and his dumplings became popular throughout the city. Nanxiang Bun Shop in Yu Yuan Park in Shanghai is still a major attraction to both local and tourist customers today.

3. I have not found this report in the *New York Times* in 1993.

4. Xiaoqing Xu and Jun Geng, "Ta Fang Taibei Shanghai Jie" (Tour around the "Shanghai Street" in Taipei), December 24, 2008, http://news.xinhuanet.com.

5. E. N. Anderson, *The Food of China* (New Haven, Conn.: Yale University Press, 1988), 196–197.

6. Bai Xianyoung (Hien-yung Pei), "The Forever Yi Xueyan," in *Bai Xianyoung zi xuan ji* (Self-Selected Anthology of Bai Xianyoung) (Guangzhou, China: Huacheng Publisher, 2009), 100.

7. Mei Wang, *Ding Tai Feng Chuanqi* (The Din Tai Fung Legend) (Taipei: Tianxia Yuanjian, 2000), 31.

8. Ibid., 42.

9. Ibid., 34.

10. Ibid., 42.

11. Ibid., 62.

12. Ibid., 93.

13. Ibid., 8–10.

14. "Din Tai Fung Joins MOFA Food Tour," *Taipei Times*, January 26, 2008, http://www.taipeitimes.com/News/taiwan/archives/2008/01/26/2003398879.

15. Lin Huei-Yi, *Yinshi Nannu Shipu* (Recipes of *Eat Drink Man Woman*) (Taipei: Taolue, 1994), 3.

16. Wang, *Ding Tai Feng Chuanqi*, 179.

17. "Din Tai Fung Joins MOFA Food Tour."

18. Wang, *Ding Tai Feng Chuanqi*, 170.

19. Yasmin Tong, "An Honorable House: A Loyal Son Opens a Dumpling Restaurant in Arcadia to Preserve His Family's Reputation," *Los Angeles Times*, March 20, 2002.

20. Ibid.

21. Wang, *Ding Tai Feng Chuanqi*, 161.

22. Tong, "Honorable House."

23. http://www.dintaifung.com.

24. Jack F. Williams, "Who Are the Taiwanese? Taiwan in the Chinese Diaspora," in *The Chinese Diaspora: Space, Place, Mobility, and Identity*, ed. Laurence J. C. Ma and Carolyn Cartier (New York: Rowman & Littlefield, 2003), 180.

25. http://www.shtwo.gov.cn/CHT/newsdetail.aspx?id=4261.

26. Tong, "Honorable House."

27. Li Yi, "Tai zhuming xiaolong ding tai feng denglu shencheng" (Famous Din Tai Fung from Taiwan Landed in Shanghai), November 29, 2003, http://www.dintaifung.com.

28. Li Weina, "Baimu yuan li le gengyun" (The Joyful Operation of Banmu Yuan), *People's Daily* (overseas edition), February 8, 2007.

29. "Banmu yuan lucheng fendian huanran yi xin" (The Remodeling of A & J Restaurant in Maryland), *Zhongcan Tongxun* (Chinese Restaurant News) 8, no. 5 (May 2002): 66.

SELECTED BIBLIOGRAPHY

NEWSPAPERS AND MAGAZINES

American Heritage
Appleton's Journal
Catholic World
Chicago Tribune
Cosmopolitan
Daily Alta California
Golden Hills News
Los Angeles Times
New York Times
Overland Monthly
San Francisco Chronicle

BOOKS AND ARTICLES

A-Cheng. *He Shangdi yiqi liulang: Youtai ren ha-er-bin binan ji* (Traveling with God: Jews' Exile Life in Harbin). Chongqing: Chongqing Publishing Group, 2008.

Albala, Ken. *The Banquet: Dining in the Great Courts of Late Renaissance Europe.* Urbana: University of Illinois Press, 2007.

Allen, Joseph R. *Taipei: City of Displacements.* Seattle: University of Washington Press, 2011.

Allen, Stewart Lee. *In the Devil's Garden: A Sinful History of Forbidden Food.* New York: Ballantine Books, 2002.

Anderson, Eugene N. *The Food of China.* New Haven, Conn.: Yale University Press, 1988.

Ashley, Bob, Joanne Hollows, Steve Jones, and Ben Taylor. *Food and Cultural Studies.* New York: Routledge, 2004.

Asian Pacific American Legal Center of Southern California. *The Diverse Face of Asians and Pacific Islanders in Los Angeles County.* Los Angeles: Asian Pacific American Legal Center of Southern California, 2004.

Ayers, James. *Gold and Sunshine: Reminiscences of Early California.* Boston: R. G. Badger, 1922.

Bai, Xianyong (Hsien-yung Pai) 白先勇. "Huaqiao Rong Ji 华侨荣记" (Huaqiao Rong Family Restaurant). In *Bai Xianyoung zi xuan ji* (*Self-Selected Anthology of Bai Xianyoung*), 171–180. Guangzhou, China: Huacheng Publisher, 2009.

———. *Taibei Ren* 台北人 (Taipei Residents). Guangzhou, China: Huacheng Press, 2004.

Barth, Gunther. *A History of the Chinese in the United States, 1850–1870.* Cambridge, Mass.: Harvard University Press, 1964.

Bates, J. H. *Notes of a Tour in Mexico and California.* New York: Burr Printing House, 1887.

Beck, Louis. *New York's Chinatown: A Historical Presentation of People and Places.* New York: Bohemia, 1898.

Beesley, David. "From Chinese to Chinese American: Chinese Women and Families in a Sierra Nevada Town." *California History* 67 (September 1988): 168–179.

Belasco, Warren, and Philip Scranton, eds. *Food Nations: Selling Taste in Consumer Societies.* New York: Routledge, 2002.

Benn, Charles. *Chinese Golden Age: Everyday Life in the Tang Dynasty.* Oxford: Oxford University Press, 2004.

Blodgett, Peter J. *Land of Golden Dreams: California in the Gold Rush Decades, 1848–1858.* San Marino, Calif.: Huntington Library, 1999.

Bodnar, John. *Remaking America: Public Memory.* Princeton, N.J.: Princeton University Press, 1992.

Bonner, Arthur. *Alas! What Brought Thee Hither? The Chinese in New York, 1800–1950.* Madison, N.J.: Fairleigh Dickinson University Press, 1997.

Bowles, Samuel. *Our New West.* Hartford, Conn., 1869.

Boorstin, Daniel J. *The Americans: The Democratic Experience.* New York: Vintage Books, 1965.

———. *The Americans: The National Experience.* New York: Vintage Books, 1965.

Bowring, Sir John. "Chinese Characteristics." *Catholic World* 2, no. 7 (October 1865): 102–110.

Camporesi, Piero. *Bread of Dreams: Food and Fantasy in Early Modern Europe.* Chicago: University of Chicago Press, 1996.

Cao, Xueqin. *Hong Lou Meng* (The Story of the Stone). Beijing: Renmin Wenxue Press, 1982.

Cather, Helen V. "The History of San Francisco's Chinatown." Master's thesis, University of California, 1991.

Chan, David. "The Five Chinatowns of Los Angeles." *Bridge* 2 (1973): 41–45.

Chan, Sucheng. *Asian Americans: An Interpretive History.* Boston: Twayne, 1991.

———. *This Bittersweet Soil: The Chinese in California Agriculture, 1860–1910.* Berkeley: University of California Press, 1986.

Chang, Iris. *A History of Chinese in America: A Narrative History.* New York: Viking Penguin, 2003.

Chang, K. C., ed. *Food in Chinese Culture: Anthropological and Historical Perspectives.* New Haven, Conn.: Yale University Press, 1977.

Chao, Tonia. "Communicating through Architecture: San Francisco Chinese Restaurants and Cultural Intersections, 1849–1984." Ph.D. diss., University of California, Berkeley, 1985.

Chen, Ben-chang 陈本昌. *Mei-guo Hua Qiao Can Guang Gung Ye* 美国华侨餐馆工业 (Chinese Restaurant Business in America). Taipei: Far East Book Co., 1971. (南宁: 广西教育出版社, 1995 年 12 月第1版).

Chen, Hsian-Shui. *Chinatown No More: Taiwanese Immigrants in Contemporary New York.* Ithaca, N.Y.: Cornell University Press, 1992.

Chen, Jack. *The Chinese of America.* San Francisco: Harper & Row, 1980.

Chen, Yong. *Chinese San Francisco, 1850–1943: A Trans-Pacific Community.* Stanford, Calif.: Stanford University Press, 2000.

———. *Chop Suey, USA: The Story of Chinese Food in America.* New York: Columbia University Press, 2014.

Cheng, Lucie, and Suellen Cheng. "Chinese Women of Los Angeles: A Social Historical Survey." In Lucie Cheng et al., *Linking Our Lives: Chinese American Women of Los Angeles.* Los Angeles: Asian American Studies Center, University of California, Los Angeles, and Chinese Historical Society of Southern California, 1984.

Cheong, Weng Eang. *Hong Merchants of Canton: Chinese Merchants in Sino-Western Trade, 1684–1798.* London: Curzon Press, 1997.

Cheung, Sidney, and Chee-Beng Tan. *Food and Foodways in Asia: Resource, Tradition, and Cooking.* New York: Routledge, 2007.

Chinn, Thomas W. *Bridging the Pacific: San Francisco Chinatown and Its People.* San Francisco: Chinese Historical Society of America, 1989.

Chinn, Thomas W., H. M. Lai, and Philip Choy, eds. *A History of the Chinese in California: A Syllabus.* San Francisco: Chinese Historical Society of America, 1969.

Chiswick, Barry A. "Immigrants in the U.S. Labor Market." *Annals of the American Academy of Political and Social Science* 460 (March 1982): 64–72.

Chu, George. "Chinatown in the Delta: The Chinese in the Sacramento–San Joaquin Delta, 1870–1960." *California Historical Society Quarterly* 49 (March 1970): 21–37.

Chu, Grace Zia. *The Pleasure of Chinese Cooking.* New York: Simon and Schuster, 1962.

Chu, Limin. *The Images of China and the Chinese in the Overland Monthly, 1868–1875, 1883–1935.* San Francisco: R & E Research Associates, 1974.

Chu, Louis H. "The Chinese Restaurants in New York City." Master's thesis, New York University, 1939.

Coe, Andrew. *Chop Suey: A Cultural History of Chinese Food in the United States.* New York: Oxford University Press, 2009.

Cohen, Myron L. "Being Chinese: The Peripheralization of Traditional Identity." In *The Living Tree: The Changing Meaning of Being Chinese Today,* ed. Tu Wei-ming, 88–108. Stanford, Calif.: Stanford University Press, 1994.

Conlin, Joseph R. *Bacon, Beans and Galantines: Food and Foodways on the Western Mining Frontier.* Reno: University of Nevada Press, 1987.

Coolidge, Mary. *Chinese Immigration.* New York: Henry Holt, 1909.

Counihan, Carole. *Food in the USA: A Reader.* New York: Routledge, 2002.

Counihan, Carole, and Steven Kaplan. *Food and Gender: Identity and Power.* Amsterdam: Overseas Publishers, 1998.

Counihan, Carole, and Penny Van Esterik. *Food and Culture: A Reader.* 2nd ed. New York: Routledge, 2008.

Daniels, Roger. *Asian America: Chinese and Japanese in the United States since 1850.* Seattle: University of Washington Press, 1988.

Davidson, Alan. *Coming to America: A History of Immigration and Ethnicity in American Life.* New York: Harper Perennial, 1990.

———. *Oxford Companion to Food.* Oxford: Oxford University Press, 1999.

Diner, Hasia R. *Hungering for America Italian, Irish, and Jewish Foodways in the Age of Migration.* Cambridge, Mass.: Harvard University Press, 2003.

Dong, Lorraine. "The Forbidden City Legacy." *Chinese America: History and Perspectives (1992): 125–148.*

Edwards, Clarence. *Bohemian San Francisco: Its Restaurants and Their Most Famous Recipes.* San Francisco: Paul Elder, 1914.

Ehrlich, M. Avrum (Mark Avrum). *Jews and Judaism in Modern China.* London: Routledge, 2010.

Erenberg, Lewis A. *Steppin' Out: New York Nightlife and the Transformation of American Culture.* Chicago: University of Chicago Press, 1984.

Fairbank, John K., and Edwin O. Reischauer. *China: Tradition and Transformation.* Rev. ed. Boston: Houghton Mifflin, 1989.

Faser, Evan D. G., and Andrew Rimas. *Empires of Food: Feast, Famine, and the Rise and Fall of Civilizations.* New York: Free Press, 2010.

Ferguson, Priscilla Parkhurst. *Accounting for Taste: The Triumph of French Cuisine.* Chicago: University of Chicago Press, 2004.

Fessler, Loren W., ed., and China Institute in America, Inc., comp. *Chinese in America: Stereotyped Past, Changing Present.* New York: Vantage Press, 1983.

Finkelstein, Joanne. *Fashioning Appetite: Restaurants and the Making of Modern Identity.* New York: Columbia University Press, 2014.

Flandrin, Jean-Louis, and Massimo Montanari (English edition by Albert Sonnenfield). *Food: A Culinary History from Antiquity to the Present.* New York: Penguin, 1999.

Fong, Joe Chung. "Transnational Newspapers: The Making of the Post-1965 Globalized/Localized San Gabriel Valley Chinese Community." *Amerasia Journal* 22, no. 3 (1996): 65–77.

Fong, Tim. *The First Suburban Chinatown: The Making of Monterey Park, California.* Philadelphia: Temple University Press, 1994.

Freedman, Paul, ed. *Food: The History of Taste.* London: Thames & Hudson, 2007.

Gabaccia, Donna R. *We Are What We Eat: Ethnic Food and the Making of Americans.* Cambridge, Mass.: Harvard University Press, 1998.

Gay, Malcolm. "St. Louie Chop Suey: You Are What You Eat: The Story of a Culture, Told through Its Cuisine." November 15, 2006. St. Louis Riverfronttimes.com.

Gernet, Jacques. *Daily Life in China: On the Eve of the Mongol Invasion 1250–1276.* Stanford, Calif.: Stanford University Press, 1970.

Genthe, Arnold. *Genthe's Photographs of San Francisco's Chinatown.* Reprint. New York: Dover, 1984.

Glen, Evelyn Nakano. "Split Household, Small Producer and Dual Wage Earner: An Analysis of Chinese-American Family Strategies." *Journal of Marriage and the Family* (February 1983): 35–46.

Glen, Evelyn Nakano, and Stacey G. H. Yap. "Chinese American Families." In *Minority Families in the United States: A Multicultural Perspective,* ed. Ronald L. Taylor, 115–145. Englewood Cliffs, N.J.: Prentice Hall, 1994.

Goldstein, Joyce, with Dore Brown. *Inside the California Food Revolution: Thirty Years That Changed Our Culinary Consciousness.* Berkeley: University of California Press, 2013.

Goody, Jack. *Food and Love: A Cultural History of East and West.* London: Verso, 1998.

Gray, John Henry. *China, A History of the Laws, Manners, and Customs of the People.* London: Macmillan, 1878.

Gutzlaff, Charles. *Three Voyages Along the Coast of China, in 1831, 1832, & 1833 with Notices of Siam, Corea, and the Loo-Choo Islands.* London, 1834. Reprint. Taipei: Cheng Wen Publishing, 1968.

Hall, Bruce Edward. *Tea That Burns: A Family Memoir of Chinatown.* New York: Free Press, 1998.

Halvorsen, Francine. *The Food and Cooking of China: An Exploration of Chinese Cuisine in the Provinces and Cities of China, Hong Kong, and Taiwan.* New York: J. Wiley, 1996.

Hansen, Gladys C., and William F. Heintz. *The Chinese in California: A Brief Bibliographic History.* Portland, Ore.: Richard Abel, 1970.

Harris, Jessica B. *High on the Hog: A Culinary Journey from Africa to America.* New York: Bloomsbury, 2011.

Hauck-Lawson, Annie, and Jonathan Deutsch. *Gastropolis: Food and New York City.* New York: Columbia University Press, 2008.

Hing, Bill Ong. *Making and Remaking Asian America through Immigration Policy, 1850–1990.* Stanford, Calif.: Stanford University Press, 1993.

Hirschman, Charles, and Morrison Wong. "The Extraordinary Educational Attainment of Asian Americans: A Search for Historical Evidence and Explanations." *Social Forces* 65 (1986): 1–27.

Hoexter, Corinne K. *From Canton to California: The Epic of Chinese Immigration.* New York: Four Winds Press, 1976.

Hoffman, William. *The Monitor; or Jottings of a New York Merchant during a Trip Round the Globe.* New York: Carleton, 1863.

Höllmann, Thomas O. *The Land of the Five Flavors: A Cultural History of Chinese Cuisine.* New York: Columbia University Press, 2013.

Hom, Ken. *Easy Family Recipes from a Chinese-American Childhood.* New York: Alfred A. Knopf, 1997.

Hooker, Richard J. *Food and Drink in America: A History.* New York: Bobbs-Merrill, 1978.

Howay, F. W. *The Journal of Captain James Colnett aboard the Argonaut from April 26, 1789 to November 3, 1791.* Toronto: Champlain Society, 1940.

Hsu, Madeline Y. "From Chop Suey to Mandarin Cuisine: Fine Dining and the Refashioning of Chinese Ethnicity during the Cold War Era." In *Chinese Americans and the Politics of Race and Culture,* ed. Sucheng Chan and Madeline Yuan-yin Hsu, 173–193. Philadelphia: Temple University Press, 2008.

Iness, Sherrie A., ed. *Kitchen Culture in America: Popular Representations of Food, Gender, and Race.* Philadelphia: University of Pennsylvania Press, 2001.

James, Rian. *Dining in New York.* New York: John Day, 1930.

Jenkins, Lawrence Waters. *Bryant Parrott Tilden of Salem, at a Chinese Dinner Party.* Princeton, N.J.: Princeton University Press, 1944.

Jones, Mary Ellen. *Daily Life on the Nineteenth Century American Frontier.* Westport, Conn.: Greenwood Press, 1998.

Joselit, Jenna Weissman. *The Wonders of America: Reinventing Jewish Culture, 1880–1950.* New York: Hill and Wang, 1994.

Jung, John. *Sweet and Sour: Life in Chinese Family Restaurants.* Los Angeles: Yin & Yang Press, 2011.

Kaplan, Anne R., et al. *The Minnesota Ethnic Fook Book.* St. Paul: Minnesota Historical Society, 1986.

Kaufman, Frederick. *A Short History of the American Stomach.* Boston: Mariner Books/ Houghton Mifflin Harcourt, 2009.

Kerr, J. G. *The Guide to the City and Suburbs of Canton.* Hong Kong: Kelly and Walsh, 1904.

Kindead, Gwen. *Chinatown: A Portrait of a Closed Society.* New York: HarperCollins, 1992.

Ku, Robert Ji-Song. *Dubious Gastronomy: The Cultural Politics of Eating Asian in the USA.* New York: New York University Press, 2013.

Ku, Robert Ji-Song, Martin F. Manalansan IV, and Anita Mannur. *Eating Asian America: A Food Studies Reader.* New York: New York University Press, 2013.

Kuhn, Philip A. *Chinese Among Others: Emigration in Modern Times.* New York: Rowman & Littlefield, 2008.

Kulp, Daniel Harrison. *Country Life in South China: The Sociology of Familism.* New York: Columbia University, 1925.

Kung, S. W. *Chinese in American Life: Some Aspects of Their History, Status, Problems, and Contributions.* Seattle: University of Washington Press, 1962.

Kwong, Peter. *Chinatown, New York: Labor and Politics, 1930–1950.* New York: Monthly Review Press, 1979.

———. *Forbidden Workers: Illegal Chinese Immigrants and American Labor.* New York: New Press, 1997.

———. *The New Chinatown.* 2nd ed. New York: Hill and Wang, 1996.

Lai, Him Mark, and Philip P. Choy. *Outlines: History of the Chinese in America.* San Francisco: Chinese American Studies Planning Group, 1972.

Larson, Louise Leung. *Sweet Bamboo: A Saga of a Chinese American Family*. Los Angeles: Chinese Historical Society of Southern California, 1989.

Lau, Estelle T. *Paper Families: Identity, Immigration Administration, and Chinese Exclusion*. Durham, N.C.: Duke University Press, 2006.

Laudan, Rachel. *Cuisine and Empire Cooking in World History*. Berkeley: University of California Press, 2013.

Lee, Calvin. *Chinatown USA*. New York: Doubleday, 1965.

Lee, Jennifer 8. *The Fortune Cookie Chronicles: Adventures in the World of Chinese Food*. New York: Hachette Book Group, 2008.

Lee, Robert. *Orientals: Asian Americans in Popular Culture*. Philadelphia: Temple University Press, 1999.

Lee, Rose Hum. *The Chinese in the United States of America*. Hong Kong: Hong Kong University Press, 1960.

Lei, Jieqiong 雷洁琼 (Kit King Louis). "Problems of Second Generation Chinese." *Sociology and Social Research* 16 (May–June 1932): 250–258.

———. "A Study of American-born American-reared Chinese in Los Angeles." Master's thesis, University of Southern California.

Leppman, Elizabeth J. *Changing Rice Bowl: Economic Development and Diet in China*. Hong Kong: Hong Kong University Press, 2005.

Levenstein, Harvey. *Paradox of Plenty: A Social History of Eating in Modern America*. New York: Oxford University Press, 1993.

———. *Revolution at the Table: The Transformation of the American Diet*. Berkeley: University of California Press, 2003.

Lewis, Mark Edward. *China's Cosmopolitan Empire: The Tang Dynasty*. Cambridge, Mass.: Belknap Press of Harvard University Press, 2009.

Lewis, Sinclair. *Main Street: The Story of Carol Kennicott*. New York: Harcourt, Brace and Howe, 1920.

Li, Wei. "Building Ethnoburbia: The Emergence and Manifestation of the Chinese Ethnoburb in Los Angeles' San Gabriel Valley." *Journal of Asian American Studies* 2, no. 1 (February 1999): 7–8.

———. *Spatial Transformation of an Urban Ethnic Community from Chinatown to Chinese Ethnoburb in Los Angeles*. Honolulu: University of Hawaii Press, 2009.

Liang, Jiabin (梁嘉彬). *Guangdong Shisan Hang Kao* 广东十三行考 (The Thirteen Hongs of Canton). Guangzhou, China: Guangdong People's Press, 1999.

Liang, Qichao 梁启超. *Xindalu Youji* 新大陆游记 (Diary of Traveling in the New World). Beijing: Shehui Kexue Wenxin Press, 2007.

Light, Ivan. "From Vice District to Tourist Attraction: The Moral Career of American Chinatown, 1880–1940." *Pacific Historical Review* 43 (1974): 367–394.

Lim, Imogene I., and John Eng-Wong. "The Chow Mein Sandwich: American as Apple Pie." *Radcliffe Culinary Times* 3, no. 2 (Autumn 1993): 4–5.

———. "The Chow Mein Sandwich: Chinese American Entrepreneurship in Rhode Island." In *Origin and Destinations: 41 Essays on Chinese America*, 417–436. Los Angeles: Chinese Historical Society of Southern California, 1994.

Lin, Huei-Yi 林慧懿. *Yinshi Nannu Shipu* 饮食男女食谱 (Recipes of Eat Drink Man Woman). Taipei: Taolue, 1994.

Ling, Huping. *Chinese Chicago: Race, Transnational Migration, and Community since 1870*. Stanford, Calif.: Stanford University Press, 2012.

———. *Chinese St. Louis: From Enclave to Cultural Community*. Philadelphia: Temple University Press, 2004.

———. "Reconceptualizing Chinese American Community in St. Louis: From Chinatown to Cultural Community." *Journal of American Ethnic History* 24, no. 2 (Winter 2005): 65–101.

Liu, Boji 刘伯骥. *Mei-guo Hua Ch'iao shi* 美国华侨史 (A History of Overseas Chinese in America). Taipei: Xingzhengyuan qiaowu wenyuan hui (publisher), Liming wenhua shiye youxian gongsi (distributor), 1976.

Liu, Haiming. "Chop Suey as an Imagined Authentic Chinese Food: Chinese Restaurant Business and Its Culinary Identity in the United States." *Journal of Transnational American Studies* 1, no. 1 (2009): article 12.

———. "Flexible Authenticity: Din Tai Fung as a Global Shanghai Dumpling House Made in Taiwan." *Chinese America: History and Perspectives (2011)*: 57–65.

———. "Food, Culinary Identity, and Transnational Culture: Chinese Restaurant Business in Southern California." *Journal of Asian American Studies* 12, no. 2 (June 2009): 135–162.

———. "Kung Pao Kosher: Jewish Americans and Chinese Restaurants in New York." *Journal of Chinese Overseas* 6, no. 1 (2010): 80–101.

Liu, John M. "A Centennial Retrospective of the Asian American Legacy in Orange County." *Journal of Ethnic Studies* 8, no. 2 (Summer 1980): 37–45.

Liu, John M., and Lucie Cheng. "Pacific Rim Development and the Duality of Post-1965 Asian Immigration to the United States." In *The New Asian Immigration in Los Angeles and Global Restructuring*, ed. Pual Ong, Edna Bonacich, and Lucie Cheng. Philadelphia: Temple University Press, 1994.

Liu, Junru. *Chinese Food*. New York: Cambridge University Press, 2011.

Lo, Kenneth. *Chinese Food: An Introduction to One of the World's Great Cuisines*. London: Penguin Group, 1972.

Loi, Linda. "'So We Don't End Up Like Chop Suey': Searching for 'Authentic' Chinese Food in L.A." http://www.sscnet.ucla.edu/aasc/classweb/fa1197/M163/loi5.html.

Lou, Raymond. "The Chinese American Community of Los Angeles, 1870–1900: A Case of Resistance, Organization, and Participation." Ph.D. diss., University of California, Irvine, 1982.

Lu, Shun, and Gary Alan Fine. "The Presentation of Ethnic Authenticity: Chinese Food as a Social Accomplishment." *Sociological Quarterly* 460 (Summer 1995): 535–553.

Lui, Garding. *Inside Los Angeles Chinatown*. N.p.: n.p., 1948.

Lui, Mary Ting Yi. *The Chinatown Trunk Mystery: Murder, Miscegenation, and Other Dangerous Encounters in Turn-of-the-Century New York City*. Princeton, N.J.: Princeton University Press, 2005.

Luo, Suwen 罗苏文. *Jindai Shanghai: dushi shehui yu shenghuo* 近代上海：都市社会与生活 (Modern Shanghai: Metropolitan Life and Society). Beijing: Zhonghua Press, 2006.

Lydon, Sandy. *Chinese Gold: The Chinese in the Monterey Bay Region*. Capitola, Calif.: Capitola Book, 1985.

Mai, Liqian 麦立谦 (Lai, Him Mark). *Cong huaqiao dao huaren: Ershi shiji meiguo huaren shehui fazhan shi* 从华侨到华人 二十世纪美国华人社会发展史 (From Overseas Chinese to Chinese Americans: A History of 20th Century Chinese American Social and Economic Development). Hong Kong: San Lian Press Joint Publishing H. K. Co., 1992

Mannur, Anita. "Asian American Food-Scapes." *Amerasia Journal* 32, no. 2 (2006): 1–5.

Mark, Mei Lin, and Ginger Chih. *A Place Called Chinese America*. Dubuque, Iowa: Kendall/Hunt, 1982.

Mason, Sarah R. "Liang May Seen and the Early Chinese Community in Minneapolis." *Minnesota History* (Spring 1995): 223–233.

Mason, William. "The Chinese in Los Angeles." *Museum Alliance Quarterly* 6, no. 2 (Fall 1967): 20–28.

McCollough, Chuck. "Nation's Appetite for Tortillas Heating Up Sales." *San Antonio Express*, September 12, 1993.

McLeod, Alexander. *Pigtails and Gold Dust*. Caldwell, Idaho: Caxton Printers, 1948.

McWilliams, Carey. *Southern California: An Island of the Land*. Salt Lake City: Gibbs M. Smith, 1983.

McWilliams, James E. *A Revolution in Eating: How the Quest for Food Shaped America*. New York: Columbia University Press, 2005.

Mei, June. "Socioeconomic Developments among the Chinese in San Francisco, 1848–1906." In *Labor Immigration Under Capitalism: Asian Workers in the United States before World War II*, ed. Lucie Cheng and Edna Bonacich, 370–399. Berkeley: University of California Press, 1984.

Miller, Hanna. "Identity Takeout: How American Jews Made Chinese Food Their Ethnic Cuisine." *Journal of Popular Culture*, no. 3 (June 2006): 430–465.

Mines, Cynthia. "Chinese Chain: Steaming with Success." *Retail Traffic*, May 1, 2000. http://retailtrafficmag.com/mag/retail_chinese_chain_steaming/.

Minnick, Sylvia. *Sun Samforw: The San Joaquin Chinese Legacy*. Fresno, Calif.: Panorama West, 1988.

Miscevic, Dusanka Dusana, and Peter Kwong. *Chinese Americans: The Immigrant Experience*. Southport, Conn.: Hugh Lauter Levin Associates, 2000.

Mouritsen, Ole G. *Seaweeds: Edible, Available, and Sustainable*. Chicago: University of Chicago Press, 2013.

Morley, Charles, trans. "The Chinese in California as Reported by Henryk Sienkiewicz." *California Historical Society Quarterly* 34 (1955): 301–316.

Moxham, Roy. *A Brief History of Tea: The Extraordinary Story of the World's First Drink*. Philadelphia: Running Press, 2008.

Nash, Roger. *In the Kosher Chow Mein Restaurant*. Sudbury, Ont.: Your Scrivener Press, 1996.

Nee, Victor G., and Brett de Bary Nee. *Longtime Californ': A Documentary Study of an American Chinatown*. New York: Pantheon, 1973.

Newman, Jacqueline M. *Food Culture in China*. Westport, Conn.: Greenwood Press, 2004.

Ng, Franklin. *The Taiwanese Americans*. Westport, Conn.: Greenwood Press, 1998.

Ong, Paul. "Chinese Laundries as an Urban Occupation in 19th Century California." In *The Annals of the Chinese Historical Society of the Pacific Northwest*, ed. Douglas W. Lee, 71–81. Seattle: Chinese Historical Society of the Pacific Northwest, 1983.

Pan, Lynn. *Sons of the Yellow Emperor: A History of Chinese Diaspora*. New York: Little, Brown, 1990

Park, Robert Ezra, and Herbert A. Miller. *Old World Traits Transplanted*. New York: Harper, 1921.

———. *Race and Culture*. Glencoe, Ill.: Free Press, 1950.

Pasadena City Directory. 1920.

Pearlman, Alison. *Smart Casual: The Transformation of Gourmet Restaurant Style in America*. Chicago: University of Chicago Press, 2013.

Plaut, Joshua Eli. *A Kosher Christmas: 'Tis the Season to Be Jewish*. New Brunswick, N.J.: Rutgers University Press, 2012.

Pleck, Elizabeth H. *Celebrating the Family: Ethnicity, Consumer Culture, and Family Rituals.* Cambridge, Mass.: Harvard University Press, 2000.

Pollan, Michael. *In Defense of Food: An Eater's Manifesto.* New York: Penguin. 2008.

———. *The Omnivore's Dilemma: A Natural History of Four Meals.* New York: Penguin. 2006.

Potter, David M. *People of Plenty: Economic Abundance and the American Character.* Chicago: University of Chicago Press, 1954.

Rebora, Giovanni. *Culture of the Fork: A Brief History of Everyday Food and Haute Cuisine in Europe.* New York: Columbia University Press, 2001.

Robert, Jag A. *China to Chinatown: Chinese Food in the West.* London: Reaktion Books, 2002.

Root, Waverly, and Richard de Rochemont. *Eating America: A History.* Hopewell, N.J.: Ecco Press, 1976.

Rubinstein, Murray A. "Taiwan's Socioeconomic Modernization, 1971–1996." In *Taiwan: A New History,* ed. Murray A. Rubinstein, 339–369. New York: M. E. Sharpe, 2007.

Ryan, William Redmond. *Personal Adventures in Upper and Lower California in 1848–9, with the Author's Experiences in the Mines.* 1850.

Sandmeyer, Elmer Clarence. *The Anti-Chinese Movement in California.* 1939. Reprint. Urbana: University of Illinois Press, 1991.

Saxton, Alexander. *The Indispensable Enemy: Labor and the Anti-Chinese Movement in California.* Berkeley: University of California Press, 1971.

Scafidi, Susan. *Who Owns Culture? Appropriation and Authenticity in American Law.* New Brunswick, N.J.: Rutgers University Press, 2005.

Schlosser, Eric. *Fast Food Nation: The Dark Side of the All-American Meal.* New York: Houghton Mifflin, 2001.

Shaw, William. *Golden Dreams & Waking Realities; Being the Adventures of a Gold-Seeker in California and the Pacific Islands.* London: Smoth, Elder, 1851.

Siegael, Donald. *From Lokshen to Lo Mein: The Jewish Love Affairs with Chinese Food, the Kosher Chinese Cookbook.* New York: Gefen Publishing House, 2005.

Sinn, Elizabeth. *Pacific Crossing: California Gold, Chinese Migration, and the Making of Hong Kong.* Hong Kong: Hong Kong University Press, 2013.

Smith. Andrew F. *Eating History: Thirty Turning Points in the Making of America Cuisine.* New York: Columbia University Press, 2009.

Spence, Jonathan D. "Food." In *Chinese Roundabout: Essays in History and Culture,* 165–204. New York: W. W. Norton, 1992.

Spencer, Colin. *British Food: An Extraordinary Thousand Years of History.* New York: Columbia University Press, 2003.

Spier, Robert F. "Food Habits of Nineteenth-Century California Chinese." *California Historical Society Quarterly* 37 (1958): 79–84.

Starr, Kevin. *Golden Dreams: California in an Age of Abundance, 1950–1963.* New York: Oxford University Press, 2009.

Sterckx, Roel. *Food, Sacrifice, and Sagehood in Early China.* Cambridge: Cambridge University Press, 2011.

Su, Heng'an 蘇恆安. *Culinary Arts in Late Ming China: Refinement, Secularization and Nourishment: A Study on Gao Lian's Discourse on Food and Drink.* Taipei: SMC Publishing, 2004.

Swislocki, Mark. *Culinary Nostalgia: Regional Food Culture and the Urban Experience in Shanghai.* Stanford, Calif.: Stanford University Press, 2009.

Takaki, Ronald. *Strangers from a Different Shore: A History of Asian Americans.* Boston: Little, Brown, 1989.

Tannahill, Reay. *Food in History*. London: Penguin, 1973. Reprint, New York: Three Rivers Press, 1988.

Taylor, Bayard. *Eldorado; or, Adventures in the Path of Empire: Comprising a Voyage to California, Via Panama; Life in San Francisco and Monterey; Pictures of the Gold Region, and Experiences of Mexican Travel*. New York: George P. Putnam, 1850.

To, Wing-kai. *Chinese in Boston, 1870–1965: Images of America: Massachusetts*. Boston: Arcadia, 2008.

Tom, K. "Functions of the Chinese Language Schools." *Sociology and Social Research* 25 (1941): 557–561.

Tropp, Barbara. *The Modern Art of Chinese Cooking: Techniques and Recipes*. New York: William Morrow, 1982.

Tsai, Shih-shan. *China and Overseas Chinese in the United States, 1868–1911*. Fayetteville: University of Arkansas Press, 1983.

———. *The Chinese Experience in America*. Bloomington: Indiana University Press, 1986.

Tu, Wei-ming. "Cultural China: The Periphery as the Center." In *The Living Tree: The Changing Meaning of Being Chinese Today*, ed. Tu Wei-ming, 13–18. Stanford, Calif.: Stanford University Press, 1994.

Tuchman, Gaye, and Harry G. Levine. "New York Jews and Chinese Food: The Social Construction of an Ethnic Pattern." *Journal of Contemporary Ethnography* 22, no. 3 (October 1993): 382–407.

———. "'Safe Treyf': New York Jews and Chinese Food." In *The Taste of American Place: A Reader on Regional and Ethnic Foods*, ed. Barbara G. Shortridge and James R. Shortridge, 163–184. New York: Roman and Littlefield, 1997.

Turner, Katherine Leonard. *How the Other Half Ate: A History of Working-Class Meals at the Turn of the Century*. Berkeley: University of Californian Press, 2014.

Twain, Mark. *Roughing It*. Berkeley: University of California Press, 1972.

Van Wyk, Ben-Erik. *Culinary Herbs and Spices of the World*. Chicago: University of Chicago Press, 2014.

Waley-Cohen, Joanna. "The Quest for Perfect Balance." In *Food: The History of Taste*, ed. Paul Freedman, 99–132. London: Thames & Hudson, 2007.

Wang, Gungwu. "Among Non-Chinese." In *The Living Tree: The Changing Meaning of Being Chinese Today*, ed. Tu Wei-ming, 127–146. Stanford, Calif.: Stanford University Press, 1994.

Wang, Mei 王梅. *Ding Tai Feng Chuanqi* 鼎泰豐传奇 (The Legend of Din Tai Fung). Taipei: Tianxia Yuanjian Press, 2001.

Wang, Peter Chen-main. "A Bastion Created, a Regime Reformed, an Economy Reestablished, an Economy Reengineered, 1949–1970." In *Taiwan: A New History*, ed. Murray A. Rubinstein, 320–330. New York: M. E. Sharpe, 2007.

Ward, Geoffrey C. *The West: An Illustrated History*. New York: Little, Brown, 1996.

Watson, James, ed. *Golden Arches East: McDonald's in East Asia*. Cambridge, Mass.: Harvard University Press, 1998.

Watson, James, and Melissa L. Caldwell, eds. *The Cultural Politics of Food and Eating*. Oxford: Wiley-Blackwell, 2005.

Webb, Walter Prescott. *The Great Plains*. Lincoln: University of Nebraska Press, 1959.

Weiss, Melford S. *Valley City: A Chinese Community in America*. San Francisco: R & E Research Associates, 1971.

Whitfield, Ruth Hall. "Public Opinion and the Chinese Question in San Francisco, 1900–1947." Master's thesis, University of California, Berkeley, 1947.

Williams, Jack F. "Who Are the Taiwanese? Taiwan in the Chinese Diaspora." In *The Chinese Diaspora: Space, Place, Mobility, and Identity*, ed. Laurence J. C. Ma and Carolyn Cartier, 163–190. New York: Rowman & Littlefield, 2003.

Wong, Charles C. "The Continuity of Chinese Grocers in Southern California." *Journal of Ethnic Studies* 8, no. 2 (Summer 1980): 63–82.

———. *Monterey Park: A Community Transition*. Pullman: Washington State University Press, 1998.

Wood, Ellen Rawson. *California and the Chinese: The First Decade*. 1961. Reprint, San Francisco: R & E Research Associates, 1974.

Wu, David Y. H. "Cantonese Cuisine (Yue-cai) in Taiwan and Taiwanese Cuisine (Tai-cai) in Hong Kong." In *The Globalization of Chinese Food*, ed. David Y. H. Wu and Sidney C. H. Cheung, 86–99. Honolulu: University of Hawaii Press, 2002.

Wu, David Y. H., and Sidney C. H. Cheung, eds. *The Globalization of Chinese Food*. Honolulu: University of Hawaii Press, 2002.

———. "McDonald's in Taipei: Hamburgers, Betel Nuts, and National Identity." In *Golden Arches East: McDonald's in East Asia*, ed. James L. Watson, 110–135. Stanford, Calif.: Stanford University Press, 1997.

Xu, Wenying. *Eating Identities: Reading Food in Asian American Literature*. Honolulu: University of Hawaii Press, 2007.

Yee, Alfred. *Shopping at Giant Foods: Chinese American Supermarkets in Northern California*. Seattle: University of Washington Press, 2013.

Yin, Xiao-huang. *Chinese American Literature since the 1850s*. Urbana: University of Illinois Press, 2000.

Yu, Renqiu. "Chop Suey: From Chinese Food to Chinese American Food." *Chinese America: History and Perspectives* (1987): 87–100.

———. "Imperial Banquets and the Emperor's Meals in Qing China." *Flavor & Fortune* 7, no. 2 (Summer 2000).

Yuan, Mei. *Sui Yuan Shi Tan* (Recipes of the Sui Yuan Garden). Beijing: Zhong Hua Shu Ju (中华书局) 2010.

Yuan, S. T. *Chinese American Population*. Hong Kong: UEA Press, 1988.

Zhou, Min. *Contemporary Chinese America: Immigration, Ethnicity, and Community Transportation*. Philadelphia: Temple University Press, 2009.

Zhu, Tianxin 朱天心. *Xiang wo juancun de xiongdi men* 想我眷村的兄弟们 (I Miss My Buddies in the Military Quarter). Taipei: Maitian Press, 1992.

Zhuang, Guotu. 庄国土 *Huaqiao huaren yu zhongguo de guanxi* 华侨华人与中国'的'关系 (Relationship between Overseas Chinese and China). Guangzhou, China: Guangdong High Education Press, 2001.

INDEX

ABOUT THE AUTHOR

HAIMING LIU is a professor of Asian and Asian American studies at the Department of Ethnic and Women's Studies, College of Education and Integrative Studies, California State Polytechnic University, Pomona. He was born in Beijing, China, and received his undergraduate and master's degrees from Beijing Foreign Studies University in China and his Ph.D. from the University of California, Irvine. His is the author of *The Transnational History of a Chinese American Family* (Rutgers University Press, 2005) and many articles and book chapters on Chinese American history.

Printed in the USA
CPSIA information can be obtained
at www.ICGtesting.com
LVHW040737260524
781439LV00041B/1333